Christmas at Home

Crafts for the Holidays

from McCall's Needlework & Crafts

Christmas at Home

at

Crafts for the Holidays

From McCall's Needlework & Crafts

Sedgewood® Press

New York

For Sedgewood® Press

Director: Elizabeth P. Rice
Project Editor: Barbara Benton
Associate Editor: Leslie Gilbert
Designer: H. Roberts
Production Manager: Bill Rose

Distributed by Macmillan Publishing Company, a division of Macmillan, Inc.

ISBN 0-02-609160-7
Library of Congress Catalog Card Number: 85-63428
Manufactured in the United States of America

10 9 8 7 6 5 4 3 2 1

Contents

*T*here's no place like home for the holidays . . . .

When family and friends gather together at Christmas time, home fires burn bright and their warmth is shared by all. Christmas comes alive in the harmony of carolers, the spicy scent of gingerbread, and especially in the festive trimmings that decorate the home.

A fragrant wreath that greets guests at the front door, handcrafted stockings hanging by the fire, and the dazzling Christmas tree with wonderful gifts wrapped and waiting underneath all make the home a showplace at holiday time. The beautiful "holiday best" linens that grace the dining room table at Christmas dinner make the year's most joyous meal even more memorable.

Perhaps among all the decorations there are some very special pieces, lovingly made, that carry fond remembrances of years gone by—a tablecloth embroidered by a great-grandmother in painstaking cross-stitch, or a needlepoint tree ornament made once-upon-a-time by a little girl who now has children of her own. These "handed-down" family treasures are the link between the nostalgia for holidays of yesterday and the sweet celebrations of today. They are part of the sentiment that makes Christmas eternal.

The projects in this book will help you to prepare your home for Christmas from top to bottom. There are wreaths, ornaments, and linens to embroider, warm and cuddly quilts and afghans to brighten up the long winter nights, and colorful centerpieces and wall hangings to decorate any room in the house. There are many pieces that you'll want to keep for your own Christmas home, and others that you'll want to make to give to special people.

The Christmas spirit of giving shines in every one of these handmade pieces, reminding you always of the bond that is shared when loved ones come home for the holidays.

Entrance

Even before you ring the bell, you know your stay
here will be full of Christmas cheer. A homemade
holiday wreath greets you in seasonal style!

HEART WREATH

A rope of fragrant evergreen foliage—decorated with cones, flowers, and berries—says a heart-felt hello.

SIZE: About 18″ around.

EQUIPMENT: Yardstick. Scissors.

MATERIALS: Heart-shaped wire frame, about 13½″ around; available in craft stores. Florist's wired roping of greens, about 3½″ wide, 1½ yards long. Assorted dried foliage (other greens, small flowers, cones, etc.) and artificial berries (see photograph). Red heart ornament, 1¼″ long. Green satin ribbon, ⅜″ wide, ⅜ yard long. Fine wire.

DIRECTIONS: Wire a hanging loop at center top of heart frame. Measure and mark center of roping; place center at bottom point of heart frame. Wire roping to frame. Bring ends of roping together at top of heart and tie bow of green ribbon over joining. Wire red heart ornament to hang below bow. Wire dried foliage and berries randomly to roping, referring to photograph.

CINNAMON STICK WREATH

Spicy bark of the cinnamon tree is hot-glued in a circular sweep, then ornamented with peppermint candies and a bright gingham bow.

SIZE: About 13½″ in diameter.

EQUIPMENT: Hot-glue gun. Ruler. Scissors. Cardboard, 8″ wide.

MATERIALS: Plastic foam wreath, 2″ wide, 2″ thick, and 12″ in diameter. Cinnamon sticks, 2″-3″ long, about 2½ lbs. Red/white peppermint hard candies, 1″ in diameter, 19. Red gingham lace-edged ribbon, 1¾″ wide, 2 yards long. Pipe cleaner. Fine wire. Glue sticks.

DIRECTIONS: Cut 4″ piece pipe cleaner and twist ends together for 1″ to form a loop. Apply hot glue to ends and insert into back of wreath; when dry, bend loop up for hanging. Glue cinnamon sticks one at a time around wreath with hot glue, holding each until set. Work in rows from outer edge to inner edge of wreath, overlapping rows as you go; do not cover back if wreath is to hang against a wall. Referring to photograph, glue candies randomly to wreath.

To make bow: Wrap ribbon around cardboard, then cut notches in ribbons at center of each side (Fig. 1). Slip ribbon off cardboard. Twist and tighten a piece of wire around notched ribbon (Fig. 2). Fan out bow (Fig. 3). Wire or glue bow to wreath.

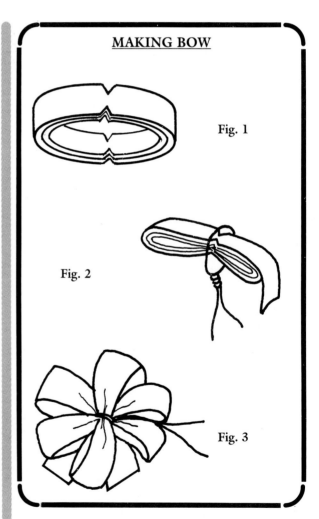

MAKING BOW

Fig. 1

Fig. 2

Fig. 3

ANGEL WREATH

A good practice piece for beginning quilters, this simple machine-stitched wreath makes an unusual window decoration.

See General Directions for enlarging a pattern.

SIZE: About 18″ in diameter.

EQUIPMENT: Pencil. Ruler. Scissors. Paper for patterns. Dressmaker's tracing (carbon) paper. Tracing wheel or dry ball-point pen. Straight pins. Sewing needle. Sewing machine. All-purpose glue.

MATERIALS: Felt, 72″ wide: blue, ¾ yd.; white, ½ yd.; small amount of yellow-orange. White, blue, and gold sewing thread. Batting.

DIRECTIONS: Enlarge patterns on paper ruled in 1″ squares; complete half-pattern. On angle pattern, short dash lines indicate where pieces overlap. Fine lines indicate additional stitching lines. Make a separate pattern for each piece. (Note: Angels and star are three layers thick.)

Angels: From yellow-orange felt, cut six hair pieces. From white felt, cut eighteen 8″ squares. Pin three layers of felt together for each angel. Position five pattern pieces (two wings, two arms, and angel body) on 8″ squares. With dressmaker's carbon, trace each piece on top layer of felt. Do not cut out pattern pieces yet. Machine-stitch along traced lines. Cut out each machine-stitched piece through all three layers, just outside stitching lines.

With three angels facing one way, and three facing the other, tack two wing and two arm pieces to each angel body following pattern. Glue hair pieces in place on each angel.

Star: From yellow-orange felt, cut three pieces 5″ square. Pin three layers together. Trace stitching lines onto top layer. Machine-stitch through all three layers. Cut out star just outside stitching line.

From blue felt, cut three 20″ squares. Pin two layers together. Using dressmaker's carbon, trace cloud lines and wreath outline on top layer. Machine-stitch the two layers together following cloud lines only. Pin third layer to first two. Machine-stitch three layers together following inner and outer wreath outlines; leave a small area open along one outside edge to stuff. Cut out wreath through all three thicknesses, just beyond inner and outer stitching lines. Fill wreath with batting, but do not overstuff. Slip-stitch opening closed.

Referring to photograph, tack star in place at center top area of wreath. Position angels around wreath, all facing the wreath center. Tack in place at feet, arm, wing, and head areas. Hang wreath as desired.

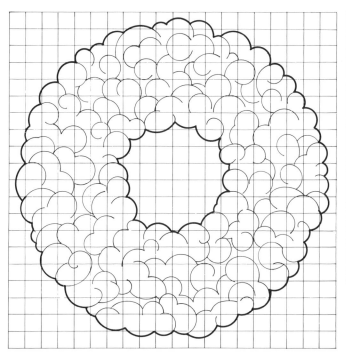

ANGEL WREATH PATTERNS

PINE CONE PLAQUE

An attractive alternative to the traditional wreath, this door plaque is a simple arrangement of pine cones and ornamental dried grasses.

See General Directions for enlarging a pattern.

SIZE: 31″ × 7″.

EQUIPMENT: Carbon paper. Tracing wheel or dry ball-point pen. Jigsaw. Sandpaper. Pencil. Drill. Serrated knife.

MATERIALS: Paper for pattern. Pine board, 1″ × 8″ × 33″. Four-inch plastic-foam ball. Dried strawflowers. Dried wheat. Dried sea oats. Pine cones. Masking tape. Florist's picks. Florist's wire. Glue. Ribbon.

DIRECTIONS: With pencil connect grid lines across plaque pattern. Then enlarge pattern by copying on paper ruled in 1″ squares. Transfer pattern to pine, using carbon paper. Cut out plaque and sand. Mark and drill ¼″-diameter hole for hanging.

Find and mark center line across diameter of plastic-foam ball. Using serrated knife, cut ball in half. Center and glue half of ball 8½″ up from bottom of plaque.

Trim stems on strawflowers to 6″ and, forming small clusters of 10 to 12 flowers, bind stems together with masking tape. To prepare pine cones cut a length of florist's wire and wrap around cone base between scale layers. Wire a florist's pick to each. Following photograph, arrange dried material to plaque by affixing to foamball, starting with tall wheat and sea oat sprays. Work bunches of strawflowers among tall sprays. Cluster pine cones. Make a loopy bow with ribbon. Attach with florist's wire to a pick and affix to foam ball.

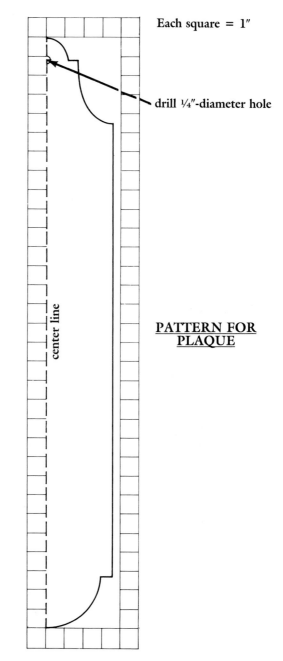

Each square = 1″

drill ¼″-diameter hole

center line

PATTERN FOR PLAQUE

STATICE WREATH

Crisp white statice flowers create a lacy Victorian effect. Finish with pine cones and a velvet bow. Extra statice can be used for spot decorations anywhere in the house.

SIZE: 14″ to 16″ in diameter, finished.

MATERIALS: Two 9″-diameter plastic-foam rings. White craft glue. Florist's tape. Florist's picks. Florist's wire. Dried statice. Pine cones. Wide velvet ribbon.

DIRECTIONS: Glue plastic-foam rings together. Wrap glued rings with floral tape. Cut dried statice into 2″ to 3″ sprigs and wire to picks. Insert statice in foam base to cover. To prepare pine cones, cut lengths of florist's wire and wrap around cones between scale layers. Wire to sticks. Insert in foam base. Make big floppy bow; attach. **Note:** Other decorations can be made similarly. Candlestick in photograph is encircled with 4″-diameter plastic-foam ring taped in place.

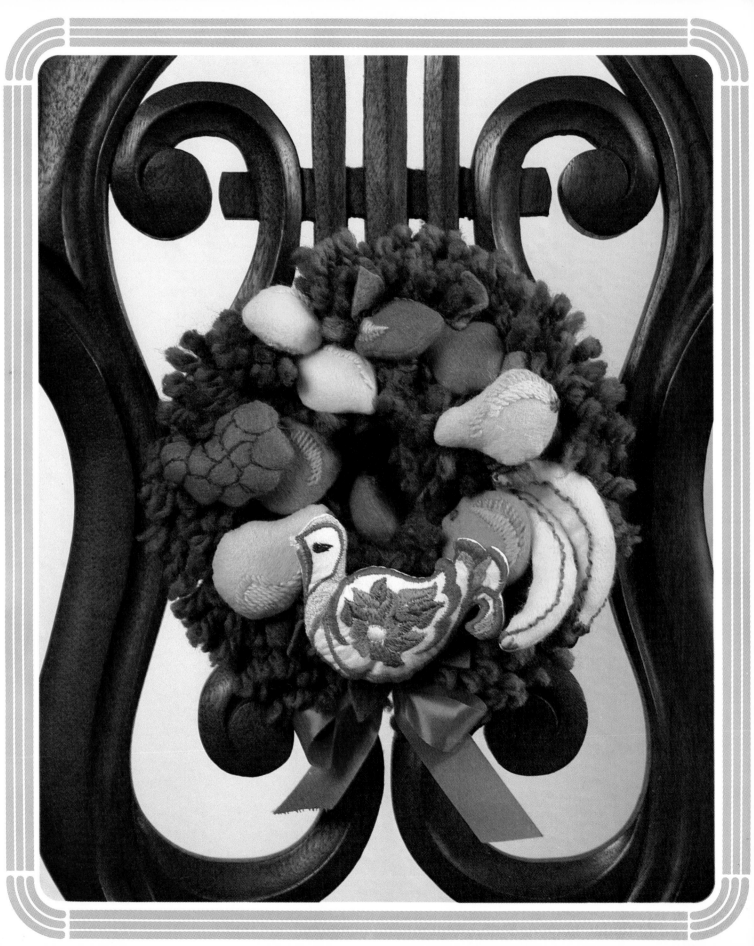

DELLA ROBBIA WREATH

Use your needlework skills to create this realistic, miniature (8″ across) wreath, reminiscent of the work of the Italian Renaissance sculptor.

SIZE: 8″ in diameter.

EQUIPMENT: Colored pencil. Pencil. Paper for patterns. Scissors. Ruler. Dressmaker's tracing (carbon) paper. Tracing wheel or dry ball-point pen. Weaving (or rug), embroidery, and sewing needles. Embroidery hoop. Sewing machine. Cardboard.

MATERIALS: Thin wire ring, 2″ in diameter. Plastic or wood ring, ½″ thick, 4¼″ inside diameter. **For Warp:** White crochet cotton, size 10, 6 yards. **For Weft:** Green heavy rug yarn, 35 yards. Felt: white and yellow, 8″ × 4″ scraps; gold, orange, red, purple, lime and olive green, 4″-square scraps. Persian yarn, 3-strand, small amounts pale yellow, gold, orange, light brown. Six-strand embroidery floss, small amounts yellow, brown, pale pink, bright pink, red, purple, blue, bright green, kelly green. Red satin ribbon ¾″ wide, ¾ yard. Green sewing thread. Fiberfill.

DIRECTIONS

Wreath: Position rings on work surface with smaller ring centered in larger ring. Cut four 6″ lengths of crochet cotton; tie them around both rings, spacing them evenly apart; be sure distance between rings remains equal all around. Using crochet cotton, wind warp as follows: Tie one end of cotton to smaller ring, carry cotton up to and around larger ring, then down and around smaller ring; continue winding around both rings 32 times, placing warp threads ¼″ apart on smaller ring and ½″ apart on larger ring, for a total of 64 warp threads. Do not wind warp too tightly; use just enough tension so that inside ring remains centered. Tie two ends together. Carefully cut and remove four original 6″ spacer cords.

Cut 128 6″ lengths of green rug yarn as follows: Wrap yarn around a 3″ piece of cardboard 128 times and cut yarn on one side. Tie 64 rya knots (Fig. 1) around outer ring, two between each loop of warp threads, with ends of knots extending to the outside. Make a second round of rya knots just inside larger ring, each tied over two adjacent warp threads and with ends facing outer ring (Fig. 2). Pull all knots taut. To weave, thread weaving needle with 1 yard rug yarn; work two full rounds of plain weave (Fig. 3) close to rya knots. Start by weaving under first thread and weave around to beginning. Weave a second round, starting it by going under first two threads and then continuing over one, under one as shown. To end, weave the end of yarn in on back. Push woven rounds toward outer ring with fingers. Work another round of rya knots, then two more rounds of plain weave as before. Wrap smaller ring tightly with rug yarn. Tie two ends together.

Fruits and Partridge: Using sharp colored pencil, draw lines across patterns, connecting grid lines. Enlarge by copying on paper ruled in ½″ squares. Heavy lines indicate pattern lines; fine lines are embroidery. Transfer the following outlines to felt, using dressmaker's carbon and dry ball-point pen: 4 yellow bananas, 4 yellow lemons, 4 gold pears, 4 oranges, 6 red apples, 4 purple cherries, 2 bunches purple grapes, 2 white partridges, 8 lime green leaves, 4 olive green leaves. Transfer embroidery lines to the following pieces for fronts: 2 bananas, 2 lemons, 2 pears, 2 oranges, 3 apples, 1 bunch grapes and 1 partridge. Separating the Persian yarn and using two strands in needle and following color key, fill in outlined areas on lemons, pears, oranges and apples with satin stitch (see General Directions for Stitch Details); with brown, work backstitch "seams" on bananas and straight-stitch "stems" on pears, oranges and apples. With two strands of embroidery floss in needle and following color key, embroider leaves on partridge with satin leaf stitch and remainder of outlined areas in satin stitch. Embroider lines on grapes in outline stitch, using brown floss.

Cut out leaves and set aside. Cut out all other felt shapes, adding ¼″ seam allowance around edges. With right sides facing and raw edges even, stitch fronts and backs of fruits and partridge together, making ¼″ seams and leaving an opening for turning. Trim seams and turn each to right side; stuff evenly with fiberfill, using eraser end of pencil if necessary. Slip-stitch openings closed.

Pinch leaves at base end and, using sewing thread, tack one lime green and one olive green leaf to each apple top; tack remaining leaves in clusters to one side (bottom) of wreath. Tack bird over leaves; tack fruit all around wreath. Refer to photograph. Tie bow with red satin ribbon; tack to center bottom of wreath.

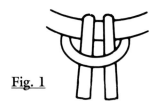

Fig. 1

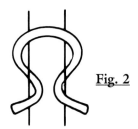

Fig. 2

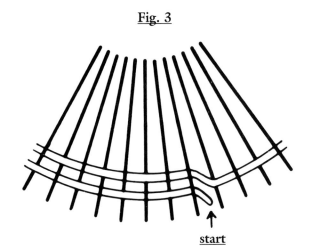

Fig. 3

start

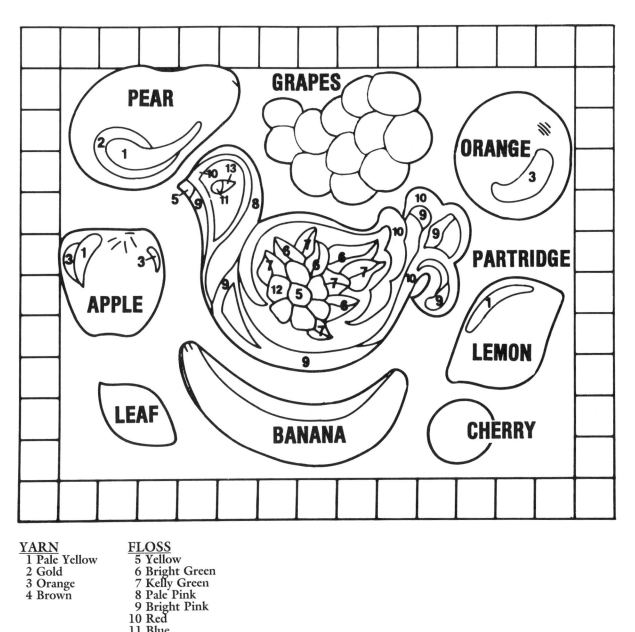

YARN
1 Pale Yellow
2 Gold
3 Orange
4 Brown

FLOSS
5 Yellow
6 Bright Green
7 Kelly Green
8 Pale Pink
9 Bright Pink
10 Red
11 Blue
12 Purple
13 Brown

Family Room

Curl up in front of the fire with a warm holiday afghan, then just sit back and admire the beautiful samplers on the family room wall. Or sneak a peek in the stockings—some of the gifts may be for you!

SNOWFLAKE AFGHAN

Snowflakes seem to float on an afghan of single- and double-crocheted hexagons—worked in white and two reds.

See General Directions for crochet.

SIZE: 42″ × 54″, plus fringe.

MATERIALS. Worsted-weight yarn, 4 4-oz skeins each of white and scarlet red, 3 skeins of flame red. Aluminum crochet hook size K (6½ mm).

GAUGE: 1 motif is 8″ across from point to point.

MOTIF (make 53): With white, ch 6; sl st in first ch to form ring.

Rnd 1: Ch 4 (counts as dc, ch 1), (dc in ring, ch 1) 11 times, sl st in 3rd ch of ch 4—12 sps.

Rnd 2: Ch 4, dc in first sp, ch 2, dc, ch 1, dc in same sp, * sk next sp; in next sp work dc, ch 1, dc, ch 2, dc, ch 1, dc, repeat from * 4 times, sl st in 3rd ch of ch 4—6 points.

Rnd 3: Sl st across to ch-2 sp; ch 4, dc, ch 2, dc in same sp, ch 1, work dc in same sp until there are 2 lps on hook; change to flame by pulling lp through 2 lps on hook. * Working over white strand, with flame, work dc, ch 1, dc in sp between points, changing to white in 2nd dc. Cut flame, leaving end to be darned in later. With white, work dc, ch 1, dc, ch 2, dc, ch 1, dc in ch-2 sp of next point, changing to flame in last dc. Repeat from * around, end with flame, sl st in 3rd ch of ch 4. Cut white; do not cut flame.

Rnd 4: With flame, ch 4, dc in sp between flame and white, changing to scarlet. * Working over flame strand, with scarlet, work dc, ch 1, dc, ch 2, dc, ch 1, dc in next ch-2 sp, changing to flame; working over scarlet, with flame, work dc, ch 1, dc in sp between white and flame pat, work dc, ch 1, dc in space between flame and white pat, change to scarlet; repeat from * around, end flame pat in last sp before last flame pat, sl st in 3rd ch of ch 4.

Rnd 5: With flame, ch 1; working over scarlet strand, sc in same ch with sl st, sc in ch-1 sp, sc in dc, changing to scarlet; * with scarlet, working over flame strand, work sc in dc, sc in ch-1 sp, sc in dc, 3 sc in ch-2 sp, sc in dc, sc in ch-1 sp, sc in dc, changing to flame; with flame, working over scarlet strand, work (sc in dc, sc in ch-1 sp, sc in dc) twice, changing to scarlet; repeat from * around, end sl st in first sc. End off. Weave in ends on back of work.

HALF MOTIF (make 6): With scarlet, ch 6; sl st in first ch to form ring.

Row 1: Ch 5, dc in ring, (ch 2, dc, ch 1, dc in ring) twice. Ch 5, turn.

Row 2: Dc in first sp, dc, ch 1, dc, ch 2, dc, ch 1, dc in next sp, sk next sp, dc, ch 1, dc, ch 2, dc, ch 1, dc in next sp, dc, ch 1, dc in last sp. Ch 5, turn.

Row 3: Dc in first sp; change to flame. * Working over scarlet strand, with flame, dc, ch 1, dc in sp between dc's; change to scarlet. Working over flame strand, sk ch-1 sp, work dc, ch 1, dc, ch 2, dc, ch 1, dc in next ch-2 sp; change to flame; sk ch-1 sp; repeat from * once. With flame, dc, ch 1, dc in sp between dc's; change to scarlet, dc, ch 1, dc in last sp. Cut yarn.

Row 4: Join scarlet in sp at beg of row 3, ch 5, dc in sp, change to flame. * With flame, dc, ch 1, dc in sp before flame pat, dc, ch 1, dc in sp after flame pat, change to scarlet. With scarlet, dc, ch 1, dc, ch 2, dc, ch 1, dc, in next ch-2 sp, change to flame; repeat from * once; with flame, dc, ch 1, dc in sp before flame pat, dc, ch 1, dc in sp after flame pat, change to scarlet. With scarlet, dc, ch 1, dc in last sp. Cut yarn.

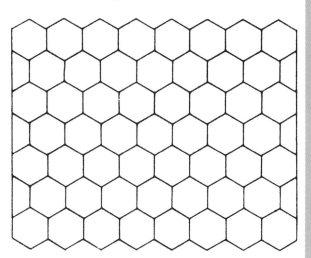

Row 5: Matching colors, work sc in each ch-1 sp and each dc and 3 sc in each ch-2 sp across last row, changing colors as before. End off.

FINISHING: Following diagram for placement of motifs, sew motifs and half motifs tog with matching yarns through back lps of sc. With scarlet, work 1 row of dc around entire outer edge, working dc in each sc, 3 dc in each outer point; on half motifs, work 3 dc in first end sp, 2 dc in each sp across edge, 3 dc in last end sp.

Fringe: Cut scarlet in 12″ lengths. Holding 5 strands tog, fold strands in half, knot in first dc at one end of afghan. Knot a fringe in every 3rd dc across. Repeat fringe on other end.

HOUSE AND TREE AFGHAN

Gold beads and metallic yarn add luster to a holiday afghan of knitted diamonds joined with crochet.

See General Directions for knitting and crochet.

SIZE: 58″ × 88″.

MATERIALS: Worsted-weight yarn 3½-oz. pull skeins: 9 skeins royal blue, 2 skeins each red, off-white, and green. Knitting needles No. 8 (5 mm). Crochet hook size J or 10 (6 mm). Metallic gold yarn for embroidery, 1 ball. Two yds. ⅛″ red ribbon. 304 small gold beads; 16 smaller gold beads. Tapestry needle.

GAUGE: 9 sts = 2″; 6 rows = 1″.

AFGHAN: **MOTIF** (make 16 house motifs and 16 tree motifs): With royal, cast on 3 sts. K 1 row, p 1 row.

Row 3: Cast on 1 st, k across to last st, k in front and back of last st.

Row 4: Purl. Repeat rows 3 and 4 until there are 51 sts, following charts for house and tree designs. When knitting in designs, use separate balls of royal each side of designs. Do not carry colors across back of work.

Row 51: Sl 1, k 1, psso; k across to last 2 sts, k 2 tog.

Row 52: Purl. Repeat rows 51 and 52 until 3 sts remain. Bind off.

EMBROIDERY: With gold metallic yarn, embroider red stitches around outline of house in duplicate st. Embroider both rows of door mat with gold. With white yarn, cross 2 straight stitches over window for panes. With gold metallic yarn, embroider green stitches around outline of tree in duplicate st. Embroider star on top of tree as shown on chart.

FINISHING: Block pieces. Sew smaller gold beads to each door of house for doorknob. Sew 19 gold beads to each tree, one on star, one at each end of branches, one at each inner angle of tree, four down center.

    For wreaths, with 1 strand each of green and gold metallic yarn, ch 12; sl st in first ch to form ring. Sew a wreath to each door. Cut red ribbon at an angle 1½″ long, tie a knot at center of piece; sew ribbon to wreath.

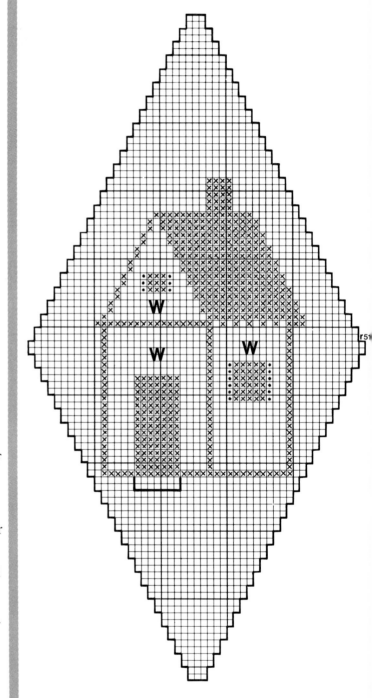

⊠ **Red**
● **Green**

Edging: With royal and size J hook, work 1 row sc around each piece, working 3 sc in each point and 24 sc on each side between points.

Joining: Motifs are joined in diagonal rows, beg at lower left corner of afghan. Attach royal with sl st in point (center sc of 3 sc) on right side of a tree motif; ch 3, sl st in top point of another tree motif; working down right side of first motif to join it to top left side of 2nd motif, * ch 3, sk 1 sc on first motif, sl st in next sc, ch 3, sk 1 sc on 2nd motif, sl st in next sc, repeat from * to left side point of 2nd motif, ch 3, dc in bottom point of first motif, ch 3, sl st in right-hand point of a house motif (this is single house motif at bottom left corner of afghan). Ch 3, sl st back in bottom point of first motif, ch 3, join top right-hand edge of house motif to lower left-hand edge of first motif as first 2 motifs were joined, end ch 3, sl st in point of first motif, ch 3, sl st in point of house motif, ch 2, dc in point of first motif, ch 2, sl st in bottom point of a 3rd tree motif, ch 3, sl st in point of first motif. Now join lower right side of 3rd tree motif to top left side of first motif, end ch 3, sl st in side point of 3rd tree motif, ch 5, sl st in top point of first motif.

You have now joined house motif to first row of tree motifs. The next row will be 5 house motifs, then 7 tree motifs, 7 house motifs, 5 tree motifs, 3 house motifs, 1 tree motif. Each motif point has 3 sl sts in center sc. At inner joinings of motifs (joinings not at the edge of afghan), work ch 5 at joining of 2 motifs. When next 2 motifs are joined to that corner, ch 2, sl st in 3rd ch of ch 5, ch 2, sl st in corner of 4th motif. This creates a + pattern between motifs. At joinings at edge of afghan, work ch 2, dc in point, ch 2 to give the same effect.

Edging: When all motifs have been joined, join royal in point at left side of first house motif, ch 4 (counts as dc, ch 1); dc in same point, * ch 3, sl st in top of dc for picot, sk next sc, dc, ch 1, dc in next sc, repeat from * around. At inner corners of afghan, work dc in center of motif joinings to finish + pattern.

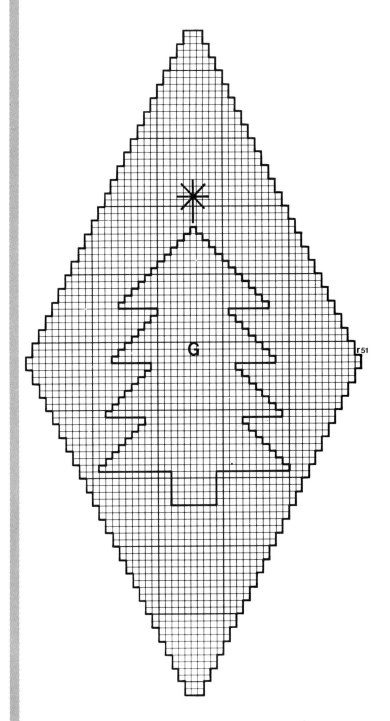

r51

G

SNOWMAN—TREE— WREATH AFGHAN

Alternating Christmas designs are crocheted right into their squares. Finishing touches are embroidered.

See General Directions for crochet and embroidery.

SIZE: 44″ × 60″.

MATERIALS: Worsted-weight yarn: 3½-oz. skeins—4 skeins red, 5 skeins green, 1 skein black; 3-oz. skeins—6 skeins white. Small amounts of yellow, mint, pale blue. Crochet hooks sizes I and H. Tapestry needle.

GAUGE: 7 sc = 2″; 4 rows = 1″ (size I hook).

AFGHAN: SNOWMAN SQUARE (make 10): With red and size I hook, ch 32.

Row 1: Sc in 2nd ch from hook and in each remaining ch—31 sc. Ch 1, turn each row.

Row 2: Sc in each sc.

Row 3 (right side): Sc in 12 sc; pull up a lp in next sc, drop red to wrong side of work, finish sc with white (always change colors in this way, by working last sc of one color until there are 2 lps on hook, then drawing lp of new color through 2 lps on hook). With white, sc in 5 sc, changing to red in last sc (use another skein of red; do not carry unused color across work); with red, sc in last 13 sc.

Beg with row 4, following chart for snowman, work to top of chart.

Edging: Rnd 1: With size H hook, join green in upper right-hand corner of square, ch 6, dc in same corner st, * ch 1, sk next st, dc in next st, repeat from * to next corner, (dc, ch 3, dc) in corner st, repeat from first * around square, end ch 1, sl st in 3rd ch of ch 6 at beg of rnd.

Rnd 2: Ch 1, sc in same ch as sl st, (sc, ch 2, sc) in corner sp, sc in each dc and ch-1 sp around, working (sc, ch 2, sc) in each corner sp. Join; end off.

Work 5 wreath squares and 5 tree squares, making background white and following charts for color changes.

EMBROIDERY: Embroider 3 large black cross-stitches on snowman's face for eyes and nose. With red, embroider mouth in back-

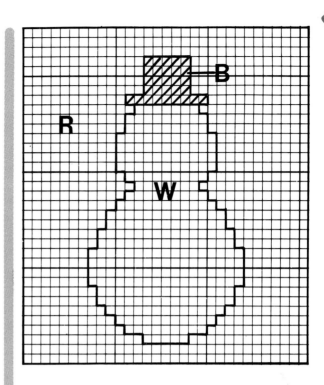

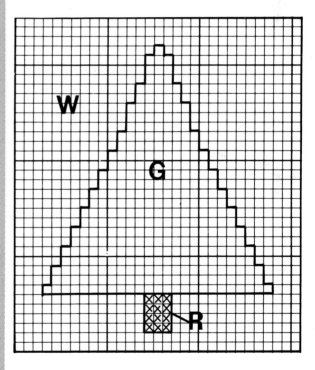

stitch. With black, embroider 3 French knots on body for buttons. With red, embroider French knots on wreaths for berries. Embroider French knots on trees for lights, 2 in yellow, 2 in mint, 1 in blue.

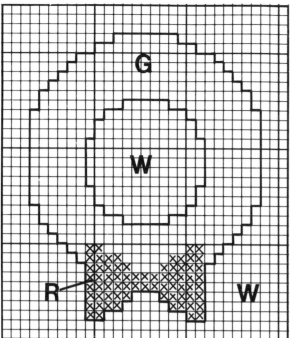

FINISHING: Arrange squares in 5 rows of 4 squares each alternating snowman squares in checkerboard fashion with tree and wreath squares; have wreath squares along sides of afghan, tree squares on the 2 inner panels. Sew squares tog through back lps of sc.

BORDER: Rnd 1: With green and size H hook, sc in each st around afghan, working (sc, ch 2, sc) in each corner. Join with sl st in first sc. End off.

Rnd 2: Join white in corner, ch 6, dc in corner sp, * ch 1, sk next st, dc in next st, repeat from * around, working (dc, ch 3, dc) in each corner sp. Sl st in 3rd ch of ch 6 at beg of rnd. End off.

Rnd 3: Join green in corner, (sc, ch 2, sc) in corner, * sl st in dc, ch 1, repeat from * around, working (sc, ch 2, sc) in each corner. Join; end off.

FIR TREE AFGHAN

Snow-touched trees in two directions zigzag across an afghan that's worked in mosaic knitting (not for beginners). A snowflake border adds contrast in both pattern and color.

See General Directions for Knitting.

SIZE: 42″ × 58″.

MATERIALS: Worsted-weight yarn, 3-oz. pull skeins: 6 skeins white, 4 skeins green, 3 skeins red. Three circular knitting needles, No. 11 (8 mm).

GAUGE: 4 sts = 1″; 5 rows = 1″ (garter st).

Notes: Entire afghan is worked in mosaic knitting; that is, garter st stripes using one color for 2 rows and second color for 2 rows. Design is formed by slipped sts. Sl all sl sts as if to purl. Always have yarn in back of sl sts on right-side rows, in front of sl sts on wrong-side rows.

Each row of chart represents 2 rows of knitting. When following chart for center section, read from right to left on right-side rows, to center and back. On wrong-side rows, it is not necessary to follow chart as the same sts are knitted and the same sts slipped as on right-side rows. On every row that begins and ends with a marked square, k all the marked sts and sl all the unmarked sts. On every row that begins and ends with an unmarked square, k all the unmarked sts and sl all the marked sts.

When following chart for border, read chart from corner to center st, then back on same row to next corner, repeat around. On next row, p all k st, sl all sl sts. Color to be knitted or purled is shown on chart.

AFGHAN: **Center Section:** With a circular needle and white cast on 117 sts.

Row 1: Following Chart 1, with green, work to center st, then follow chart back on same row, working center st only once.

Row 2 (wrong side): Following same row of chart, k the k sts, sl the slipped sts, being sure to carry unused green in front of slipped sts.

Work to top of chart, then repeat from marks at sides of chart to top. Bind off with green.

BORDER: With green, using 3 circular needles, pick up and k 1 st in each st at top and bottom of center section. 1 st in each garter st stripe on sides.

Rnd 1: With green, knit around.

Rnd 2: With green, purl around, inc 2 sts at each corner. Follow Chart 2 to outer edge, inc 2 sts every other rnd. Corners are continuous. Rnds are separated on chart for clarity. When outer edge of chart is reached, bind off.

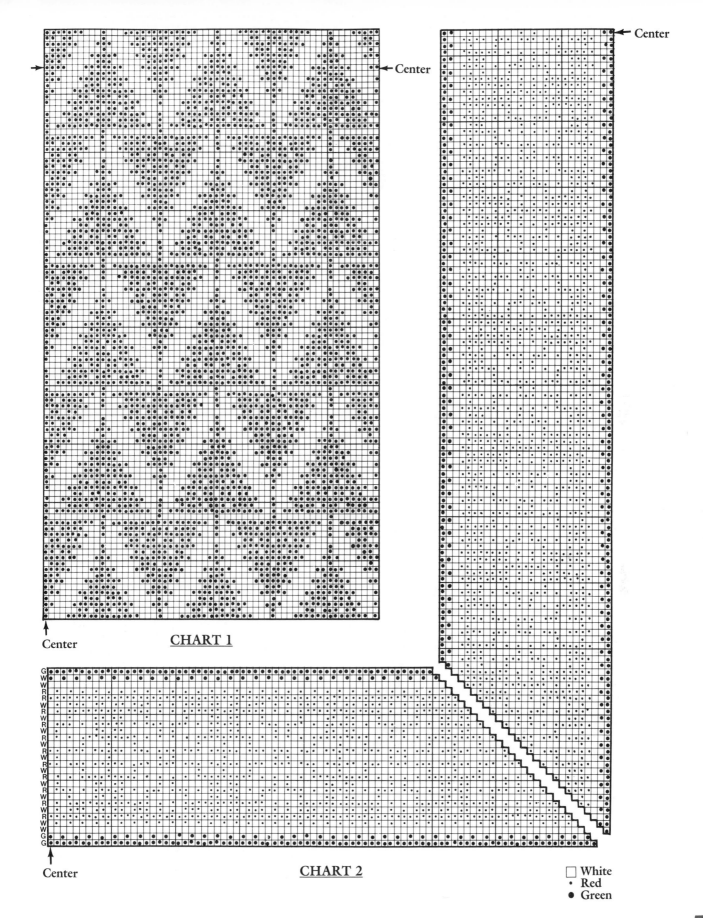

← Center

CHART 1

Center

Center

CHART 2

Center

□ White
· Red
● Green

33

CHRISTMAS WALL HANGING

Eighteen different symbols of Christmas—knitted in stockinette stitches—go into this festive wall hanging. You can add a triangle at the bottom for family names.

See General Directions for knitting, embroidery, and crochet.

SIZE: 45″ long, plus 11″ long triangle for family names and 5″ tassel (optional).

MATERIALS: Worsted-weight yarn, 3½-oz. skeins: 3 skeins red, 3 skeins green, 1 skein each white, yellow, and black, few yards of beige. Knitting needles, No. 10. For embroidery, 6-strand embroidery floss, white, black, and yellow. Metallic gold and silver yarns. Embroidery and tapestry needles. For lining and extension at bottom for embroidering names, 2 yds. red flannel. Matching sewing thread. Red fringe braid, 1½ yds. Red tape for hanging piece. 30″ curtain rod.

GAUGE: 4 sts = 1″.

WALL HANGING: Each motif is knitted separately in stockinette st (k 1 row, p 1 row). Carry unused design colors across back of work if desired, since back will be lined. First, knit each motif according to chart. When motifs are finished, block them, and work embroidery. Sew motifs tog vertically in 3 long strips, then sew strips together.

FIRST STRIP

Madonna and Child: With green, cast on 30 sts. Following chart, k to top of chart. Bind off.

Embroider Madonna's halo in gold outline st, headband in gold blanket st and duplicate st, eye in black duplicate st, mouth in red straight st. Embroider around Infant's head and swaddling clothes in gold outline st. Work some duplicate sts in gold on clothes. Embroider black dots for eyes, red mouth. On lower curve of Madonna's arm, embroider some sts with silver in duplicate st.

Moon and Stars: With red, cast on 30 sts. Following chart, work to top of chart, bind off. Embroider stars with gold sts, moon with red embroidery floss.

Poinsettia: With green, cast on 30 sts. Following chart, work to top of chart. Bind off.

Heart: With green, cast on 30 sts. Following chart, work to top of chart. Bind off.

Angel: With red, cast on 30 sts. Following chart, work to top of chart. Bind off. Embroider eye black, mouth red. With gold, embroider sleeve and back of robe in outline st; work 2 rows of sts near bottom of robe in duplicate st; embroider light in straight sts.

Girl Skater: With green, cast on 30 sts. Following chart, work to top of chart. Bind off. With white embroidery floss, embroider skates in outline st, snowflakes in 2 cross-sts. Embroider black eyes, red mouth.

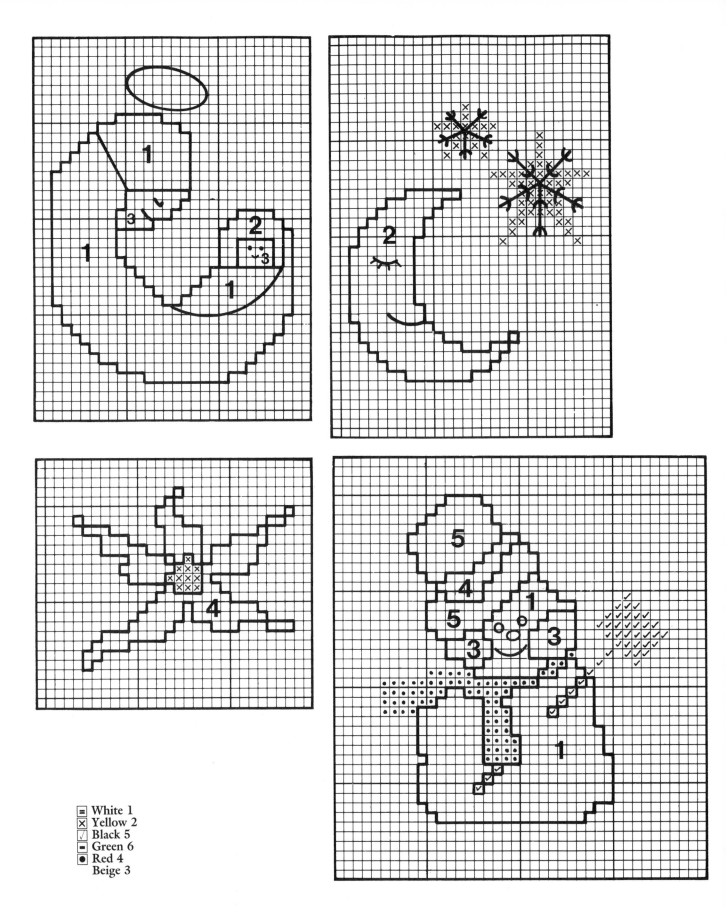

SECOND STRIP

Snowflake: With red, cast on 40 sts. Following chart, work to top of chart. Bind off.

Snowman: With green, cast on 40 sts. Following chart, work to top of chart. Bind off. Embroider cheeks with beige yarn in satin st. Embroider snowflakes with white yarn. With black yarn, embroider broom handle in straight sts, broom in satin st. Work gold straight sts on broom. Embroider black eyes, yellow nose, red mouth.

Tree: With red, cast on 40 sts. Following chart, work to top of chart. Bind off. With white yarn, embroider candles in straight st. With yellow yarn, make small st above each candle; embroider star at top of tree.

Boy and Girl: With green, cast on 40 sts. Following chart, work to top of chart. Bind off. With white yarn, embroider snowflakes.

Reindeer: With red, cast on 40 sts. Following chart, work to top of chart. Bind off. With black yarn, embroider trees in straight sts. With white yarn, make straight sts along top of branches; embroider hill in outline st; embroider snowflakes.

THIRD STRIP

Candle: With green, cast on 30 sts. Following chart, work to top of chart. Bind off. With yellow embroidery floss, make straight sts around flame.

Bells: With red, cast on 30 sts. Following chart, work to top of chart. Bind off. With gold, embroider lower edge of yellow bell in duplicate st. With silver, work lower edge of white bell in same way.

Stocking: With green, cast on 30 sts. Following chart, work to top of chart. Bind off. With white and red yarns, embroider candy canes and lollipop.

Santa: With green, cast on 30 sts. Following chart, work to top of chart. Bind off. With black yarn, embroider eyes. With red yarn, embroider cheeks, nose and mouth.

Wreath: With red, cast on 30 sts. Following chart, work to top of chart. Bind off. With red yarn, embroider berries in duplicate st or French knots.

Boy Skater: With green, cast on 30 sts. Following chart, work to top of chart. Bind off. Embroider as for girl skater.

FINISHING: Sew strips tog. With red, work 1 rnd sc around wall hanging, working 3 sc in each corner. Join; end off. Cut flannel 2″ wider and 14″ longer than knitted piece. Turn under 1″ seam allowance at top and side edges. Baste flannel to back, then stitch top and side edges. At lower edge, form point at center by bringing 2 halves of bottom edge tog. Stitch center seam. Turn under row edge at top of triangle and stitch. To hold knitting in place on lining, stitch across wall hanging on edges of red motifs.

To form heading at top, cut flannel 2″ wider than knitted piece and 6″ deep. Turn under 1″ at each end of strip and stitch. Turn under ½″ along both long edges, place edges tog; baste edges to top of wall hanging; stitch in place. Stitch fringe braid across fold edge of heading on front; stitch again ½″ below first row. Put curtain rod through heading. Attach red braid to ends of rod for hanging piece. Stitch fringe braid across lower edge of wall hanging. With white embroidery floss, embroider names on triangular extension at bottom of wall hanging. Add flower trims, if desired. Make 5″ tassel from red yarn. Sew to bottom point.

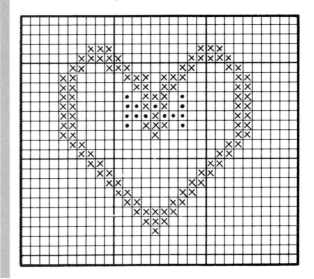

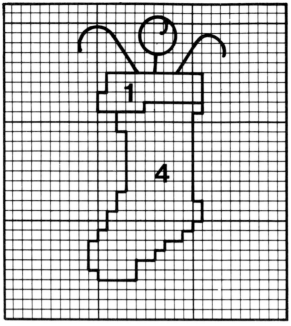

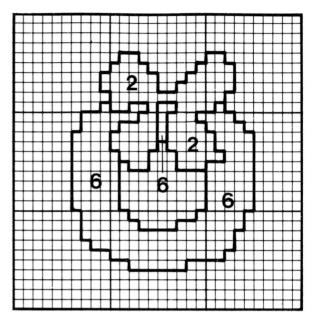

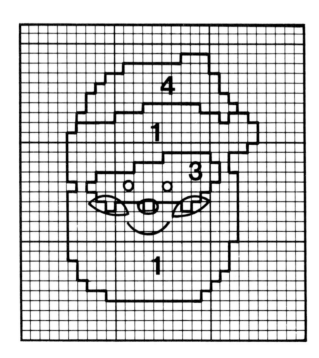

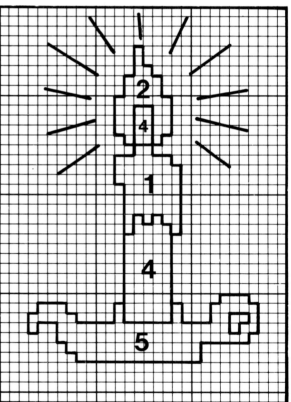

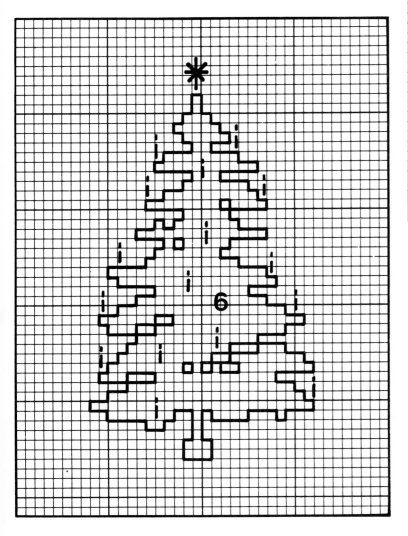

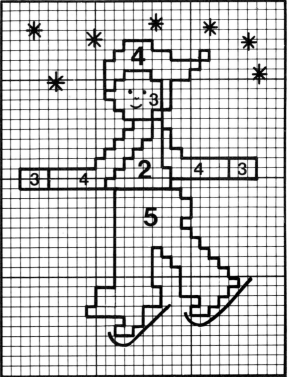

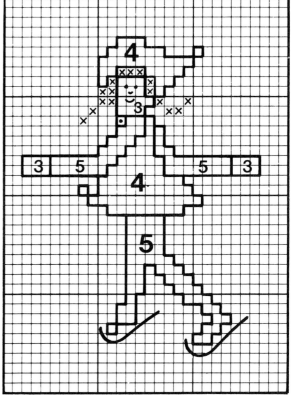

- ▣ White 1
- ☒ Yellow 2
- √ Black 5
- ▬ Green 6
- ⦿ Red 4
- Beige 3

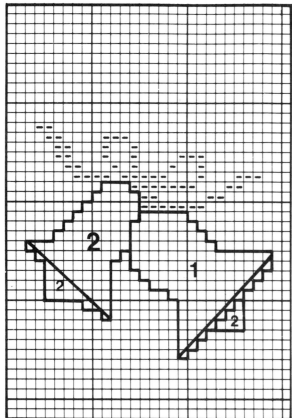

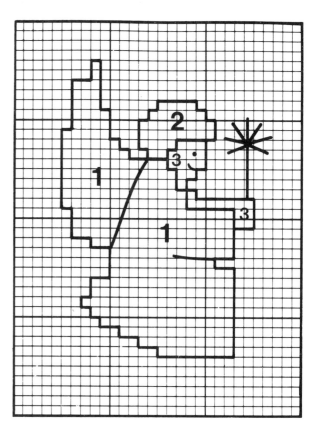

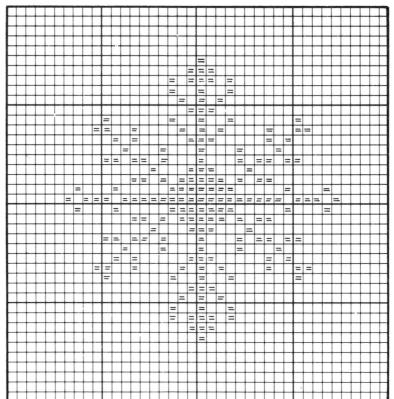

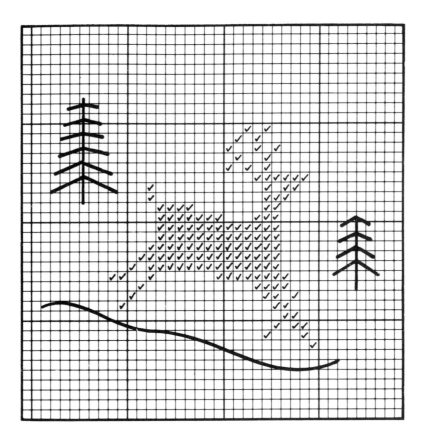

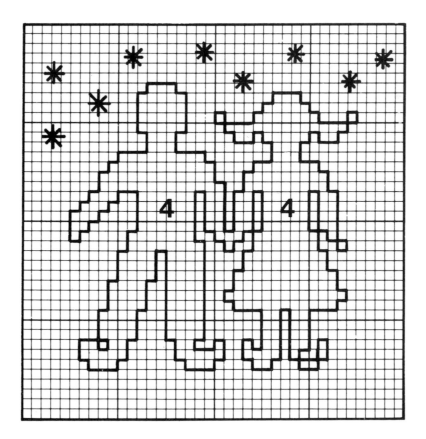

NEEDLEWORK SANTAS

The tiny stockings—perfect size for decorating a tree or wreath—are needlepoint, while Santa and his reindeer friends are mostly cross-stitch embroidery.

TINY STOCKINGS

See General Directions for needlepoint and embroidery

SIZE: About 6″ high.

EQUIPMENT: Pencil. Ruler. Scissors. Masking tape. Tapestry and sewing needles. Sewing machine. Pin.

MATERIALS: For each: Mono needlepoint canvas 8″ × 9″ piece; 18 mesh-to-the-inch. Six-strand embroidery floss; 2 skeins of first color listed in color key, one skein of other floss colors, plus small amounts black, red, and gold (Tree Stocking only) metallic threads. Velveteen, 5″ × 8″ piece, and gingham, two 5″ × 8″ pieces, to match or contrast with needlepoint. Sewing thread.

DIRECTIONS: Prepare canvas for each stocking as directed. Place canvas with 8″ edges at top and bottom.

For Wreath Stocking: Measure 1½″ down and 3″ in from upper right corner of canvas for first stitch; mark mesh with pin. Work design in needlepoint (continental or diagonal stitch), following chart and color key; first stitch is indicated by arrow. Each symbol or blank square on chart represents one stitch; different symbols represent different colors;

large areas of one color are indicated by a number. Disregard heavy lines and large dots while working needlepoint. Use all 6 strands of floss in needle; for metallic threads, use number of strands needed to cover canvas. When needlepoint is completed, embroider details over work. Backstitch eyes and mouth with black and red floss; make a French-knot berry at each large dot with red metallic thread. Block stocking if necessary.

For Tree Stocking: Measure 3″ down and 3″ in from upper right corner for first stitch; mark mesh. Beginning at arrow, work tree, Santa, and holly leaves in needlepoint and embroider details; see Wreath Stocking. Counting squares on chart, mark outline of stocking on canvas. Fill in background with mosaic stitch; see detail. Block if necessary.

FINISHING: Cut out canvas stocking ¼″ outside needlepoint all around. Use canvas piece as pattern to cut two lining pieces from gingham and one backing piece from velveteen. Turn margin at top edge of canvas stocking to wrong side, slashing as necessary; pin. Using floss in background color, overcast canvas edge. Turn top edge of velveteen piece ¼″ to wrong side. With right sides facing, stitch canvas and velveteen pieces together, making ¼″ seam and leaving top open; turn to right side. Stitch gingham pieces together in same manner, leave wrong side out, but

turn top edge ¼″ to outside. Place gingham lining inside canvas/velvet stocking. Using embroidery floss to match stocking background or lining, braid a 4″ length with three groups of 6 strands each; tie ends together to form loop for hanging. Insert braided loop end ¼″ into upper left corner between lining and stocking; slip-stitch edges together, securing loop.

COLOR KEY

2	Yellow
•	White
√ 1	Green
	Beige
╱	Red
■	Maroon
	Red Metallic
●	Black Metallic

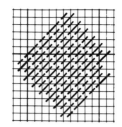

MOSAIC STITCH: Take long and short stitches alternately in diagonal rows. In each row, work a short stitch into end of a long stitch and a long stitch into end of a short stitch.

COLOR KEY

2	Light Green
•	White
	Beige
√ 1	Green
╱	Red
■	Maroon
✕	Gold Metallic
●	Black Metallic

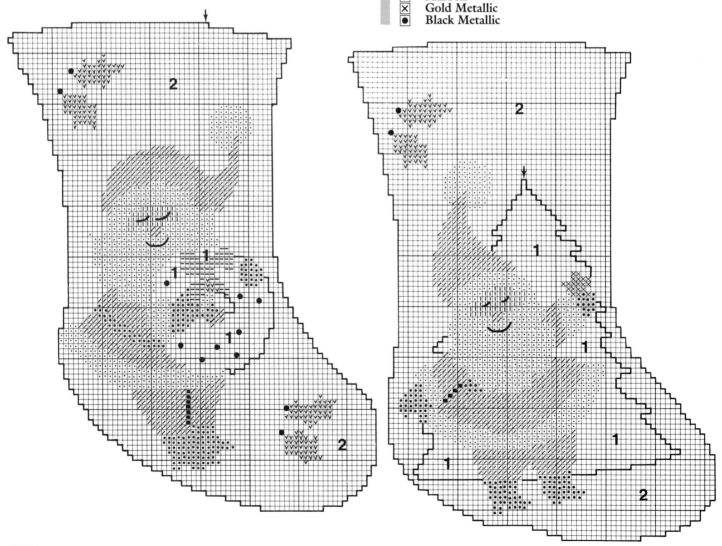

Reindeer B

Reindeer A

COLOR KEY

⊠	Gold
◱	Dark Gold
✔	Brown
▭	Light Green
◿	Dark Green

⊂	Orange
◫	Peach
	Pink
●	Red
▲	Maroon

N	Lavender
◯	Light Blue
▤	Medium Blue
	Dark Blue
◼	Black

| ⊡ | White |
| ⊡ | Ecru (pearl cotton) |

SANTA AND FRIENDS

SIZE: Design area, approx. 7½" × 9".

EQUIPMENT: Ruler. Embroidery and regular scissors. Sewing, tapestry, and darning needles. Straight pin. Embroidery hoop.

MATERIALS: Aida fabric, 11 threads-to-the-inch, 12" × 14" piece white. Six-strand embroidery floss, one skein each color listed in color key. Mercerized knitting and crochet cotton, one skein ecru. Scrap of gold metallic thread.

DIRECTIONS: Prepare fabric as directed. Measure 2½" down and in from upper left corner for placement of first stitch; mark fabric thread with pin. Place fabric in hoop. Using two strands of embroidery floss or pearl cotton in needle throughout, work outer red line of border, then lettering and figures, etc., in cross-stitch, following chart and color key and beginning at stitch marked by arrow on chart. Each symbol on chart represents one cross-stitch worked over one "square" of fabric; different symbols represent different colors; heavy lines indicate details to be worked after all embroidery is completed; heavy circles indicate French knots to be worked over cross-stitches. When cross-stitch is completed, embroider details as follows (refer to illustration): With two strands of gold floss in needle, backstitch Reindeer B's antlers; with two strands of brown floss, backstitch Reindeer A's antlers, straight-stitch a mouth for Reindeer A and a mouth for doll, and make French knot eyes and nose for doll; using two strands of black floss, make eyes for Santa and both reindeer and a nose for Reindeer B, and backstitch zigzag trim on Santa's coat; using four stands of red floss, make nose for Reindeer A and, using two strands of red floss, straight-stitch mouth for Reindeer B; using all six strands of pink floss in needle, make three French knots for Santa's nose; using all six strands of light green floss in needle, chain-stitch collar on Reindeer A, as shown in illustration; with three strands of gold metallic thread, make French knot for bell in center of Reindeer A's collar; using all six strands of white floss in needle, make ½" turkey work loops for Santa's beard, then cut loop ends. For sack's tie, using 12 strands of maroon floss and following illustration, make a straight stitch over neck of sack from right to left; make a second loose straight stitch from sack to Santa's mitten; run stitch under fabric and up through top left corner of mitten; cut 1" end. Backstitch inner border using two strands light blue floss for light lines and two strands dark blue for heavy lines; work over one square of fabric except at each corner, where light blue is worked over two squares. For each reindeer's tail, use 20 strands of white floss in a darning needle; pull floss from front to back through bottom left corner of blank square, leaving ⅜" end; pull floss up through bottom right corner of square and back through top left corner, securing tail; knot thread. For Santa's tassel, use 18 strands of pearl cotton in darning needle; knot thread, then pull thread up from back of work at tip of Santa's cap; make loop ¾" long and thread needle back through fabric one square below first stitch; secure loop with two straight stitches crossing top of loop; cut bottom of loop to make tassel. After all embroidery is completed, remove fabric from hoop. Steam-press gently on padded surface. Mount and frame as desired.

CHRISTMAS SAMPLER

Embroider a "recipe" for a merry Christmas! Favorite toys and holiday goodies add to the fun.

See General Directions for embroidery.

SIZE: Design area, 11¾″ × 8½″.

EQUIPMENT: Masking tape. Ruler. Tapestry needle. Embroidery hoop and scissors.

MATERIALS: Aida fabric, 14″ × 11″ piece white, 14 threads-to-the-inch. Six-strand embroidery floss, one skein of each color listed in color key.

DIRECTIONS: Prepare fabric as directed. To begin embroidery, measure 1⅛″ in from left 11″ edge and 1¼″ down from top 14″ edge; mark thread with pin. Place fabric in hoop. Work each cross-stitch over a "square" of one horizontal and one vertical fabric thread, using two strands of floss in needle. Start first stitch at pin, with top motif of left border; follow chart and color key to complete cross-stitches, indicated on chart by symbols. After cross-stitches are completed, work backstitches, indicated by heavy lines on chart, using two strands of floss in needle: Work the first four lines of phrase, boat sails, teddy bear's nose, Santa's hair, beard and pompon, doll's shoes, rocking horse's body, and lollypop sticks in black; work MERRY CHRISTMAS outlines, Jack-in-the box's mouth, Santa's mouth, doll's nose and mouth, gingerbread men's mouths, and house sides and red roof tile edge in red; work Santa's nose in flesh; work rocking horse's reins and green roof tile edge in green; work yellow roof tile edge in yellow; work pink roof tile edge in pink.

After all embroidery is completed, remove fabric from hoop. Finish, following general directions; frame as desired.

<u>**COLOR KEY**</u>

◨ Dark Green	· Pink	= Blue
● Light Green	▯ Flesh	✕ Brown
▱ Red	◩ Yellow	◼ Black

WINTER WALL HANGING

Choice fabric scraps go into this appliqué creation, which you embroider for detail interest then quilt for a textured effect.

See General Directions for appliqué, embroidery, and quilting.

MATTED SIZE: 22½" × 28".

EQUIPMENT: Paper for patterns. Tracing paper. Pencil. Ruler. Dressmaker's tracing (carbon) paper. Scissors. Tailor's chalk. Tracing wheel or dry ball-point pen. Straight pins. Sewing and embroidery needles. **For Mat:** X-Acto knife; metal straight edge.

MATERIALS: Unbleached muslin, 36" wide, ½ yard. Batting, 18" × 24". Blue cotton print fabric for sky, 36" wide, ¼ yard. White embroidered cotton for snow background, 36" wide, ½ yard. Large and small pieces of print and plain fabrics as illustrated or as desired which are suitable for the appliqués. Six-strand embroidery floss; three skeins dark brown, two skeins red-brown, one skein each white, black, red, blue, green, flesh, yellow, tan, orange, and purple or as desired. Sewing thread to match fabrics. Print fabric for mat, 36" wide, ¾ yard. Mounting cardboard and mat board (same size as matted size given above). Rubber cement. Double and single-faced masking tape.

DIRECTIONS:

To Make Patterns: Enlarge complete pattern below by copying on paper ruled in 1" squares. The heavier lines on pattern indicate pieces to be cut out and appliquéd. The finer lines indicate what is to be embroidered. Trace pattern for each appliqué piece.

To Make Background: Using separate patterns, cut fabric background piece for sky and pieces for ground, adding ¼" to top, sides, and bottom edges. Cut batting and muslin for backing, both 18" × 24". Place the muslin under batting; place background fabrics on top of batting, overlapping the lower pieces of background on upper pieces ¼". Turn top edge of lower fabrics under ¼" and, with running stitch and double strand of thread, sew together through all layers where they overlap.

Quilt background with double strand of matching sewing thread using tiny running stitches. Use a random pattern for quilting or select a pattern appropriate to the design.

To Make Appliqués: Place separate patterns on the particular fabric for a specific part of the scene. Insert carbon between and, with tracing wheel or dry ball-point pen, transfer the outline to the fabric. Cut the individual pieces out of fabric, adding ¼″ all around each piece. Fold under ¼″ along each edge of each piece; press. Using double strand of matching sewing thread, appliqué each piece in place on background with tiny running stitches, going through all layers. Cut the separate pieces for each building and sew pieces for each together before appliquéing complete structure to background.

To Embroider: Work with all six strands of floss in needle. Embroider through top background layer of fabric only; do not work through all layers. Follow illustration for colors of floss to be used or work in colors desired. Embroider all tree trunks and heavy branches in satin stitch; work thinner branches in outline stitch. Fill in windows with white satin stitch; make outlines in straight stitch in contrasting colors. Outline barn door in wide outline stitch. Work weather vane in

S. HESSE

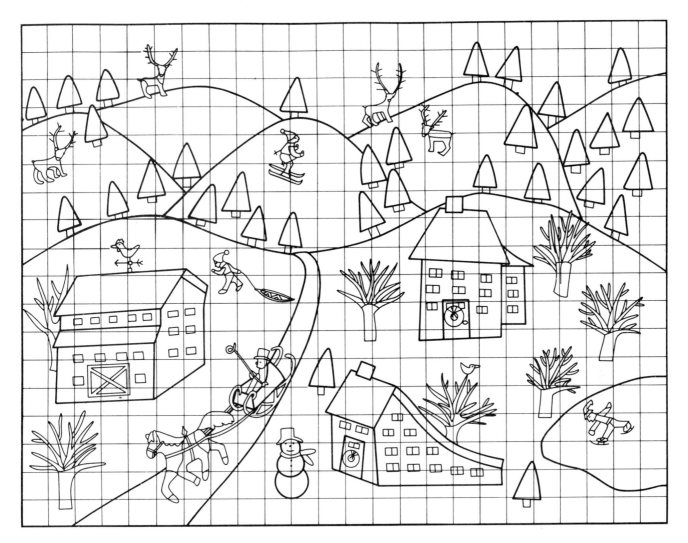

straight stitches, rooster in satin stitch. Both wreaths are in satin stitch with bows in straight stitch. Embroider horse in satin stitch, reins in outline stitch. Make runners of horse-drawn sleigh in outline stitch, as well as man's whip, belt, and hat brim. All men's bodies and clothes are in satin stitch, single straight lines indicate straight stitch. Sled is in outline stitch, rope is in long chain stitches. Skiis are in outline stitch. Ski poles and skate blades are in chain stitch. Reindeers' bodies and features are in satin stitch, antlers are in outline stitch; straight lines indicate straight stitch. Make snowman's mouth in chain stitch, hat, scarf, details in satin stitch.

To Make Mat: Cut opening 17½″ × 23¼″ in center of mat board using X-Acto knife and straight edge. Spread rubber cement over one surface of mat and cover with fabric; pull excess fabric over outer edge to other side and cement in back to secure. Clip into center of fabric and cut out 1½″ away from inner edges of mat. Clip into corners to edge of mat; fold fabric over to back and cement. Tape finished fabric scene to center of mounting cardboard. Place double-faced masking tape around edge of mounting cardboard; place mat over picture and cardboard and press to secure. Frame if desired.

CHRISTMAS TREE WALL HANGING

No room for a big tree? All you need for this one—made of twenty pieced blocks, individually quilted—is a bare wall.

See General Directions for quilting stitch.

SIZE: 71″ × 57″.

EQUIPMENT: Pencil. Ruler. Scissors. Thin, stiff cardboard. Sewing needle. Sewing machine (optional). Iron.

MATERIALS: Closely woven cotton or cotton-blend fabric, 45″ wide (with yardage in parentheses): solid shades of bright green (⅜), dark green (⅝), olive (⅔), white and red (⅛ each); small-scale prints of blue (2), green (⅝), blue-green (½), light, dark, and medium brown, and yellow with red (⅛ each). Muslin, 80″ wide, 1⅔ yards. Dacron batting with glazed finish. White sewing thread.

DIRECTIONS: Wall hanging is made up of 20 pieced blocks. Blocks are pieced and quilted separately, in one operation, then arranged and joined for complete design.

Patterns: To make blocks, cut cardboard patterns as follows, labeling each one: Piece A—1¾″ square; piece A-B—3½″ square. The remaining pieces are strips, all 1¾″ wide; cut in following lengths: Piece B—3½″; C—5¼″; D—7″; E—8¾″; F—10½″; G—12¼″; H—14″. Use patterns for cutting patch pieces as follows; if pattern edges begin to fray, discard and cut duplicates.

Patch Pieces: Using cardboard patterns, cut patch pieces for each block as indicated. Lay fabric out flat, wrong side up. Lay pattern on fabric, with edges following grain. Using sharp, hard pencil, draw around pattern; hold pencil at an outward angle, with point firmly against edge of pattern. Position remaining patterns to be cut from same fabric at least ½″ from each other. Cut out patches ¼″ from marked line, which will be stitching line.

(Note: Before cutting patches from blue print fabric, cut strip 8″ × 72″ and set aside, to be used later for binding edges.)

Assembling Block. For each block, cut muslin and one layer of batting, both 15″ square. Baste these two pieces together. Begin piecing and quilting from center of block outward, following Diagram I or II as indicated and making either Center 1 or Center 2 (see Diagram III).

Center 1 Blocks: With ruler and pencil, mark two corner-to-corner diagonal lines on batting, crossing at center of square. Lay piece A-B right side up in center of batting, with corners touching diagonal lines; do not turn under seam allowance, but baste piece in place. Lay strip B to right or left of A-B piece (following Diagram I or II); turn B over onto A-B so that right sides are together and stitch ¼″ from outside long edge through all thicknesses on marked seam line. Turn B back to right side and press very lightly along seam. Lay a C strip above the two pieces

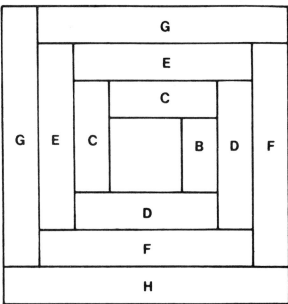

DIAGRAM I

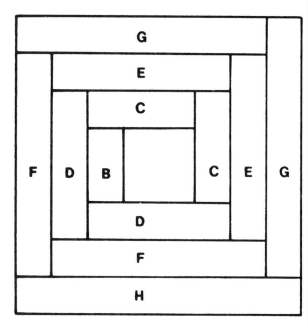

DIAGRAM II

joined, then turn over so that right sides are together and a long edge of C strip matches combined top edges of A-B and B pieces. Stitch C in same manner as before; turn back to right side and press. Add second C piece to center, following Diagram I or II. Add lower D piece. Continue adding pieces in sequence,

working around in a counterclockwise direction if following Diagram I or a clockwise direction if following Diagram II. When H piece has been added, finished patchwork should measure 14½" square, incuding the outside seam allowance. Stitch all around block to secure, ½" from edge of muslin and batting, ¼" from edge of patchwork.

Center 2 Blocks: Draw a horizontal and vertical line through center of batting. To begin center design, place designated A square, right side up, in upper left quadrant of batting, with piece overlapping center lines by ¼" (seam allowance). Baste piece in place, without turning under seam allowance. Place second A piece over first A piece, right sides together; stitch along right edge through all thicknesses on marked seam line. Turn second A piece over to right side, so it lies in upper right quadrant of batting; press lightly. Place designated B piece over A pieces, right sides together; stitch along lower edge on marked seam line. Turn B piece over to right side and press, completing Center 1. Add second B piece and all other pieces in sequence; see directions for Center 1 Blocks.

Make 20 blocks for hanging as follows; see Diagram IV.

Blocks 1, 20: Using patterns, cut and assemble pieces in this order, referring to Diagrams II and III (Center 1): blue print A-B, blue-green print B, blue-green print C, green print C, green print D, blue print D, blue print E, blue-green print E, blue-green print F, green print F, green print G, blue print G, blue print H.

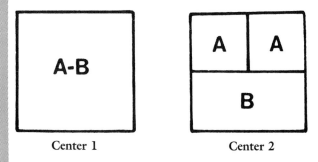

Center 1   Center 2

DIAGRAM III

Blocks 2, 13: Cut and assemble pieces in this order, referring to Diagrams I and III (Center 2): white A, red A, yellow B, bright green B, bright green C, blue-green print C, blue-green print D, dark green D, dark green E, green print E, green print F, olive F, olive G, blue print G, blue print H.

Blocks 3, 16: Cut same pieces as Block 2, but follow Diagram II to assemble; begin with red A.

Blocks 4, 17: Cut same pieces as for Block 1, but follow Diagram I to assemble.

Blocks 5, 9: Same as Block 2, but begin with red A.

Blocks 6, 10: Cut and assemble pieces in this order, referring to Diagrams I and III (Center 2): red A, white A, yellow B, bright green B, bright green C, olive C, olive D, dark green D, dark green E, dark green E, dark green F, olive F, olive G, bright green G, bright green H.

Blocks 7, 11: Cut same pieces as Block 6, but follow Diagram II to assemble and begin with white A.

Blocks 8, 12: Same as Block 3, but begin with white A.

Block 14: Same as block 6, but begin with white A.

Block 15: Same as block 7, but begin with red A.

Block 18: Cut and assemble pieces in this order, following Diagrams II and III (Center 1): light brown A-B, blue-green B, blue-green C, light brown C, light brown D, green print D, green print E, dark brown E, dark brown F, blue print F, blue print G, medium brown G, medium brown H.

Block 19: Cut same pieces as Block 18, but follow Diagram I to assemble.

Assembling Quilt: When all 20 blocks are completed, set them out in 5 horizontal rows of 4 blocks each, following Diagram IV. Turn blocks as necessary to make the design; see color illustration for position of center pieces.

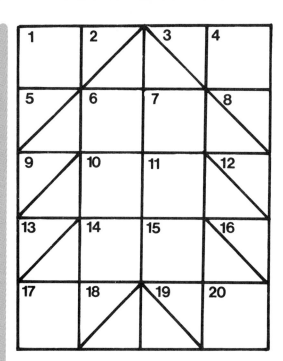

DIAGRAM IV

Stitch blocks together in rows, then stitch rows together, following seams already stitched around edge of blocks. Hanging should measure 71″ × 57″, including seam allowance around outside edges.

For hanging loops, cut 5 pieces from blue print fabric 3″ × 6″. Fold each in half lengthwise, right side inward, and stitch ¼″ from long edges. Turn strips to right side and press, with seam centered on one side. Fold strips in half widthwise, center seam inward. Stitch strips to back of hanging, matching raw edges at top and making ½″ seams; place one at each end and where blocks join.

To bind edges, use the 8″ × 72″ strip cut previously from blue print fabric to cut four strips 2″ wide, two 57½″ long and two 71″ long. Place longer strips on sides of hanging, right sides together and raw edges flush; stitch ½″ from outer edge. Fold strips around edges of hanging to back, making ½″ border; turn in raw edges ¼″, and slip-stitch folded edges to muslin. Turn in ends of shorter strips ¼″ and press. Bind top and bottom edges of hanging in same manner as sides, using shorter strips and enclosing ends of loops.

FILET CROCHET STOCKING

Create a feeling of old-time Christmas elegance with this unusual stocking made of ecru cotton mesh, set off with red velvet cuff and lining.

See General Directions for crochet.

SIZE: 23″ long.

EQUIPMENT: Steel crochet hook No. 8, or size required to obtain gauge. Straight pins. Tailor's chalk. Sewing machine.

MATERIALS: Pearl cotton No. 5, 4 balls ecru. Red velvet, ¾ yd. Matching sewing threads.

GAUGE: 3 sps or bls = 1″; 4 rows = 1″.

FILET PIECE: Beg at top of stocking, ch 68.

Row 1: Dc in 4th ch from hook (counts as 2 dc), (ch 2, sk 2 ch, dc in next ch) 21 times, dc in last ch—21 sps. Ch 3, turn.

Rows 2 and 3: Ski first dc, dc in next dc, (ch 2, dc in next dc) 21 times, dc in top of ch 3. Ch 3, turn.

Row 4 (right side): Sk first dc, dc in next dc, (ch 2, dc in next dc) 10 times, dc in each of next 2 ch, dc in next dc (1 bl made), (ch 2, dc in next dc) 10 times, dc in top of ch 3. Ch 3, turn.

Row 5: Sk first dc, dc in next dc, (ch 2, dc in next dc) 9 times, dc in each of next 2 ch, dc in next dc (1 bl made), ch 2, sk 2 dc, dc in next dc (sp over bl made), dc in each of next 2 ch, dc in next dc (1 bl made), (ch 2, dc in next dc) 9 times, dc in top of ch 3. Ch 3, turn.

Continue to work from chart, keeping 2 dc at each side edge, reading chart from right to left on even-numbered rows and from left to right on odd-numbered rows, to end of row 58.

Row 59 (wrong side): Sk first dc, dc in next dc, (ch 2, dc in next dc) 21 times, ch 1, 2 dc in top of ch 3. Keep dc's and ch's at inc edge loose so as not to tighten edge of stocking.

Row 60: Sk first dc, dc in next dc, (ch 2, dc in next dc) 22 times, dc in top of ch 3—1 sp inc at beg of row. Ch 3, turn.

Rows 61–70: Continue to inc 1 sp at front of foot every other row as for rows 59 and 60.

Row 71 (wrong side): Work even in pat—27 sps.

Row 72: Work in pat across 26 sps, sk last sp, dc in next dc—1 sp dec. Turn.

Row 73: Sl st in next dc, ch 3, dc in next dc (1 sp dec), work in pat across 25 sps, ch 1, 2 dc in top of ch 3. Ch 3, turn.

Row 74: Sk first dc, dc in next dc, (ch 2, dc in next dc) 25 times, sk last sp, dc in next dc—1 sp dec. Turn.

Following chart, continue to dec 1 sp at heel edge of stocking every row to row 89, inc 1 sp at front edge of stocking every 4th row twice more; then work even on front

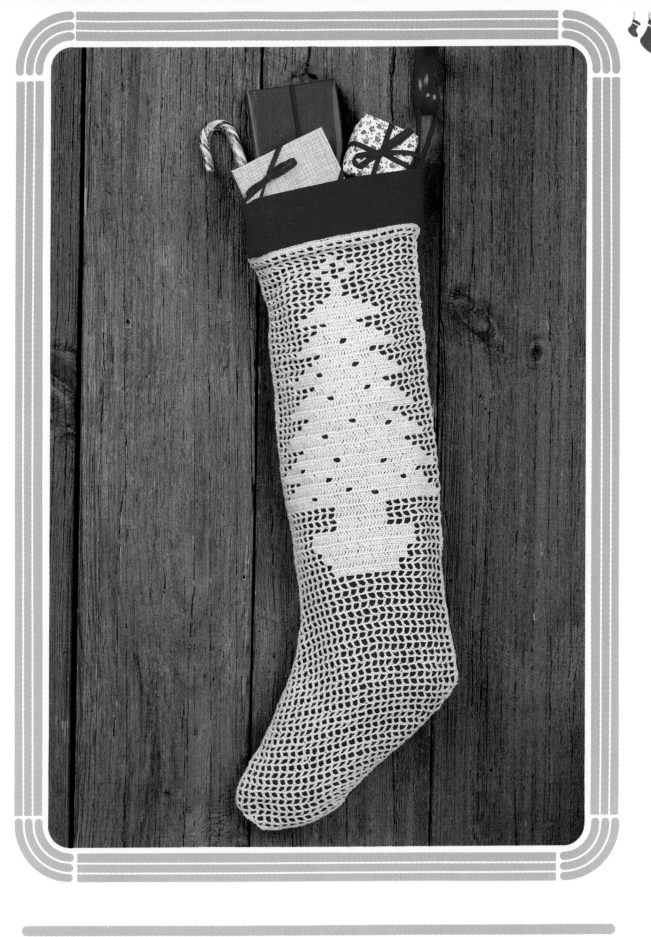

edge for 4 rows and dec 1 sp at front edge every row 3 times. At end of row 89, ch 1, turn. Sc in each st across last row. End off. Join thread in first ch at top of stocking, sc in each ch across. End off.

RED VELVET STOCKING: Fold velvet in half lengthwise, right side in. Using crocheted stocking as pattern, mark outline of stocking on velvet with tailor's chalk, so that nap runs from bottom to top. Set crocheted stocking aside. Pin velvet layers together 1/4" inside outline to prevent fabric from shifting. Cut out through both layers, adding 1/4" all around for seam allowance, for two stockings. With right sides facing, machine-stitch velvet stockings together around side and bottom edges, making 1/4" seams. Clip into seam

allowance at curves; turn to right side. Cut 2½"-deep velvet strip for cuff, wide enough to fit around stocking top, plus ½". Also cut 1⅛" × 10" strip for hanging loop. Stitch cuff ends together 1/4" from edges. Pin cuff to velvet stocking, right sides facing, with top edges even, matching seams at side above heel; stitch 1/4" from top edge. Baste raw cuff edge 1/4" to wrong side. Fold cuff to inside of stocking, overlapping, cuff/stocking joining; slipstitch in place.

For hanging loop: Fold strip in thirds lengthwise; topstitch ⅛" from each fold. Fold strip in half with ends even. Pin loop bottom to inside of cuff over side seam; tack securely in place.

To Finish: Pin crocheted stocking to velvet stocking front, so that crocheted edges are even with seams all around; slip-stitch in place.

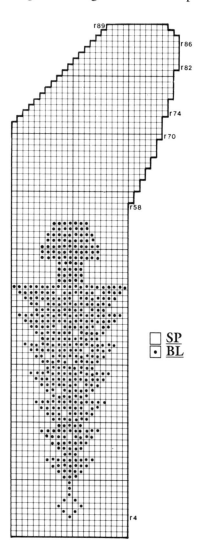

□ SP
· BL

BATIK STOCKINGS

The batik process, involving hot wax and paint, is an art form in many cultures. Once you learn the method here, you can use batik for many other practical and creative projects.

See General Directions at end of book for enlarging a pattern and for quilting stitch detail.

SIZE: 21″ long.

EQUIPMENT: Pencil. Ruler and yardstick. Paper for pattern. Tracing paper. Graph paper. Black waterproof marking pen. Tape. Scissors. Newspaper, waxed paper, brown paper bags. Hot plate. Double boiler. Stirring rods, such as inexpensive chopsticks. Immersible thermometer. Salt or baking soda (to extinguish fire, should it occur). Blunt knife. Tjanting tool (wax pen, used to apply hot wax to fabric in a continuous line) with fine spout. Thin wire for cleaning spout. Clean rag for catchcloth. Plastic cups. Natural-bristle paintbrushes: small, medium, and large. Rubber gloves. Plastic pail. Benzine. Detergent. Iron. Ironing board. Straight pins. Sewing needle. Sewing machine.

MATERIALS: Acrylic paint: white, gray, and assorted colors. Paraffin wax and beeswax. Polyester batting. To make three stockings: 45″-wide fabric, ¾ yard each: White crepe-backed satin; red cotton; green cotton velveteen. Red bias tape ½″ wide, 1½ yards. Red sewing thread.

GENERAL DIRECTIONS FOR BATIK STOCKINGS: Prepare patterns, following directions for completing stocking below; piece together paper for patterns and tracings as necessary. Darken lines with waterproof marker. Mark small section of one pattern on scrap of tracing paper for test sample. Wash satin fabric in warm water and detergent to pre-shrink and remove sizing; let dry; iron. Cover work surface with newspaper, then waxed paper and pattern. Place satin piece right side up and centered over pattern with design lines showing through; tape edges to secure. Using pencil, lightly transfer outline of stocking, then dotted lines for quilting. Leave pattern and satin piece in place.

Waxing Process: Work in a well-lighted, well-ventilated room. (Before beginning, use sample pattern and satin scrap to test waxing process below.) For best results, use ½ paraffin and ½ beeswax.

Place hot plate on work surface. Fill bottom of double boiler with 1½″ water; put wax in top of boiler. Place double boiler on hot plate (never over flame). Melt wax to about 80°C (170°F), stirring occasionally. Keep wax from overheating; when wax starts to smoke, it is too hot. Take great precautions not to spill or get water near pot of hot wax. Water will cause splattering and you can be severely burned! If fire occurs, extinguish flame with salt or baking soda, not water.

Work close to hot plate, keeping wax fluid at a constant temperature with dial control, if your hot plate has one, or by turning heat on and off as necessary. Fill tjanting tool with melted wax. Test wax first on satin scrap. Wax is ready for application when it makes a dark transparent mark on cloth; fabric should absorb wax immediately. If yellowish-white crust forms, wax is not hot enough; reheat and apply again to underside of fabric.

Trace design lines smoothly and evenly with spout of tjanting tool to transfer designs to fabric; do not trace pencil lines. If spout of tool clogs, clear passage with thin wire. Use catchcloth beneath tool to prevent wax from dripping on fabric. Should drips occur, carefully scrape both sides of fabric with a blunt knife or your fingernail, then fold and rub the area between your fingers. When all design lines have been transferred, remove pattern, then retape fabric piece in place.

To Paint Fabric: Tape fabric scrap to work surface for test sample. Place a small amount of each color paint, except white, into individual cups. Blend in water until paints have the consistency of ink. Mix paints together in additional cups to obtain desired colors (see color illustration). Use paintbrush to test colors on sample; if too pale, blend in more paint; if too dark, add a few drops of white; for muted colors, add a few drops of gray (**Note:** Colors will appear darker when wet.) Paint small areas of design first, then medium-sized areas, following illustrations for colors, or as desired. Paint background areas on stocking or quilt last, extending them to marked outlines. Let fabric dry thoroughly before removing from work surface.

To Remove Wax: To protect ironing board, cover section with paper bag. Place painted piece on ironing board between layers of paper bags; set iron for cotton. As the heat of the iron is applied to fabric, wax will melt and be absorbed by paper. Replace paper as it becomes saturated with wax. Repeat until all wax is absorbed and no wax shows on paper. Since heat is a color-fastening agent, iron entire piece well. To remove all wax, clean fabric thoroughly: Wearing rubber gloves, soak fabric for a few minutes in plastic pail filled with benzine; wring out. Wash in cold water and detergent to remove all benzine; let dry; iron.

To Quilt: Cut out painted front piece, lining, and batting. Lay lining flat, wrong side up. Place batting, then front piece on top, matching edges; baste lengthwise, crosswise, and diagonally. Quilt around each design, parts of designs, and quilting lines; use doubled red thread.

To Complete Stocking: Read General Directions for Batik Stockings above. Enlarge and trace stocking pattern. To prepare name band, mark on graph paper a 7″ × 2″ rectangle. Using markings on graph paper as a guide, write or print desired name within rectangle, spacing letters evenly. If name is too long, use nickname or initials. Transfer name to tracing, centering it within band. For three stockings, cut satin fabric into three pieces 15″ × 27″ Transfer outline to each piece; wax, omitting snowman's eyes, then paint, following directions above; remove wax. Use small paintbrush to carefully paint over "windowpane dividers" on background in paler shade (see illustration); let dry, then press fabric again. Cut out painted stocking front, adding ¾″ seam allowance at sides and bottom, and ½″ at top. Cut red cotton lining and batting same size as front piece. Assemble pieces, then quilt, following directions above. Work double-cross eyes on snowman, using same thread as for quilting.

From velveteen, cut stocking back same size as front. Pin back to front with wrong sides facing and edges even. Make French seam: Stitch sides and bottom, making ¼″ seams; turn stocking to wrong side. Stitch sides and bottom again, making ½″ seams; turn to right side. Cut bias tape to fit top edge of stocking, plus ½″. Unfold one long edge of tape; press under one short edge ¼″. With right sides facing and raw edges even, pin tape to stocking top, starting at pressed edge and lapping ends; stitch along fold. Press tape and ¼″ of stocking top to inside and slip-stitch. Cut 3″ length of bias tape for hanging loop. Press tape in half lengthwise; topstitch close to long open edges. Stitch loop to inside of stocking at top right corner.

Ornaments

Deck the halls!
Special decorations make Christmas even more
wonderful! There are more than a dozen different
techniques represented in this collection of
ornaments, tree skirts, candles, and crèche figures.
All full of down-home country charm!

NEEDLEPOINT ORNAMENTS

Stitch a tiny troupe of needlepoint folk to ornament your tree—Santa, soldier, elf, angels, and skater. Trim them with beads, bells, bits of felt, cotton, lace, and bright red yarn.

SIZES: Tree-top angel, 8"; other figures, 4½"-6½".

EQUIPMENT: Pencil. Ruler. Masking tape. Paper for patterns. Embroidery and regular scissors. Tapestry and sewing needles. Straight pins. **For Skater:** Wire cutters. Pliers. **For Tree-top Angel:** Sewing machine. Steam iron.

MATERIALS: Mono needlepoint canvas, 12 mesh-to-the-inch, 36" wide, ¾ yard for all figures and tree-top angel (or 15" × 9" piece for each figure, and 29" × 10" piece for tree-top angel). Red Persian-type yarn, one 12-yard skein of each color in color keys, unless otherwise indicated in parentheses. Metallic thread, one spool each of gold, silver, and pink. Sewing thread. Polyester fiberfill. All-purpose white glue. **For Elf:** Dark green felt, piece 3" × 4". One ⅜" jingle bell. Two round ¼"-diameter silver beads. **For Santa:** White ⅝"-diameter pompon. **For Soldier:** Scrap of black felt. Black six-strand embroidery floss. Gold metallic flat braided trim ⅜" wide, piece 2" long. **For Little Angel:** White flat lace trim ⅜" wide, 1¼ yards. Inexpensive jeweled chain, 1½" long. **For Skater:** Black felt, piece 3" × 4". Two small steel paper clips (1¼" long). **For Tree-top Angel:** White ruffled lace trim ⅜" wide, ¾ yard. Cotton fabric for lining, piece 6" × 12". Silver metallic round braided trim 1/16" diameter, piece 4½". Two pink ½"-diameter pompons. Clear or silver sequins, ⅛" diameter.

GENERAL DIRECTIONS FOR NEEDLEPOINT ORNAMENTS: With pencil, mark a 2" margin all around canvas. Mark two 5" squares inside margin for each figure (one for front and one for back), placing squares 1" apart; mark two 12" × 6" rectangles, 1" apart, for tree-top angel front and back; reserve extra space on canvas for angels' wings (or use scrap of finer mesh canvas, if desired). Tape canvas edges to prevent raveling. Do not cut out individual pieces until directed.

To Work Needlepoint: Cut yarn and metallic thread into 18" lengths. Separate strands of yarn and work with two strands in needle throughout. Use enough strands of metallic thread in needle to equal thickness of two strands of Persian-type yarn. When starting first working strand, leave 1" of yarn on back of canvas and cover it as work proceeds; your first few stitches will anchor it in place. To end strand or to begin a new one, run yarn under a few stitches on back of work; do not make knots. Work needlepoint on all pieces in either continental or diagonal stitch (see stitch details, next page); work embroidery (see General Directions for embroidery at end of book). Begin each piece in upper right corner of marked area on canvas by counting squares in from corresponding chart outline; maintain indicated spaces between pieces. Each square on chart represents one mesh on canvas; different symbols represent different colors (see color keys); letters in blank areas also represent colors, for clothing; blank areas without letters represent pale pink, for flesh, unless otherwise indicated. Work each piece of each figure, following chart, color keys, and individual directions.

When all pieces are completed, block entire canvas if necessary, following directions in back of book. Disregarding pencil guidelines, cut out pieces, three canvas meshes beyond last row of stitches all around.

To Assemble Dolls: Fold canvas margins to back of work on each piece. Place bodies together, wrong sides facing and matching folded edges; whipstitch together, using matching yarn and working through last row of needlepoint on each edge; leave straight edge open, at top or bottom. Stuff body firmly with fiberfill; stitch opening closed. Assemble head pieces as for body. Fold arm, leg, and foot pieces in half vertically; stitch and stuff as for body. Slip-stitch head to neck edge; wrap yarn around joining several times and secure at neck back. Slip-stitch arms to shoulders with long seams facing back. For elf, soldier, and Santa, slip-stitch legs to bottom straight edge of body. For skater, stitch one leg to body in same manner; stitch second leg to panty edge at opposite side. For little angel, stitch feet, centered, to bottom edge of body with short seams at front and back and folded edges touching. See individual directions for assembling tree-top angel.

To Finish: Using sharp colored pencil, draw lines across patterns, connecting grid lines. Enlarge patterns (see General Directions at end of book) by copying on paper ruled in

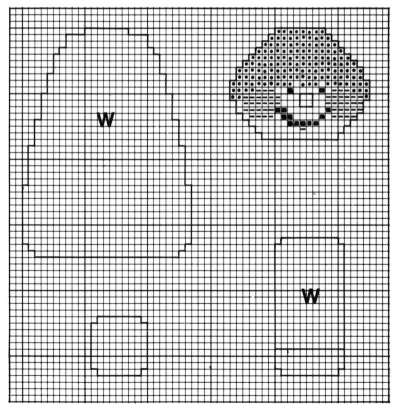

W White
☐ Pale Pink
⊟ Pink
⊙ Burnt Orange
◼ Black

LITTLE ANGEL

½″ squares; complete half patterns, indicated by dash lines. Cut out patterns and use to finish figures, following individual directions.

Hanger: From metallic thread, cut a 5″ length for each hanger. Use sewing needle to thread length through top of hat or "curls"; remove needle and tie ends of thread together.

ELF: Read General Directions above.

To Stitch: Work body front and back, two arms, and two legs, working each second piece as for first. Work needlepoint on head front, leaving nose blank. To work head back, work hat back same as front; work bottom three rows (neck) with pale pink; work hair between, using burnt orange. Fill in nose with pale pink satin stitch; for mouth, work a straight stitch, using rose. Cut out completed pieces and assemble, following General Directions above.

To Finish: Cover hair with turkey work "curls" (see Stitch Details), in matching yarn. Using enlarged patterns A and B, cut from dark green felt one A (collar) and three B's (hat trim and cuffs). Place collar around neck, overlapping ends at center back; glue in place, or tack invisibly with matching thread. Place one B, pointed edge up, around bottom of hat; tack or glue as for collar. Cut remaining B's in half widthwise for cuffs. Place one cuff around each "wrist" and "ankle" and secure. Sew jingle bell to top of hat. Sew a silver bead to toe of each foot. Make hanger and attach, following General Directions.

SANTA: Read General Directions above.

To Stitch: Work body front and back and two arms, working second pieces as for first, except omitting belt buckle on body back. To work legs, turn canvas and chart sideways, so that bottom of boot is facing you; work two legs, beginning each where indicated by arrows. Turn canvas back to original position. Work needlepoint on head front, leaving nose blank. To work head back, work hat back same as front; work bottom three rows (neck) with pale pink; work area between

with white. Fill in nose with rose satin stitch. Cut out pieces and assemble, following General Directions.

To Finish: For "fur" trim, use white yarn to make matching turkey work loops (see Stitch Details) over white needlepoint stitches around sleeve and pants cuffs and band on jacket; also work three rows of loops below bottom of hat. For mustache, cut a narrow strip of fiberfill; tie a piece of white yarn around center; tack in place below nose. Cut fiberfill for beard and back of hair; glue in place. Cut a thin wisp of fiberfill and glue it below hat on forehead. Trim hair to shape. Stitch a small white pompon to top of hat. Make hanger and attach, following General Directions.

SOLDIER: Read General Directions above.

To Stitch: Work body front and back, two arms, and two legs; work second pieces as for first, except omitting belt buckle on body back and reversing stripe on second leg. Work needlepoint on head front, leaving nose blank. To work head back, work hat back same as front; work bottom three rows (neck) with pale pink; work hair between with burnt orange. Fill in nose with pale pink satin stitch; use two strands of black floss in needle to work mouth in outline stitch. Cut out pieces and assemble, following General Directions.

To Finish: Cover hair with turkey work "curls" (see Stitch Details), in matching yarn. Use enlarged pattern to cut hat brim from black felt. Place brim around bottom of hat front; tack at side seams. Use gold metallic thread to sew a ¼″ gold bead to each end of brim. To make hat band, wind gold thread back and forth around beads until band is desired thickness. Stitch six ¼″ gold beads (circles on chart) to front of jacket. Referring to color photograph, wind gold thread around beads as shown. Stitch ⅛″ bead to each outer sleeve below stripes. To make epaulets, cut flat gold trim into two equal lengths; cut across each corner, forming pointed ends. Fold each piece in half widthwise with a drop of glue between; hold between fingers until dry. Glue one epaulet to each shoulder with pointed end at neck edge. Make hanger and attach, following General Directions.

LITTLE ANGEL: Read General Directions above.

To Stitch: Work gown front and back, two arms, and two feet, working each second piece as for first. Work needlepoint on head front, leaving nose blank. To work head back, work bottom three rows (neck) with pale pink; work hair above with burnt orange. Fill in nose with pale pink satin stitch. Cut out pieces and assemble, following General Directions.

To Finish: Cover hair with turkey work "curls" (see Stitch Details), in matching yarn. For halo, arrange jeweled chain on top of head; tack ends to "curls." For ruffles: Cut flat lace trim into two equal lengths. To trim hem, use white thread and long running

DIAGONAL STITCH

CONTINENTAL STITCH

stitches to gather one piece of lace until it fits around bottom edge of gown; slip-stitch in place. Cut second piece of lace in half widthwise. Gather one piece to fit around neck for collar; tack in place at center back. In the same manner, cut remaining lace in half and make cuffs. For wings: Place scrap canvas over enlarged small wing pattern and mark shape; cut out. Coat wing edges with white glue and let dry; repeat several times. Using gold metallic thread, whipstitch wing edges, working several stitches in each mesh. Tack to doll at center of back. Make hanger and attach, following General Directions.

SKATER: Read General Directions above.

To Stitch: Work body front and back, two arms, and two legs, working each second piece as for first. Work needlepoint on head front, leaving nose blank. To work head back, work bottom three rows (neck) with pale pink; work hair above with burnt orange. Fill in nose with pale pink satin stitch; for mouth, work a straight stitch, using bright pink. Cut out pieces and assemble, following General Directions.

To Finish: Trim doll with turkey work loops (see Stitch Details), as follows: Cover hair with "curls" in matching yarn; work white "ruffles" around each cuff and around neck and leg joinings; work a bright pink "pompon" on each skate by making several loops through one stitch on toe. Use enlarged pattern to cut skirt from black felt; also cut two ⅛" × 3¾" strips for suspenders. Place skirt around doll, overlapping ends at center back; glue. Tuck suspenders into waist edges, criss-crossing them at center back; glue at waist and at criss-cross point to secure. To make each skate blade: Following diagram, cut paper clip with wire cutters, discarding sections indicated by dash lines. Use pliers to curl curved end inward (see photograph). Starting at heel of doll and working toward toe, slide straight edge of paper clip through bottom of foot. Make hanger and attach, following General Directions.

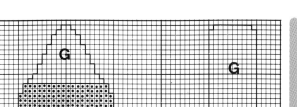

ELF

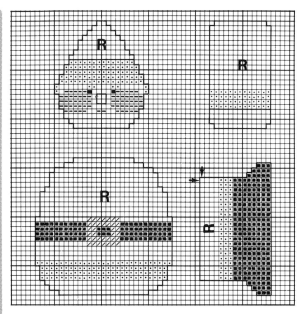

SANTA

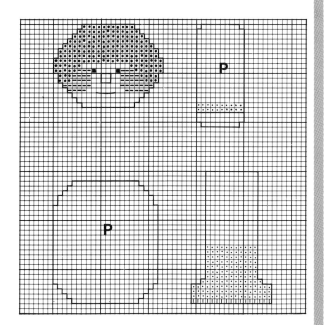

SKATER

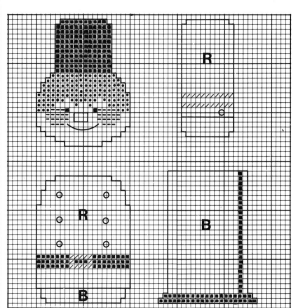

SOLDIER

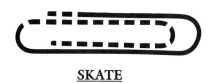

SKATE

· White		⊘ Gold metallic thread	
☐ Pale Pink		⊓ Silver metallic thread	
═ Rose		B Light Blue	
● Burnt Orange		G Bright Green	
⬕ Brown		P Bright Pink	
■ Black		R Red	

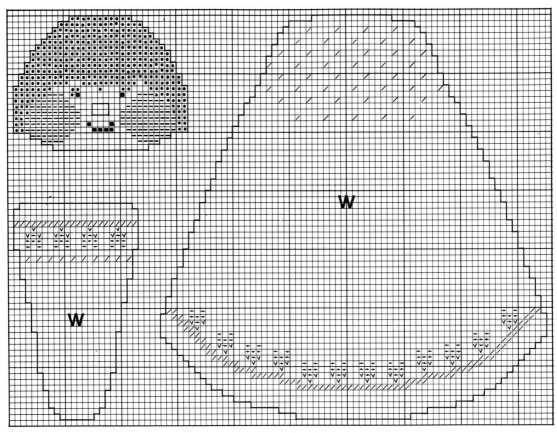

TREE-TOP ANGEL

W White
☐ Pale Pink
⊟ Pink
⊙ Burnt Orange
☑ Bright Green
◼ Black
⊕ Pink metallic thread
◫ Gold metallic thread

TREE-TOP ANGEL: Read General Directions above.

To Stitch: Work gown front and back and four sleeves, working second, third, and fourth pieces as for first. Work head front and back as for Little Angel. Cut out completed pieces, following General Directions.

To Assemble: Fold canvas margins to back on each piece. Assemble head and two sleeves, following General Directions. Use one gown piece to trace two linings on cotton fabric, adding ¼″ all around each for seam allowance; cut out linings and set aside. Stitch needlepoint gowns together, leaving curved hem edge open. Cut ruffled lace trim into two equal lengths. Starting at side seam of gown, pin one length of lace under folded hem edges, so that lace extends beyond hem; slip-stitch in

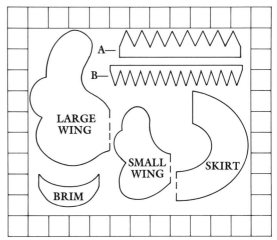

place. Pin linings together with right sides facing and edges even; machine-stitch around side and neck edges, making ¼″ seams; press hem ¼″ to wrong side. Insert lining into gown, wrong sides facing, matching neck and side seams. Working from inside lining, stitch through neck edges to secure. Slip-stitch lining to gown along one (back) edge of hem between side seams, matching folded edges. Stuff front.

ANGEL TRIMS

These quick-stitch angels add to any holiday decor:
The "I love you" angel picture is perfect for a mantel;
"Noel" angel, trimmed with jingle bells, hangs on an
inside door; while smaller angel ornaments accent
your wreath or tree.

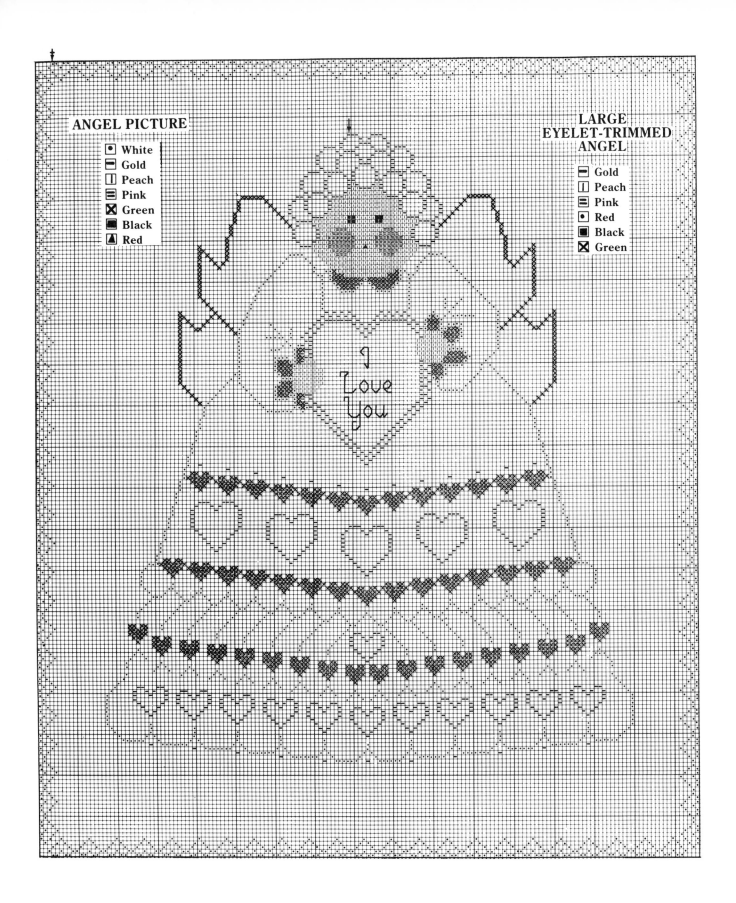

ANGEL PICTURE

- ☐ White
- ☐ Gold
- ☐ Peach
- ☐ Pink
- ☒ Green
- ☐ Black
- ◢ Red

LARGE EYELET-TRIMMED ANGEL

- ☐ Gold
- ☐ Peach
- ☐ Pink
- ☐ Red
- ☐ Black
- ☒ Green

I Love You

See General Directions for enlarging a pattern and for embroidery.

ANGEL PICTURE

SIZE: Design area, 11⅞″ × 13¾″.

EQUIPMENT: Pencil. Ruler. Scissors. Masking tape. Sewing and tapestry needles. Straight pin. Embroidery hoop.

MATERIALS: Aida fabric, 14 threads-to-the-inch, 15″ × 17″ piece red. Six-strand cotton embroidery floss: 2 skeins green; one skein each white, pink, peach, black; small amount red. Fine gold metallic thread. Heavy cardboard, piece 13″ × 15″. Green twisted cord ⅜″ diameter, 1¾ yards. Glue.

DIRECTIONS: Prepare fabric as directed. Measure 1⅝″ down and 1¾″ in from upper left corner of fabric for placement of first stitch; mark fabric thread with pin. Work border and angel in cross-stitch, following chart and color key and beginning at stitch marked by dagger on chart. Work each cross-stitch over one "square" of fabric, using three strands embroidery floss or two strands metallic thread in tapestry needle. Work "I Love You" in backstitch with black. After all embroidery is completed, remove fabric from hoop. Steam-press gently on padded surface.

To mount, center cardboard on wrong side of embroidered piece. Wrap excess fabric to back and glue in place. Cut twisted cord to fit perimeter, plus 1″; glue in place, overlapping ends at center bottom.

EYELET-TRIMMED ANGELS

SIZE: Small angel, 6¾″. Large angel, 13¼″.

EQUIPMENT: Pencil. Ruler. Scissors. Masking tape. Paper for pattern. Dressmaker's tracing (carbon) paper. Tracing wheel or dry ball-point pen. Sewing and tapestry needles. Sewing machine. Steam iron. Embroidery hoop. Straight pins.

MATERIALS: Even-weave Aida fabric, 14 threads-to-the-inch, white: 10″ square for small angel; 16″ square for large angel. Six-strand cotton embroidery floss: 2 skeins green; one skein each red, peach, pink, black. Fine gold metallic thread. Closely woven cotton fabric with holiday print: 8″ square for small angel; 13″ square for large angel. Piping: red for small angel; green for large angel. Pre-gathered white eyelet trim: 1″ wide, ½ yard for small angel: 2″ wide, ¾ yard for large angel. Satin ribbon: ⅛″ wide, ½ yard red for small angel; ⅜″ wide, ½ yard green for large angel. Jingle bells: five ⅜″ diameter for small angel; five ⅝″ diameter for large angel. Batting. Lightweight non-woven interfacing. Sewing thread to match fabrics and trims.

DIRECTIONS: **For each:** Draw lines across pattern, connecting grid lines. Enlarge pattern by copying on paper ruled in 1″ squares; complete half-pattern indicated by dash line. Using dressmaker's carbon and tracing wheel or dry ball-point pen, transfer pattern outline to wrong side of Aida fabric, including dot on pattern. Do not cut out shape, but baste a line down center of shape, between two rows of squares.

Prepare fabric edges as directed. Starting at top of basted center thread, measure ⅜″ down and one thread to the left for small angel and ½″ down and ⅜″ to the left for large angel; mark fabric thread with pin, for placement of first stitch. Work design by following chart and color key and beginning at stitch marked by arrow on chart (do not work border around large angel). Use three strands of embroidery floss or two strands of metallic thread throughout. Work each cross-stitch over one "square" of fabric. Work "NOEL" or "LOVE" in backstitch with black, centered in heart; see Contents for stitch details. Using red, work mouth with a straight stitch for small angel, a cross-stitch for large angel. After all embroidery is completed, remove fabric from hoop. Press gently on a padded surface.

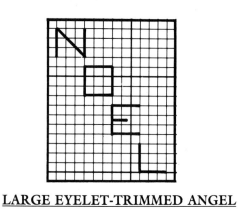

LARGE EYELET-TRIMMED ANGEL

Cut out embroidered front ¼″ beyond basted outline. Cut same-size back from print fabric, and one same-size lining each from batting and interfacing. Baste batting to wrong side of embroidered front. Baste interfacing to wrong side of back. Pin piping to right side of angel front around sides and top between dots, matching all raw edges. Baste in place; remove pins. With right sides facing, place angel front and back together, enclosing piping. Stitch with ¼″ seam, using zipper-foot attachment; leave bottom open;

SMALL EYELET-TRIMMED ANGEL

| ⊟ Gold | ⊟ Pink | ■ Black |
| Ⅱ Peach | ● Red | ☒ Green |

RED ORNAMENT

⊟ Gold
Ⅱ Peach
⊟ Pink
■ Black
☒ White
● Green

GREEN ORNAMENT

⊟ Gold
Ⅱ Peach
⊟ Pink
■ Black
● White
☒ Red

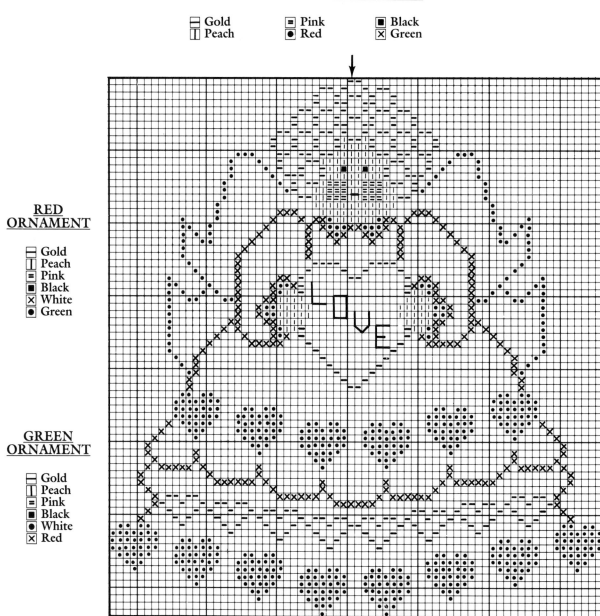

turn. Cut eyelet trim to fit around bottom opening, plus 1"; pin in place with right sides facing and unfinished edges even; stitch with ¼" seam. Press seam allowance up, so trim extends below angel. Topstitch all around, close to bottom fold. Tie satin ribbon in bow; tack to center top of angel. Tack jingle bells, evenly spaced, across bottom as shown.

ANGEL ORNAMENTS

SIZE: Each 5½" long.

EQUIPMENT: Pencil. Ruler. Scissors. Masking tape. Paper for pattern. Dressmaker's tracing (carbon) paper. Tracing wheel or dry ball-point pen. Sewing and tapestry needles. Sewing machine. Steam iron. Embroidery hoop. Straight pins.

MATERIALS: Even-weave Aida fabric, 14 threads-to-the-inch, 10" square red or green. Six-strand cotton embroidery floss: one skein each peach, pink, black, red, white, plus green for red ornament only. Fine gold metallic thread. Closely woven cotton fabric, 8" square holiday print. Piping, red or green, to contrast with Aida fabric. Satin ribbon ⅛" wide, ½ yard to match piping. Fiberfill. Sewing thread to match fabrics and trims.

DIRECTIONS: **For each:** Draw lines across pattern, connecting grid lines. Enlarge pattern by copying on paper ruled in 1" squares; complete half-pattern indicated by dash line.

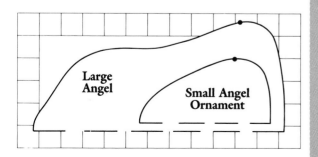

Using dressmaker's carbon and tracing wheel or dry ball-point pen, transfer pattern outline to wrong side of Aida fabric, centering on piece; ignore dots on pattern. Do not cut out shape, but baste to mark outline on right side; also baste a line down center of shape, between two rows of squares.

Prepare fabric edges as directed. Starting at top of basted center thread, measure ⅜" down; mark first fabric thread to the left with pin, for placement of first stitch. Work design following chart and color key and beginning at stitch marked by arrow on chart. Use three strands of embroidery floss or two strands of metallic thread throughout. Work each cross-stitch over one "square" of fabric. Work "JOY" or "NOEL" in backstitch with black, centered in heart. Work straight-stitch mouth with red. After all embroidery is completed, remove fabric from hoop. Steam-press gently on padded surface.

 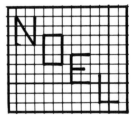

Cut out embroidered front ¼" beyond basting. Cut same-size back from print fabric. To attach piping to ornament front, begin at center top; pin piping to right side of front, matching raw edges of piping and front all around. Baste in place; remove pins. With right sides facing, place ornament front and back together, enclosing piping. Stitch with ¼" seam, using zipper-foot attachment; leave 3" opening. Turn to right side; stuff firmly; slip-stitch opening closed.

Cut a 6" length of satin ribbon; tack ends to center top of ornament for hanging loop. Tie remaining ribbon into bow; tack to center top as shown.

THE TWELVE DAYS OF CHRISTMAS

Simple motifs in soft country colors are fun and easy to stencil. Shown here on muslin, "framed" in embroidery hoops, and edged with ruffles of lace and plaid, the designs are ideal for pictures, pillows, and cards!

See General Directions for enlarging a pattern.

SIZE: Framed picture 13″ in diameter.

EQUIPMENT: Pencil. Ruler. Black quick-drying fine-tipped felt pen. Scissors. Paper for patterns. White paper. Tracing paper. Stencil paper (enough to cut out about fifty-five 9″ squares). X-acto knife. Masking tape. Glass, 12″ square with filed or masked edges. Paper towels. Old newspapers. Small jars with lids. Stencil brushes, at least one for each color paint. Staple gun. Sewing machine. Iron.

MATERIALS (for 12 pictures): Medium-weight unbleached muslin, 80″ wide, ¾ yard. Taffeta, 36″ wide, 1¼ yards red/green plaid. Medium-weight nonwoven fusible interfacing, at least 22″ wide, 1¾ yards white. Heavy-weight non-woven interfacing, at least 25″ wide, 1¾ yards white. Red sewing thread. Lace trim, 1¾″ wide, 8¾ yards off-white. Satin ribbon, ⅛″ wide, 6 yards off-white. Twelve wooden embroidery hoops, 8″. Acrylic paint in muted colors, one small jar each: barn red, Christmas red, yellow, pale blue, royal blue, holly green. Red pencil or crayon. White crafts glue. Water-repellant spray.

DIRECTIONS

Preparing Stencils: Draw lines across patterns, connecting grid lines. Enlarge patterns by copying on paper ruled in 1″ squares; use a separate piece of paper at least 12″ square for each design. Strengthen heavy lines of design (stencil outlines) with black marking pen. Mark a 9″ square around each design for guidelines, leaving equal margins all around on each.

Following individual directions below, use enlarged patterns to make and label one stencil for each color in each design; make additional stencils as directed: For each stencil, cut a 9″ square from stencil paper. Align edges of stencil paper with marked guidelines on pattern and trace individual sections of design. Reserve patterns for tracing inking lines later.

To cut out stencil, place white paper then stencil paper on glass; tape in place. Holding X-acto knife like a pencil, carefully cut out marked sections, starting with smallest first; cut toward you, turning the glass as you cut and lifting blade only after an entire area has been cut out; change blades often. If your knife should slip, mend cut area on both sides of stencil with tape, trimming with X-acto knife.

Preparing Muslin: From muslin, cut twelve 12″ squares. From fusible interfacing, cut twelve 10″ squares. Fuse interfacing to center of muslin pieces on wrong side with edges parallel, following manufacturer's directions. Use pencil to mark a 9″ square on right side of each muslin piece for guidelines, leaving 1½″ margins on each side. Cut and prepare an additional muslin square for test sample. Cover work surface with newspapers and tape muslin, marked side up, tautly in place.

Stenciling: Place ½ teaspoon of each color paint into individual jars; stir two or three tablespoons of water into each until paint has the consistency of ink; seal jars when not in use. Test paints on sample before beginning work; stencil each color on designs separately, following individual directions below: Tape stencil in place on muslin, lining up edges of paper with guidelines on fabric; press stencil flat with free hand while working; do not move stencil while working, or paint will smear. To stencil, dip brush into paint; then pounce brush on paper towel until almost dry. Holding brush like a pencil, perpendicular to surface, brush over cutout area with a circular motion, working over edge of stencil for a clean line. For a soft, antique effect, use paint sparingly, so that fabric will show through in some areas; to create deeper tones for shading (see photograph), press down with

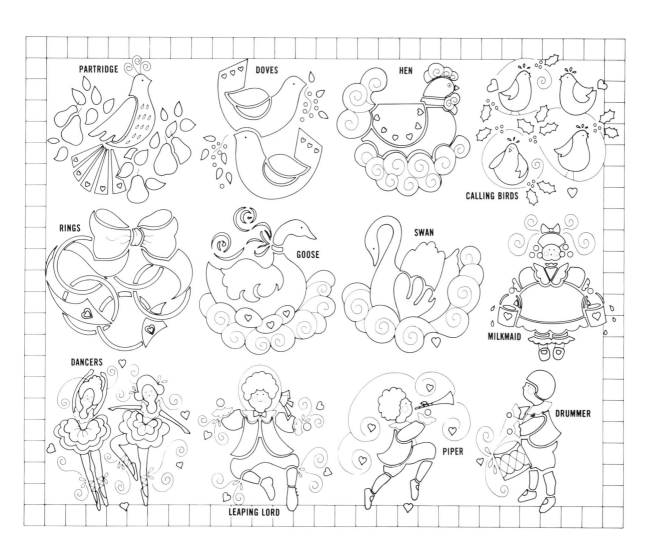

brush, or repaint area when dry. Allow paint to dry, remove tape, then carefully lift stencil from fabric. Wash and dry brushes thoroughly between color changes.

Partridge: Make four stencils: wing; tail and pears; body and hearts; leaves. Stencil wing with royal blue. Stencil tail and pears with yellow, body and hearts with Christmas red, leaves with holly green.

Doves: Make three stencils: bodies and wings; hearts and berries; leaves. Stencil bodies and wings with royal blue. Stencil hearts and berries with Christmas red, leaves with holly green.

Hen: Make four stencils: head and body; nest and beak; wing; comb, neck, tail, and hearts. Stencil head and body with pale blue. Stencil nest and beak with yellow, wing with holly green. Stencil remaining areas with Christmas red.

Calling Birds: Make five stencils: bodies, including outer wing line; wings only; combs; leaves; berries and hearts. Stencil bodies, then wings, with yellow. Stencil combs with pale blue, leaves with holly green, berries and hearts with Christmas red.

Rings: Make three stencils: rings; hearts and inside of bow; ribbon. On scrap of stencil paper, trace hearts again; mark a second heart 1/16″ outside each; cut out shapes on outermost lines. Stencil rings with yellow, hearts and inside of bow with Christmas red. Form two tiny loops with masking tape and use to tape heart shapes, centered, over stenciled hearts. Holding down edges of heart shapes, stencil ribbon with holly green.

Goose: Make four stencils: head and body, including outer wing line; wing only; nest; ribbon and hearts. Stencil head and body with royal blue, wing with holly green, nest with yellow, ribbon and hearts with Christmas red.

Swan: Make four stencils: swan, including outer wing line; wings only; water; heart. Stencil swan with pale blue. Stencil wings with pale blue, water with deep royal blue. Stencil heart with Christmas red.

Milkmaid: Make six stencils: hair bow, hearts, and lace trim on clothing; skirt and pantalets; face and hands; hair; blouse and water; buckets and shoes. On scrap of stencil paper, trace hearts again; cut out shapes on marked lines. Stencil bow, hearts, and lace trim with Christmas red. Stencil skirt and pantalets with holly green. Stencil skin with pale barn red, hair with yellow, blouse and water with light pale blue. Form two tiny loops with masking tape and use to tape heart shapes over stenciled hearts with edges even. Holding down edges of heart shapes, stencil bucket and shoes with deep pale blue.

Dancers: Make six stencils: faces, arms, and legs; hair and shoes; two complete skirts; middle layers of skirts; top layers of skirts; hearts. Stencil skin with pale barn red, hair and shoes with yellow. Applying royal blue in deepening shades as shown, stencil complete skirts first, middle layers second, and top layers last. Stencil hearts with Christmas red.

Leaping Lord: Make five stencils: vest, ties, shoes, and hearts; sleeves; knickers; face, hands, and legs; hair. Stencil vest, ties, shoes, and hearts with Christmas red. Stencil sleeves with pale blue, knickers with holly green, skin with pale barn red, hair with yellow.

Piper: Make five stencils: vest, shoes, and hearts; sleeves; knickers, face, hands, legs, and insteps; hair and pipe. Stencil vest, shoes, and hearts with red. Stencil sleeves with pale blue, knickers with holly green, skin with pale barn red, hair and pipe with yellow.

Drummer: Make five stencils: vest, shoes, and heart; sleeves and drum; knickers; face, hands, legs, and insteps; hair. Stencil vest, shoes, and heart with Christmas red. Stencil sleeves with light pale blue, drum with deep pale blue. Stencil knickers with holly green, skin with pale barn red, hair with yellow.

Inking (for each): When stenciling is complete, place tracing paper over enlarged pattern. Use black marker to trace fine lines of design (inking lines), extending them around stencil outlines as shown in illustration; also trace eyes and other facial features, if any;

trace guidelines. Tape tracing then stenciled fabric to window with right sides facing you, matching guidelines. Using black marker, trace inking lines onto fabric; mark all facial features except cheeks. "Rouge" cheeks with red pencil or crayon. When all marking is complete, remove fabric and tracing. To protect designs, spray muslin with water-repellant spray, following manufacturer's directions.

To Finish Each Picture: Separate rings of embroidery hoop. Place outer ring on heavy-weight interfacing. Use black marker to trace around outside of ring to mark a circle on interfacing; cut out on marked line and set aside. Center design over inner ring of hoop. Replace outer ring as shown with screw at top; tighten screw. Trim excess fabric close to hoop. Fold one end of lace trim ½″ to wrong side. Starting at top of hoop with folded end, staple right side of lace to back of outer ring, so that lace extends beyond hoop as shown; overlap folded end 1″ and cut away excess. From taffeta, cut a 3¼″ strip twice as long as circumference of inner ring of hoop. Press short edges then one long edge of strip ⅛″ to wrong side twice; topstitch close to outer folds. Press one end of strip ½″ to wrong side. Staple strip to outer ring as for lace, except folding ½″ pleats every 1″. Glue interfacing circle over back of hoop, covering raw fabric edges.

For hanging loop, cut 18″ length from satin ribbon. Fold length in half with ends even; knot ends together 3″ from fold, forming hanging loop. Slip one ribbon end under each side of screw on embroidery hoop from back to front; loop will extend above screw. Tie ends into a bow in front of screw as shown.

PATCHES
AND LACE

Here's a quick and simple way to use up leftover fabrics.
Adorable teddy, seven inches tall, waves Merry
Christmas. Other ornaments are lace-trimmed to match.
Make the patchwork first, then cut out the shapes.

See General Directions for enlarging a pattern.

SIZE: 3″–7″ high.

EQUIPMENT: Pencil. Ruler. Scissors. Paper for patterns. Dressmaker's tracing (carbon) paper. Tracing wheel or dry ball-point pen. Sewing needle. Sewing machine.

MATERIALS: Closely woven cotton fabrics in coordinating prints and solids: reds for candy canes and bell; greens for tree; browns for bear. Satin ribbon ⅛″ wide, small amounts assorted colors, including red and green. Ecru or white lace trim ⅜″ wide: 1 yd. for bear, ⅜ yd. each for others. Gold thread, for all except bell. Fiberfill for stuffing. Matching sewing thread. **For bell:** Two jingle bells ⅜″ diameter. **For bear:** Three black pompons, one ⅜″ diameter, two ¼″ diameter.

DIRECTIONS: To make patchwork fabric, cut coordinating prints and solids into 1½″-square pieces; arrange squares as desired (see photograph), then stitch together in rows with right sides facing, raw edges even, and making ⅛″ seams; stitch rows together to obtain patchwork fabric 4″ × 6″ for each candy cane, 6″ × 8″ for tree, 3″ × 8″ for bell, and 8″ × 12″ for bear. Press fabric smooth.

Enlarge ornament patterns by copying on paper ruled in ½″ squares; complete half-patterns indicated by dash lines. Heavy lines are pattern outlines, dotted lines topstitching. Use dressmaker's carbon and tracing wheel or dry ball-point pen to transfer ornament front and back to wrong side of patchwork fabric, reversing pattern for back; center pattern along a row of squares. Cut out, adding ¼″ seam allowance. Stitch front and back together with right sides facing, edges even, and making ¼″ seams; leave opening for turning. Turn to right side; stuff with fiberfill, using eraser end of pencil to reach into narrow areas. Turn raw edges at opening under ¼″; slip-stitch closed. Stitch bear's ears. Cut lace trim to fit around ornament plus ¼″; slip-stitch to ornament edges, covering seams; overlap ends ¼″. For hanger, cut 5″ length of gold thread (green ribbon for bell); tie ends together and tack to center top of ornament. For tree, cut five 4″ lengths of assorted ribbons; tie into bows and tack to tree at top and intersection of squares. For bear, cut 9″ length of red ribbon; tie around neck in bow. Glue on ⅜″-diameter pompon nose and ¼″-diameter eyes. For candy canes, cut two 5″ lengths from ribbon, one green and one red; tie around canes as shown. For bell, tack a green ribbon bow to front and back at base of hanging loop. Tack on jingle bells at center bottom on each side.

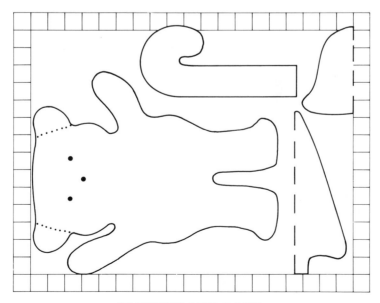

PATCHES AND LACE

PATCHWORK ORNAMENTS

All-time favorite patchwork patterns are sewn on a small scale for six of the sweetest ornaments you'll find anywhere. To make them extra special, fill with potpourri.

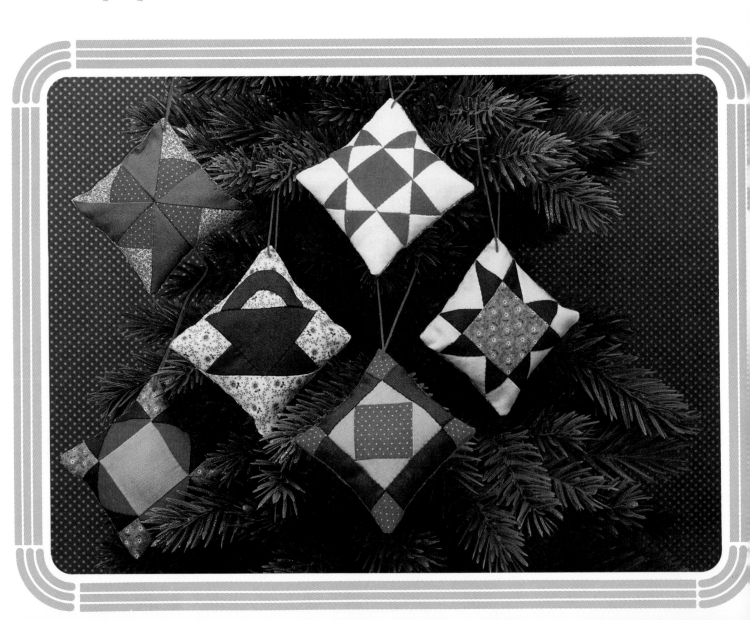

SIZE: Each ornament, 3″ square.

EQUIPMENT: Pencil. Ruler. Tracing and graph paper. Thin, stiff cardboard. Glue. Scissors. Straight pins. Sewing needle. Large-eyed embroidery needle. Knitting needle. Sewing machine. Iron.

MATERIALS: Closely woven cotton fabric scraps of the following colors and patterns: red solid; white-on-red dotted; red print; light, medium, and dark green solids; light green print; ecru solid; ecru print. Sewing threads to match fabrics. Cotton cording 1/16″ diameter, 1½ yards red. Polyester fiberfill or cotton balls.

GENERAL DIRECTIONS FOR PATCHWORK ORNAMENTS: Mark patterns on graph paper, following individual directions below. Glue graph paper to cardboard; let dry; cut carefully along marked lines for templates. Use templates to mark pieces as directed: Place template on wrong side of fabric with right angles, two parallel edges, or one straight edge on straight of goods. Draw around template with sharp pencil held at an outward angle. Mark as many pieces as needed of one color at a time, leaving ½″ between two pieces. Cut out pieces ¼″ outside pencil lines for seam allowance; pencil lines will be stitching lines. To join two pieces, place them together with right sides facing, matching one edge; stitch on marked line; press seam to one side, under darker color. Join pieces to form a block 3½″ square, following individual directions, diagrams, and color illustration.

To Assemble (for each): Cut 3½″ fabric square for back. Pin patchwork front and back together, wrong sides out; stitch ¼″ from edges all around, leaving 2″ opening in one edge; turn to right side. Stuff until plump, poking stuffing into corners with knitting needle. Turn raw edge ¼″ to inside; slip-stitch opening closed. **For hanging loop:** From cording, cut 9″ length. Use embroidery needle to thread cord through one corner (top) of ornament; remove needle and knot ends together.

EVENING STAR (middle right, in photograph): Read General Directions above. Make templates: Divide a ¾″ square in half diagonally for triangle shape and label it A. Divide a 1 1/16″ square in half diagonally for triangle B. C, ¾″ square. D, 1½″ square. From solid dark green fabric, cut eight of A. From solid ecru fabric, cut four each of B and C. From green print fabric, cut one of D.

Following diagram, join A's to B's. Join C's to two A-B-A pieces. Join third and fourth A-B-A pieces to D. Join pieces as shown, completing block. Assemble ornament and attach hanging loop, following General Directions.

SQUARE IN DIAMOND (bottom left): Read General Directions above. Make templates for A, B, C, and D: See directions above for Evening Star. From solid dark green fabric, cut eight of A. From solid red fabric, cut four of B. From green print fabric, cut four of C. From solid light green fabric, cut one of D.

Following diagram, join pieces to form block as directed for Evening Star, except reversing position of A-B-A pieces as shown. Assemble ornament and attach hanging loop, following General Directions.

WINDMILL (top left): Read General Directions above. Make template for B: See directions above for Evening Star. Divide a 1½″ square in half diagonally for triangle E. From red print and dotted fabrics, cut four each of B. From solid medium green fabric, cut four of E.

Following diagram, join B's at short edges. Join B-B pieces to long edge of E's. Join B-B-E pieces as shown, completing block. Assemble ornament and attach hanging loop, following General Directions.

OHIO STAR (top right): Read General Directions above. Make templates: Divide a 1″ square in quarters diagonally for triangle shape and label it F. G, 1″ square. From solid ecru fabric, cut eight of F and four of G. From solid red fabric, cut one of G and eight of F.

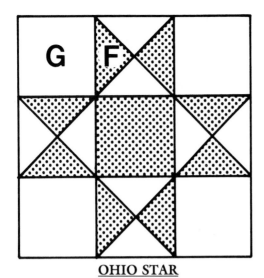

OHIO STAR

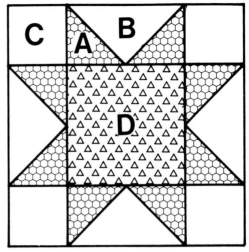

EVENING STAR

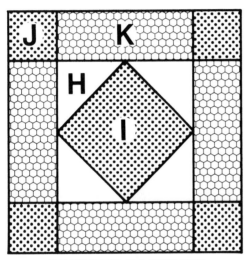

DIAMOND IN SQUARE

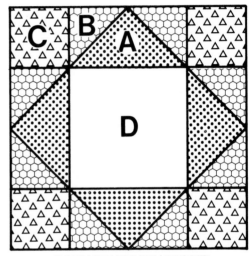

SQUARE IN DIAMOND

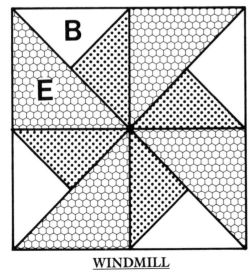

WINDMILL

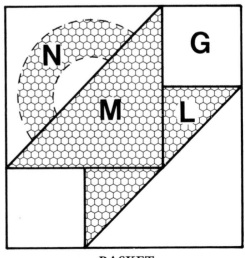

BASKET

Following diagram, join F's. Join G's to F's as shown to form three strips. Join strips, completing block. Assemble ornament and attach hanging loop, following General Directions.

DIAMOND IN SQUARE (bottom right): Read General Directions above. Make templates: Divide a ⅞″ square in half diagonally for triangle shape and label it H. I, 1¼″ square. J, ⅝″ square. K, 1¾″ × ⅝″ rectangle. From solid light green fabric, cut four of H. From red dotted fabric, cut one of I and four of J. From solid dark green fabric, cut four of K.

Following diagram, join H's to I. Join J's to ends of two K's. Join third and fourth K's to H's. Join pieces as shown, completing block. Assemble ornament and attach hanging loop, following General Directions.

BASKET (middle left): Read General Directions above. Make template for G: See directions above for Ohio Star. Divide G in half diagonally for triangle L. Divide a 2″

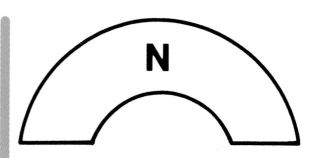

square in half diagonally for triangle M. Trace actual size pattern N and make template. From ecru print fabric, cut two each of G and M. From solid dark green fabric, cut two of L and one of M; also cut one of N, referring to instructions for appliqué in General Directions at end of book.

Following diagram, join G's to L's. Following directions for hand-appliqué, pin, baste, and stitch N to one ecru print M, with straight edges even and side margins equal; see dash lines on diagram. Attach M's as shown, completing block. Assemble ornament and attach hanging loop, following General Directions above.

NORTH POLE EVENING

Here's a cozy setting from the North Pole! Mrs. Claus and her famous husband have an evening at home. Each little figure, about ten inches tall, is of fabric scraps and is easy to make, too.

edges in front and turning down top corners for collar. If too large, trim; if too small, adjust pattern and recut. Turn in seam allowance all around edges and stitch in place; at armholes, slash edges before turning. Fit shirt on Santa, overlapping fronts; tack fronts to hold or sew on snaps. For hat, fold piece in half, wrong side out, and stitch along curved edge. Cut strip of fake fur ¾″ × 6¾″. Trim fur to short pile. With wrong side of hat still facing out, pin fur strip around rim, matching edges; stitch with ¼″ seam. Trim seam to ⅛″, turn hat to right side; turn up fur cuff. Tack pompon to tip of hat. For each slipper, turn in long straight edge of top piece and topstitch. Lightly gather curved edge between X's for toe. Starting at center of toe, glue seam allowance of slipper top to underside of cardboard sole; let dry. Turn in seam allowance of red fabric sole and press, cutting in at curves; glue to underside of cardboard sole. Paint edge of sole red. For sweater and socks, see directions following. Dress Santa, putting socks and slipper on Santa's left foot, as illustrated. Reserve unfinished sock for Mrs. Santa. Glue toy to left hand. Make brush: Paint toothpick yellow. Cut two 1″ lengths of string; glue to one end of toothpick. Wrap thread tightly around glued section and tie, for ferrule. Unravel string, then twist together for brush. Dip end of brush into paint. Using sharp scissors, poke two holes in underside of Santa's right hand. Insert toothpick handle through holes and glue in place.

Mrs. Santa's Body: Make as for Santa, omitting paunch; cut muslin pieces as follows: body 5″ × 8″, legs 3½″ × 5½″ each, arms 2½″ × 5″ each; also cut 10″-diameter circle for head. Make feet about 1″ long; leave legs straight and attach to bottom of body for standing doll, or make legs similar to Santa's for sitting doll. Make arms, turning in top edge; slipstitch arms closed and do not attach to body yet. Paint hands. For head, paint smiling mouth, then knot thread and make "dimple" at corners of mouth as for nostrils. Omit eyebrows. For hair, cut semicircle 8″ in

diameter from white fake fur; cut in half for two quarter circles. Pin a quarter circle to one side of head, with one straight edge forming a center part and other straight edge along hairline from center front to back. Pin second quarter circle to other side of head in same manner. Pin curved edges to back of head, snipping out segments for a neat fit. Slipstitch hair to head along edges. Comb hair to sides and back; swirl excess to form bun at nape and tack in place. Insert head into shoulders in upright position (or turned slightly to right) and slip-stitch in place.

Mrs. Santa's Clothes: For underskirt, cut piece 6½″ × 24½″ from white cotton fabric (or measure doll from waist to ankles for width). Turn under one long edge ¼″ twice and topstitch, for hem. Lay piece flat, with hemmed edge at bottom. Starting and ending ¼″ from ends, paint green and orange design freehand across piece, just above stitching; see diagram and photograph. Fold piece in half and stitch ends together; turn to right side. Machine-baste around top, ¼″ from raw edge. Place underskirt on doll, pull up basting to gather top, and slip-stitch to doll's waist. For dress, cut piece 5½″ × 25″ from white-dotted red fabric (or 1″ narrower than underskirt) for skirt; cut piece 3″ × 8½″ from red/white gingham (or piece 1″ longer than circumference of doll's waist) for bodice. Turn under one long edge of skirt ¼″ twice and topstitch, for hem. Gather other long edge to length of bodice; stitch to bodice; press seam up. Press under top edge of bodice ¼″; run line of basting through doubled fabric. Wrap dress around doll, wrong side out; bring edges

HEM DIAGRAM

loosely together in back and mark a seam line. Stitch back seam from hem to neck; trim seam if necessary. Turn right side out; place on doll. Pull up basting at neck; end off. For each sleeve, cut piece 4½" square from gingham. Turn in two opposite edges ¼" and press. Fold piece in half, bringing raw edges together, and stitch, forming tube. Run line of basting through doubled fabric at each end of tube; pull one end to gather tightly; end off. Turn sleeve to right side. Insert arm into sleeve, with top at closed end. Pull basting to gather other end around "wrist"; end off. Slip-stitch sleeve to dress. For collar, cut four from gingham. Pair pieces and stitch together, leaving opening along inner edge. Trim seams to ⅛", turn collar to right side, press, and slip-stitch closed. Place the two collar pieces on doll and slip-stitch inner edges to top of bodice. For apron, cut 6¾" × 14½" skirt and 1¼" × 20" waistband/ties from sheer white-on-white checked fabric. Turn under short edges of skirt ⅛" twice; topstitch. Turn under one long edge ⅛", then 1½"; topstitch for hem. Gather opposite edge to 4". Center waistband/ties over top of skirt, right sides, facing and matching raw edges; stitch in place with ¼" seam. Turn waistband up and topstitch. Turn under remaining edges of waistband/ties ⅛" twice; topstitch all around. At each end, fold a corner down against opposite side; stitch in place. Tie apron on doll. Insert toothpick "knitting needles" in Mrs. Santa's hands; see directions for Santa and photograph.

CAT: Make two pompons from gray yarn, 2½" and ¾" in diameter. For body, trim larger pompon to oval shape, then trim away one side of oval for flat surface, making underside of reclining cat. Trim away another section for neck area, then sew on smaller pompon for head. Trim away more yarn to refine cat shape, as desired. Cut two triangles about ¼" × ½" from gray felt for ears; cut tiny strip from pink felt for mouth. Glue ears, mouth, and plastic eyes to head. Wrap yarn in a spiral around 3" length of pipe cleaner, gluing as you go; let dry, then brush lightly to "fluff." Sew tail to underside of body. Tie ribbon bow around neck.

SOFA: Cut two sofas and two cushions from print fabric, adding seam allowance. Cut one sofa from cardboard and two from batting, following lines of pattern. Lightly glue a layer of batting to each side of cardboard sofa. Stitch fabric pieces together, leaving bottom edge open; turn to right side. Insert padded cardboard through opening. Stuff in extra batting on one (front) side. Turn in opening at bottom and slipstitch closed. Stitch cushion pieces together, leaving opening in center of curved edge. Turn to right side. Stuff plumply, turn in open edges, and slip-stitch closed. Pin curved edge of cushion against center front of sofa, about 1½" above bottom. Bend sofa arms forward, enclosing entire curve of cushion with sofa. Slip-stitch cushion and sofa together.

RUG: Cut 1"-wide strip about 2 yards long from each of three fabrics; if piecing for length, join sections on the bias in a different place for each strip. Double-fold each strip and press. To braid, stack strips at one end; stitch together. Pin joined ends to a firm surface. Begin braiding by folding right-hand strip over middle strip, then left-hand strip over middle, keeping double edges to center. Continue braiding, always folding alternate outside strips over middle strip; pin strips together at end of braid. Working on a flat surface, wind braid around itself to make round or oval rug; start in center with joined end, overlapping edge, and work outward, sewing adjacent sides together. When rug is almost size desired, cut off excess braid, then taper-trim each strip and rebraid to make narrow tail end. Tuck in tail through loop of adjoining braid and tack securely.

SANTA'S SWEATER AND SOCKS:

MATERIALS: Sport-weight yarn, 1 oz. red. Knitting needles No. 2. Four white sew-on beads. Yarn needle.

GAUGE: 5 sts = 1"; 7 rows = 1".

SWEATER: BACK: Beg at lower edge, with No. 2 needles, cast on 28 sts. Work in ribbing of k 2, p 2 for 4 rows. Work in stockinette st (k 1 row, p 1 row) for 2″ above ribbing, end p row.

Shape Armholes: Bind off 5 sts at beg of next 2 rows, then dec 1 st each edge once—16 sts. Work even in stockinette st for ½″ above bound-off sts, end p row.

Shape Shoulders: Bind off 4 sts at beg of next 2 rows. Bind off remaining 8 sts.

LEFT FRONT: Beg at lower edge, with No. 2 needles, cast on 18 sts. Work as for back until piece measures 2″ above ribbing, end p row.

Shape Armholes: Bind off 5 sts at beg of next row, then dec 1 st at same edge once. Work even for ½″, end p row.

Shape Shoulders: Bind off 4 sts at beg of next row. Bind off remaining 8 sts.

RIGHT FRONT: Work as for left front, reversing shapings.

SLEEVES: Beg at lower edge, with No. 2 needles, cast on 20 sts. Work in ribbing of k 2, p 2 for 4 rows. Work in stockinette st for 3½″ above ribbing, end p row.

Shape Armholes and Cap: Bind off 4 sts at beg of next 2 rows, then dec 1 st each side every other row twice. Bind off remaining 8 sts.

FINISHING: Sew shoulder, side, and sleeve seams. Set in sleeves. Sew beads on left front edge, first one at bottom edge, remaining beads ¾″ apart. Fold out top edges of fronts, p side showing, for lapels. Sew in place.

SOCKS (make 1½): Beg at top edge, with No. 2 needles, cast on 18 sts. Work in ribbing of k 2, p 2 for 6 rows. Work in stockinette st for 2″ above ribbing, end p row.

Next Row: *K 1, k 2 tog, repeat from * across. P 1 row. Cut yarn, leaving a 4″ end. Thread yarn needle and draw through remaining 12 sts; fasten securely to wrong side. Sew back seam.

Work another sock the same for 2″ above ribbing. Leaving sts on needle, cut yarn 18″ long. Roll end into a ball; glue or sew securely, letting ball hang about 2″ from work. Divide remaining sts onto toothpick "needles."

CANDY CANE CHERUBS

Three playful angels have found a new use for candy canes! These cherubs, about seven inches tall, are sewn of felt and fabric scraps, then softly stuffed.

See General Directions for enlarging a pattern and for embroidery.

SIZE: About 7 " high.

EQUIPMENT: Pencil. Scissors. Ruler. Paper for patterns. Dressmaker's tracing (carbon) paper. Tracing wheel or dry ball-point pen. Sewing and embroidery needles. Sewing machine (optional).

MATERIALS: **For All:** Felt 9″ × 12″ pieces white and flesh tone; scraps of light blue and green. Cotton fabric: red/white narrow striped, piece 9″ × 12″; scraps of solid red, red dotted, green striped. Small amount long-pile fake fur, desired color(s) for hair. Narrow gold braid trim, 1 yard. Satin ribbon ¼″ wide: ¾ yard red; scrap green. Cardboard scrap. Six-strand embroidery floss: scraps of brown, red. Pink crayon. Sewing thread to match felt and fabrics. Fiberfill for stuffing.

DIRECTIONS: **For Each:** Using sharp pencil, draw lines across patterns, connecting grid lines. Enlarge patterns by copying on paper ruled in 1″ squares; complete half patterns indicated by dash lines. Using dressmaker's carbon and tracing wheel or dry ball-point pen, mark the following pieces on felt: two bodies on white; wings on blue; two arm/hand pieces, one or two legs/feet, and two heads on flesh, transferring face to one head only. Mark two hair pieces on fur and two candy canes on red-striped, both on wrong side of fabric. Cut out pieces, adding ¼″ seam allowance to candy cane.

Place body front and back together with arms and legs between pieces (see photograph). Stitch all around body, ⅛″ in from edges, securing arms and legs; before closing body, stuff lightly with fiberfill.

With two strands of floss in embroidery needle, embroider brown eyes and red mouth with fly stitch. "Rouge" cheeks with crayon. Whipstitch head front to back, stuffing lightly as you go. With right sides facing, whipstitch hair pieces together along long curved edge; turn to right side and place over head; tack to secure. Cut 4″ length of gold braid; stitch ends together; place over hair and tack to secure. Slip-stitch head in place, overlapping

front of body. Cut 1½″ length of red or green ribbon; tack to body at neck with straight stitch across center. For apron, cut fabric as follows: 4″ × 2¼″ for striped apron; 3″ × 1½″ for solid apron; 2″ square for dotted apron. Turn all edges under ⅛″ twice and stitch in place. Gather one (top) edge to fit across waist (see photograph); tack to body at waist. Stitch wings to back down center.

With right sides facing and edges even, stitch candy canes pieces together, making ¼″ seam and leaving 1″ open for turning. Trim seam allowance and clip into curves. Turn to right side; stuff fully; turn in raw edges at opening and slip-stitch closed.

FINISHING: For cherubs with print aprons, wrap hand(s) around candy cane as shown; slip-stitch in place. Make straight-stitch fingers, using matching sewing thread.

For swing, cut two 1″ × 3″ rectangles of green felt and one ¾″ × 2″ rectangle of cardboard. Center cardboard between felt; whipstitch to close. Cut 18″ length of gold braid; using embroidery needle, thread down through one side of skirt (X on pattern), through seat at one short end, and back up through seat and skirt; tie ends around candy cane. Wrap hands around braid; tack in place with straight-stitch fingers. Fold feet up at heels and tack in place. Fold body (dotted line on pattern) to form seated position; tack to secure.

For hangers, cut 6″ length of ribbon; tack ends to center back of candy cane.

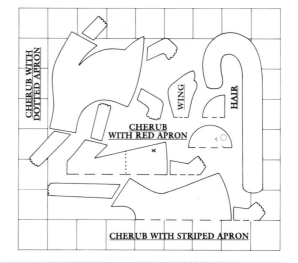

BALSA TRIMS

Light as air, these balsa wood trims are easy to cut and quick to decorate with a dot or a dash from a felt-tipped pen. Tree is thirteen inches tall.

See General Directions for enlarging a pattern.

EQUIPMENT: Paper for patterns. Pencil. Ruler. Scissors. X-Acto knife. Hole punch. Compass.

MATERIALS: Balsa wood sheets 1/8" or 1/16" thick; see individual directions for amounts. Black or brown felt-tipped pen with fine point. Crystal clear acrylic spray. White craft glue. Taffeta ribbon: green, blue, and white tartan plaid, 5/8" and 1 1/2" wide. See additional materials in individual directions.

DIRECTIONS: Enlarge patterns below by copying on paper ruled in 1" squares; complete half-patterns and quarter-patterns indicated by dash lines. Using patterns, cut out shapes carefully with knife. Plan desired dot design (see photograph) and mark lightly with pencil on the wood. Ink in design with pen by pressing tip into wood, making an indentation at the same time. In some cases, it will be easier to ink the design after assembling item. Assemble individual items, following directions below. Spray items with acrylic.

DRIED FLOWER HOLDER: You will need one sheet of balsa wood 1/8" × 3" × 36"; dried flowers; plastic modeling clay, 1/2 pound, or rock; can 2 3/4" diameter, 4" tall; florist's styrofoam; ribbon 1 1/2" wide, 1 yard.

Cut four pieces of balsa wood each 3" × 6" and one piece 2 3/4" × 3" for bottom. Mark and ink in the designs on the sides. Glue the four sides together and to the base with butt joints to form box; let dry.

Put clay or rock in bottom of can. Glue can to inside bottom of box, as a weight. Fill space above can with florist's foam. Insert dried flowers into foam. Tie ribbon around box.

GIFT BOX: You will need one sheet of balsa wood 1/8" × 4" × 36".

From balsa wood, cut four pieces each 4" × 5" for sides and two pieces each 4" × 3 3/4" for inside lid and box bottom and one piece 4" × 4 1/4" for outside lid. Mark and ink in designs on sides and outside lid. Glue the sides and bottom together with butt joints to form box; let dry. For the lid, glue the smaller piece to center of larger piece on unmarked side; let dry and place on box.

TREE: You will need styrofoam cone 12" tall; styrofoam disk 3" in diameter, 1" thick; three sheets of balsa wood, each 1/16" × 4" × 48"; ribbon 5/8" wide, about 2 yards.

Glue the disk to the base of cone; let dry. Wrap ribbon around disk to cover; pin and glue to secure. Cut about 80 branch pieces from balsa wood, using pattern A. With pen, dot the notched edge of each as illustrated. For each piece, cut a sliver of balsa wood 1/16" × 3/8" and glue on back about 1/4" below short, straight edge. Insert pin through wood from front to back, just above sliver.

Pin a row of pieces around bottom of cone, overlapping so that styrofoam is well covered.

Working from bottom to top, continue to pin rows around cone, overlapping rows as you go. For final row, pin four pieces without the sliver in back around top of cone. Tie remaining ribbon into bow; pin to tree top.

ORNAMENTS: For each ornament, you will need a piece of balsa wood $1/16'' \times 3'' \times 4''$ and ribbon $5/8''$ wide for hanging.

For each, cut three pieces of pattern B. To vary designs, cut notches in the center of one piece or punch one or two holes near the ends of pieces (see photograph). Crisscross the pieces at centers and glue together. Decorate with dots. Hang individually or as a group from ribbon.

MEDALLION: You will need one sheet of balsa wood $1/8'' \times 4'' \times 48''$ and one sheet $1/16'' \times 4'' \times 48''$; corrugated paper $6''$ square; ribbon $5/8''$ wide, $5/8$ yard.

With compass, cut two half-circles $8''$ in diameter and two half-circles $6''$ in diameter from $1/8''$ balsa. Cut $6''$-diameter circle from corrugated paper. Glue the balsa half-circles together to make $6''$ and $8''$ circles. Glue the $6''$ balsa and paper circles to either side of the $8''$ balsa circle, centering all pieces; let dry.

From $1/16''$ balsa, cut 12 of piece B. Glue six pieces to $6''$ balsa circle with points touching so that notches form a star in center as illustrated.

Cut six of piece C; punch holes in centers; glue between pieces B. Cut six of piece D and glue one behind each piece C. Cut 12 of piece E; glue two together as shown in Diag. 1. Glue to each remaining piece B as in Diag. 2. Turn medallion to back. Glue other end of each piece B to paper circle, so that each three-part end will extend beyond $8''$ circle and be directly behind piece D; see photograph. Mark and ink in designs. With $10''$ of ribbon, make hanging loop; glue in place. With remaining ribbon, tie bow and glue to top of loop.

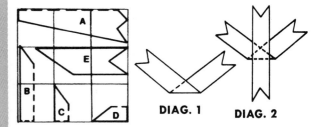

DIAG. 1   DIAG. 2

TREETOP ANGEL

Crochet a lacy treetop angel, then stiffen her wings and skirt (shell-stitched) with a solution of water and all-purpose glue.

See General Directions for crochet.

SIZE: 8″ high.

MATERIALS: Mercerized knitting and crochet cotton, 1 ball white. Steel crochet hook No. 6. Absorbent cotton. All-purpose glue.

GAUGE: 8 sc = 1″.

ANGEL: SKIRT: Ch 16; sl st in first ch to form ring.

Rnd 1: Ch 2 (counts as first dc), 2 dc in same ch with sl st, ch 1, 3 dc in same ch (shell made), * ch 1, sk 1 ch, dc, ch 1, dc in next

ch (V made), ch 1, sk 1 ch, 3 dc, ch 1, 3 dc in next ch, repeat from * twice, ch 1, sk 1 ch, V in next ch, ch 1, sl st in top of ch 2 at beg of rnd—4 shells, 4 V's.

Rnds 2–4. Sl st to center of first shell, shell in ch-1 sp of first shell, * ch 1, V in ch-1 sp of next V, ch 1, shell in ch-1 sp of next shell, repeat from * around, end V in ch-1 sp of last V, ch 1, sl st in top of ch 2 at beg of rnd.

Rnd 5: Sl st to center of first shell, * shell of 4 dc, ch 1, 4 dc in ch-1 sp of shell, ch 1, 2 dc, ch 1, 2 dc in ch-1 sp of V, ch 1, repeat from * around. Join.

Rnds 6–8: Sl st to center of first shell, * shell of 4 dc, ch 1, 4 dc in ch-1 sp of shell, ch 1, 2 dc, ch 1, 2 dc in ch-1 sp of small shell, ch 1, repeat from * around. Join.

Rnds 9 and 10: Sl st to center of first shell, shell of 5 dc, ch 1, 5 dc in ch-1 sp of shell, * ch 1, shell of 5 dc, ch 1, 5 dc in ch-1 sp of next shell, repeat from * around, ch 1; join.

Rnd 11: * Ch 3, sc in 3rd dc of shell, ch 3, sc in ch-1 sp of shell, ch 3, sc in 8th dc of shell, ch 3, sc in sp between shells, repeat from * around. Join; end off.

WINGS: **Row 1:** Ch 12; dc in 4th ch from hook (V made), * ch 1, sk 1 ch, 3 dc, ch 1, 3 dc in next ch (shell), ch 1, sk 1 ch, dc, ch 1, dc in next ch, repeat from * once—3 V's. Turn.

Row 2: Sl st to center of first V, ch 4, dc in V, * ch 1, shell in shell, ch 1, V in V, repeat from * once. Turn each row.

Rows 3 and 4: Repeat row 2.

Row 5: Sl st to center of first V, ch 2, dc, ch 1, 2 dc in V, * ch 1, 4 dc, ch 1, 4 dc in next shell, ch 1, 2 dc, ch 1, 2 dc in next V, repeat from * once.

Row 6: Sl st to center of first small shell, ch 2, dc, ch 1, 2 dc in shell, * ch 1, 4 dc, ch 1, 4 dc in next shell, ch 1, 2 dc, ch 1, 2 dc in next small shell, repeat from * once.

Row 7: Sl st to center of first shell, ch 2, 4 dc, ch 1, 5 dc in first shell, * ch 1, 5 dc, ch 1, 5 dc in next shell, repeat from * across.

Row 8: Work as for rnd 11 of skirt across. End off.

Work 2nd wing the same. Sew tog across row 1.

HEAD AND BODY: Ch 4; sl st in first ch to form ring.

Rnd 1: 7 sc in ring.

Rnd 2: 2 sc in each sc around—14 sc.

Rnd 3: * Sc in next sc, 2 sc in next sc, repeat from * around—21 sc.

Rnds 4–11: Sc in each sc around.

Rnds 12 and 13: * Pull up a lp in each of next 2 sts, yo and through 3 lps on hook, repeat from * until 7 sts remain.

Rnd 14: Sc in each sc around.

Rnds 15 and 16: * Sc in next sc, 2 sc in next sc, repeat from * around until there are 16 sc in rnd.

Rnds 17–26: Work even on 16 sc. End off. Stuff head and body.

HAIR: Cut 3″ strands of cotton. Holding 12 or more strands tog, sew around center of strands and sew to head, beg at center of forehead. Sew 4 more bunches of strands across top center of head to back.

ARMS (make 2): Ch 13, Sc in 2nd ch from hook and in each remaining ch. Ch. 1, turn. Work 4 more rows of 12 sc. End off. Sew last row to starting ch. Sew arms to sides at shoulders. Tack "hands" tog.

FINISHING: Sew wings to back of body. Dilute glue with a little water. Stiffen hair, wings and skirt with glue.

MUSICAL TREE SKIRT

A music-loving family will especially appreciate this crocheted tree skirt. The staff is worked into the background, the notes and bells crocheted separately and sewn on (make extras to trim the tree!).

See General Directions for crochet.

SIZE: 15″ from center to edge.

MATERIALS: Worsted-weight yarn, three 3½-oz. skeins white, 1 skein green. Mercerized knitting and crochet cotton, 1 ball each of white and red. Crochet hook size G (4¼ mm). Steel crochet hook No. 1. Starch.

GAUGE: 7 sts = 2″; 2 dc rows = 1″.

SKIRT: Beg at center, with white yarn and size G hook, ch 40.

Row 1: Dc in 4th ch from hook, * 2 dc in next ch, dc in each of next 2 ch, repeat from * across. Ch 3, turn.

Row 2: Sk first dc, dc in each of next 2 dc, * 2 dc in next dc, dc in each of next 3 dc, repeat from * across, end dc in next dc, dc in turning ch. Ch 3, turn.

Row 3: Sk first dc, dc in each of next 3 dc, * 2 dc in next dc, dc in each of next 4 dc, repeat from * across, end dc in next dc, dc in turning ch. Ch 3, turn.

Row 4: Sk first dc, dc in each of next 4 dc, * 2 dc in next dc, dc in each of next 5 dc, repeat from * across, end dc in next dc, dc in turning ch. Ch 3, turn.

Rows 5–15: Work in same way, skipping first dc and increasing 12 sts each row, with 1 st more between incs each row, ending each row with dc in next to last st, dc in turning ch. At end of row 15, drop white. Join green, ch 1, turn.

Row 16 (right side): With green, sc in each dc across. End off.

Row 17 (right side): Pick up white in back lp of first sc, ch 2; working in back lps, hdc in 16 sc, 2 hdc in next sc, * hdc in 17 sc, 2 hdc in next sc, repeat from * across, hdc in each of last 2 sc. Ch 2, turn.

Row 18: Sk first hdc, hdc in each of next 17 hdc, 2 hdc in next hdc, * hdc in each of next 18 hdc, 2 hdc in next hdc, repeat from * across, hdc in next hdc, hdc in turning ch. Drop white; join green; ch 1, turn.

Row 19: With green, sc in each hdc and turning ch. End off.

Row 20: Repeat row 17 but inc in every 20th sc.

Row 21: Repeat row 18 but inc in every 21st sc.

Row 22: Repeat row 19.

Row 23: Repeat row 17 but inc in every 22nd sc.

Row 24: Repeat row 18 but inc in every 23rd sc.

Row 25: Repeat row 19.

Row 26: Repeat row 17 but inc in every 24th sc.

Row 27: Repeat row 18 but inc in every 25th sc.

Row 28: Repeat row 19.

Row 29: Pick up white in back lp of first sc, ch 3; working in back lps of sc, dc in each of next 24 sc, 2 dc in next sc, * dc in each of next 25 sc, 2 dc in next sc, repeat from * across. Ch 3, turn.

Row 30: Work in dc, inc in every 27th dc.

Row 31: Work in dc, inc in every 28th dc. End off.

Edging: Join green in first st of row 31, * sl st in next dc, sk 1 dc, 4 dc in next dc, sk 1 dc, repeat from * across, sl st in last st. End off.

APPLIQUES: BELLS (make 3): Use double strand of mercerized cotton. Beg at top of bell with red and No. 1 hook, ch 11, sl st in 8th ch from hook (for hanger), ch 4.

Row 1: Sc in 2nd ch from hook, sc in each ch across—6 sc. Ch 1, turn.

Row 2: 2 sc in first sc, sc in 4 sc, 2 sc in last sc. Ch 1, turn.

Row 3: 2 sc in first sc, sc in 6 sc, 2 sc in last sc. Ch 1, turn.

Row 4–12: Sc in each sc. Ch 1, turn each row.

Row 13: 2 sc in first sc, sc in 8 sc, 2 sc in last sc. End off. Join white. Ch 2, turn.

Row 14: Hdc in each sc across, 2 hdc in last sc. Ch 2, turn.

Row 15: Hdc in each hdc, 2 hdc in turning ch. End off. Join red. Ch 1, turn.

Row 16: 2 sc in first hdc, sc in each hdc across, 2 sc in turning ch. Ch 1, turn.

Rows 17 and 18: Sc in each sc. Ch 1, turn.

Row 19: Sk first sc, sl st in next sc, sc in next 5 sc, hdc in next sc, 2 dc in each of next 2 sc, hdc in next sc, sc in next 5 sc, sk 1 sc, sl st in next sc. End off.

For second bell, work the same through row 18.

Row 19: Sk first sc, sl st in next sc, sc in next 6 sc, hdc in next sc, 2 dc in each of next 2 sc, hdc in next sc, sc in next 4 sc, sk 1 sc, sl st in next sc. End off.

For third bell, work the same through row 18.

Row 19: Sk first sc, sl st in next sc, sc in next 4 sc, hdc in next sc, 2 dc in each of next 2 sc, hdc in next sc, sc in next 6 sc, sk 1 sc, sl st in last sc. End off.

BOW: With 2 strands of red mercerized cotton and No. 1 hook, ch 83. Sl st in 2nd ch from hook; working in each ch across, work sc, hdc, 7 dc, 2 hdc, 2 sc, (2 sl sts, 2 sc, 2 hdc, 3 dc, 2 dc in each of 4 ch, 3 dc in each of 2 ch, 2 dc in each of 4 ch, 3 dc, 2 hdc, 2 sc) 2 times, 2 sl sts, 2 sc, 2 hdc, 7 dc, hdc, sc, sl st in last ch. End off.

For center knot of bow, ch 9, hdc in 3rd ch from hook and in each remaining ch. End off.

MUSICAL NOTES: Use 2 strands of red mercerized cotton and No. 1 hook.

EIGHTH NOTE (make 9): **Body:** Ch 5. In 5th ch from hook make 4 dc, 3 tr, 4 dc and 2 tr. Sl st in top of ch 5.

Stem and Flag: Ch 31. Sl st in 2nd ch from hook and in next ch, sc in next 6 ch, hdc in next 3 ch, dc in next 4 ch, ch 1, 2 sc around bar of last dc made, sc in same ch as last dc, sc in each remaining ch to last ch, sk last ch, sl st in next dc on body of note. End off.

QUARTER NOTE (make 4): **Body:** Same as for eighth note.

Stem: Ch 18. Sc in 2nd ch from hook and in each remaining ch to last ch, sk last ch, sl st in next dc on body of note. End off.

Bar: Ch 25. Sc in 2nd ch from hook and in each ch across. End off.

FINISHING: Starch and block appliques. With red mercerized cotton, sew appliques to skirt over green lines, 3 bells and bow at center front, bar to the right of bells and notes arranged on skirt about 4″ apart.

REINDEER TREE SKIRT

Santa's reindeer will encircle your tree and form a charming backdrop for gifts. This skirt is made entirely of versatile felt.

See General Directions for enlarging a pattern.

SIZE: 36″ in diameter.

EQUIPMENT: Pencil. Ruler. Scissors. Paper for patterns. Dressmaker's tracing (carbon) paper. Tracing wheel or dry ball-point pen. Straight pins. Sewing machine. String.

MATERIALS: Felt, red, 36″ square; white and brown, 72″ wide, ½ yd each; small amounts of tan, black and pink. Sewing thread to match felt. All-purpose glue.

DIRECTIONS: To make circle for tree skirt, tack one end of string in the exact center of the 36″ square of felt. Tie other end of string to a pencil with 18″ of string between tack and pencil. Swing pencil in an arc to make a circle. Cut out along this line. Enlarge pattern by copying on paper ruled in 1″ squares; complete half-pattern indicated by long dash line. Short dash lines indicate where pieces overlap. Using dressmaker's carbon and tracing wheel or dry ball-point pen, mark pattern pieces on felt for six reindeer: For each, cut brown body, head, eyes and eyebrows; tan face; pink ears; red nose; white eyes, beard and antlers. Omitting antlers, assemble each reindeer in the following order, pinning, then stitching with matching sewing thread. Stitch beard to body; face to beard; head to face; ears and nose to head; eyebrows to face. Glue eyes in place.

Place the six reindeer around edge of skirt equidistant from each other; pin. Slip antlers in place under head interlocking horns as shown in pattern; pin. Stitch reindeer and antlers to felt circle ⅛″ from edges.

To determine the size of the center opening for the tree trunk, estimate the approximate trunk diameter of the tree. Place tack with string in center of felt as before. The length of the string will be half the trunk diameter. Draw a circle the diameter of the tree trunk; cut out.

With a ruler, mark a straight line from center hole to edge of tree skirt. Cut along line for back opening of tree skirt.

Cut 1″ strips across width of white felt, to go around circumference of skirt; cut two 1″ strips for edges of slit. Fold strips in half around edges and stitch in place.

CHRISTMAS BANNER

Carolers in this wall hanging (which you appliqué, embroider, and quilt) extend an age-old holiday greeting. Hang in the foyer or family room for the benefit of arriving guests.

See General Directions for enlarging a pattern, appliqué, embroidery, and quilting.

SIZE: 23″ × 25¾″.

EQUIPMENT: Pencil. Ruler. Paper for patterns. Scissors. Dressmaker's tracing (carbon) paper. Tracing wheel or dry ball-point pen. Sewing, embroidery, and quilting needles. Straight pins. Embroidery hoop. Sewing machine.

MATERIALS: Closely woven cotton fabric, 36″ wide: dark green, ¾ yard; dark red, ⅜ yard. Cotton pieces for background: white, 17¼″ × 7¼″; white-on-black large dotted, 17¼″ × 10½″; white-on-gray small dotted, 17¼″ × 4½″. Cotton scraps for appliqués; see photograph. Batting. Gold grosgrain ribbon, ⅛″ wide, 2¾ yards. Six-strand embroidery floss: black, brown, tan, rose, dark red, white. Matching sewing threads.

DIRECTIONS: Draw lines across patterns, connecting grid lines. Enlarge patterns by copying on paper ruled in 1″ squares. Heavy lines indicate background and appliques, fine lines embroidery, dotted lines quilting. For three background patterns, continue lines separating sky, far ground, and near ground, drawing through figures. Using dressmaker's carbon and tracing wheel or dry ball-point

pen, transfer background patterns to wrong side of background pieces, following photograph. Cut out pieces ¼″ beyond marked lines. Press top edge of gray piece to right side, just inside marked line. With wrong side of both pieces facing up, overlap bottom ¼″ of black piece with top edge of gray piece; slip-stitch in place. "Wrong" sides of both pieces are now the "right" side, for muted coloring. Press under top edge of white piece (using either right or wrong side of fabric) and slip-stitch to gray piece in same manner. Ground-sky background piece should measure 17¼″ × 20″.

From red fabric, cut four strips 3⅜″ wide, two 23″ long and two 25¾″ long. Right sides facing and matching raw edges, center strips along sides of background piece. Stitch in place with ¼″ seam, press flat, then miter corners.

Appliqué: Transfer main outline of design onto background piece. Following photograph, cut and prepare individual pieces as directed for hand appliqué. (For brown and black hair, we used wrong side of fabrics.) Appliqué pieces in place as directed. Appliqué a heart (see small pattern) over each corner seam of border, ½″ from inner edge.

Embroidery: Replace pattern and transfer fine lines to piece. Following photograph for placement, transfer word pattern around red border. Place piece in embroidery hoop. Separating floss and using two strands in needle, embroider as follows: Work cheeks and eyes in satin stitch with rose and brown; work scarf fringe and highlight trees in straight stitch with dark red and white; outline other appliqués and embroider details in outline stitch with black, changing to brown for mother's hair, tan for girl's hair, dark red for scarf, white for clouds, and three strands of black to embroider girl's lower dress and words on border.

Quilting: Transfer dotted-line quilting pattern to piece. Cut same-size layer of batting. Place appliquéd piece right side up over batting and baste together with large cross-stitch. From green fabric, cut lining 24¾″ × 27½″. Place lining flat, wrong side up, and center appliquéd piece, right side up, over lining. Baste layers together lengthwise, crosswise, and diagonally. Using matching thread, starting in center, and working around and outward, quilt around figures, faces, boy's scarf, father's book; mother's cape, girl's V-shaped dress trim, trees, marked lines, and all around background, inside red border.

Finishing: Press in edge of lining ¼″, then pin excess onto red border, mitering corners. Slip-stitch in place, making ⅝″ green border. Cut gold ribbon to fit inside green border and slip-stitch in place.

APPLIQUE CHRISTMAS STORY

Free-standing, soft-sculpture crèche figures are backed by a hand-quilted panel showing the herald angel. Figures range from four and one-half inches (Babe) to fourteen inches (Joseph).

See General Directions for enlarging a pattern, appliqué, and embroidery.

CRECHE FIGURES

SIZE: Standing figures, 12½" to 14" tall. Baby Jesus, 4½" long.

EQUIPMENT: Pencil. Ruler. Paper for patterns. Sewing and embroidery needles. Dressmaker's tracing (carbon) paper. Tracing wheel or dry ball-point pen. Straight pins. Compass. Sewing machine. Iron.

MATERIALS: Closely woven cotton fabrics, 36" wide: ecru, medium blue, gold, and navy, ½ yard each; brown pinstripe, ¼ yard; scraps of brown, brown print, maroon, maroon print, and light pink. Six-strand embroidery floss: brown, peach, white. Quilt batting. Polyester fiberfill for stuffing. Sewing thread to match fabrics. Gold sport-weight yarn.

DIRECTIONS: Draw lines across patterns, connecting grid lines. Enlarge patterns by copying on paper ruled in 1" squares; complete half-patterns indicated by dash lines. Heavy lines indicate outlines and appliqués, fine lines embroidery. Using dressmaker's carbon and

tracing wheel or dry ball-point pen, transfer body outlines only to right side of ecru fabric, placing pieces ½" from fabric edges and ½" apart. Cut out bodies ¼" beyond marked lines. Following photograph, cut out individual pieces for hand appliqué. Appliqué pieces to ecru bodies, beginning with innermost pieces (underrobes) and ending with outermost

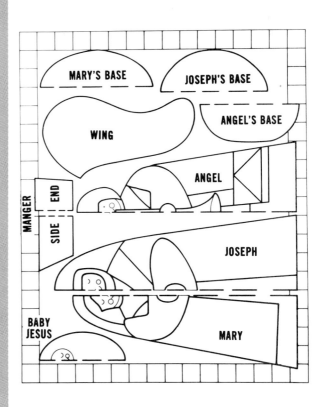

pieces (hands, hoods); prepare overlapping edges as you go, leaving overlapped edges raw; match raw outer edges of appliqués and bodies. When all pieces are appliquéd, replace patterns and transfer fine lines to figures. Using two strands of brown floss and outline stitch, stitch facial embroidery lines, except cheeks; also stitch Angel's horn detail and outline hands and lower edge of sleeves, as shown in photograph. Using two strands of white floss, stitch fine lines on Joseph's and Mary's clothing; outline top edge of Mary's sleeves as shown. Using three strands of peach floss and satin stitch, fill in cheeks of each figure.

Use ecru bodies (front) as patterns to cut same-size back from fabric, using gold for Angel, navy for Joseph, blue for Mary, and ecru for Baby Jesus. Also cut matching bases for standing figures, using patterns; add ¼" seam allowance all around. With right sides facing, raw edges even, and using thread to match back and base, stitch each front to its corresponding back, making ¼" seam and leaving bottom open. Stitch Baby Jesus to back in same manner, leaving 2" opening for turning. Pin half of each base to front piece of standing figure and stitch from seam to seam. Turn figures to right side. Stuff firmly with fiberfill. Press remaining edges ¼" to wrong side, slip-stitch opening closed. To finish Angel, use compass to make pattern for 4"-diameter circle; use to cut two halos from gold fabric and one from batting, adding ¼" seam allowance. Also cut four wings from blue and two from batting, adding ¼" seam allowance all around and reversing pattern for second and fourth pieces. Stack pairs of corresponding pieces with right sides facing, edges even, and a batting piece on top. Stitch ¼" seam around outside, leaving 2" opening for turning. Turn pieces to right side, so that batting is inside; press edges at opening ¼" to inside; slip-stitch opening closed. Slip-stitch halo and wings to back of Angel's head and body as shown, using matching thread.

To make manger, use patterns to cut four sides and four ends from brown pinstripe fabric and two each from batting, adding ¼"

seam allowance all around. Also cut two 3¾" × 4¾" rectangles for bottom and a same-size piece batting. Stitch together and finish corresponding pairs of manger pieces as for wings and halo. Using brown thread, slip-stitch end pieces to side pieces; stitch manger bottom in place. From gold yarn, cut eighty 4" pieces for hay. Tack 10 bundles of eight around inside bottom edges of manger.

HERALD ANGEL PANEL

SIZE: 21" × 26".

EQUIPMENT: Pencil. Ruler. Paper and tracing paper for patterns. Sewing, quilting, and embroidery needles. Dressmaker's tracing (carbon) paper. Tracing wheel or dry ball-point pen. Straight pins. Sewing machine. Iron.

MATERIALS: Closely woven cotton fabrics 36" wide: ecru, gold, brown, navy, ¼ yard each; light blue, medium blue, ½ yard each; maroon, ¾ yard. Six-strand embroidery floss: brown, peach. Quilt batting. Sewing thread to match fabrics.

DIRECTIONS: Draw lines across pattern, connecting grid lines. Enlarge pattern by copying on paper ruled in 1" squares; complete half-pattern indicated by dash line. Heavy lines indicate appliqués, fine lines embroidery. From light blue fabric, cut a 17" × 22" piece for background; place on flat surface with short edges at top and bottom. Center angel pattern over background; using dressmaker's carbon and dry ball-point pen, transfer heavy lines.

ACTUAL-SIZE PATTERN

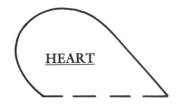

HEART

Following photograph, cut and prepare individual pieces for hand appliqué. Appliqué pieces to background as directed; cut a solid piece for horn; appliqué hand overlapping horn as shown. When all pieces are appliquéd, replace pattern and transfer fine lines to angel. Using two strands of brown floss in a needle, embroider nose, mouth, and chin in outline stitch. Make brown eyes with French knots. Fill in cheeks wtih satin stitch, using three strands of peach floss.

Cut two 3″ × 17″ and two 3″ × 22″ strips from medium blue fabric for border; also cut four 3″ squares from navy for corners. With right sides facing, raw edges even, and making ½″ seams, stitch 22″ strips to sides of background; press seams to one side. In same manner, stitch a navy square to each end of shorter strips, then stitch each resulting strip to top or bottom of background; press seams to one side. Piece should measure 21″ × 26″. Trace actual-size heart pattern; complete half-pattern indicated by dash line. Use pattern to cut out four heart appliqués as directed; appliqué one to each corner.

Cut a layer of quilt batting same size as appliquéd piece. Place piece right side up over batting and baste them together with a large cross-stitch. From maroon fabric, cut lining 23″ × 28″. Place lining flat, wrong side up, and center appliquéd piece, right side up, over lining. Baste layers together lengthwise, crosswise, and diagonally. Using matching thread and starting at center, quilt around each appliqué, close to the edge; also quilt along inside edge of border and corner strips.

Press in edge of lining ½″, then pin excess onto border, first along sides, then along top and bottom; slip-stitch in place, making a second border ½″ wide.

ANGEL

Kitchen and Dining Room

No holiday celebration is complete without the best of foods. Just follow your nose into the kitchen where you'll find yummy jams, breads, and other goodies. While you're there, feast your eyes on the handmade table decorations and serving accessories.

CHRISTMAS COOKIE TREATS

Use ginger- and sugar-cookie dough to create edible gifts and decorations! Little boxes are built with flat ginger cookies, iced with swirls and stars, then trimmed with favorite candies. The free-standing tree (over a foot tall) is made of ginger cookies, then trimmed with candies, sugar-cookie cutouts, and lots of luscious icing.

EQUIPMENT: Tracing paper. Pencil. Lightweight cardboard. Ruler. Single-edged razor blade. Aluminum foil. Sifter. Electric mixer and large mixing bowl. Rubber scraper. Rolling pin. Cookie sheets: 3 small ones or one used 3 times. Pastry blender or 2 knives. Sharp knife. Fork. Waxed paper. Spatula. Small saucepan. Pastry brush. Damp cloth. Bowl for icing. Pastry tube with tips for writing, rosettes, and thick serrated line.

MATERIALS: Gingerbread Cookies, Sugar Cookies, and Decorating Icing (see recipes following). Green and yellow vegetable food coloring. Candies for decorating: Assorted gumdrops, mint leaves, red hots, silver dragées. Tiny red candles and small white candle cups (the type used on birthday cakes). Sturdy cardboard, 2½" wide, 14" long (or mailing tube). Brown paper. Masking tape.

DIRECTIONS: Trace patterns; complete half-patterns indicated by dash lines. Make a separate pattern for each piece; cut out of cardboard. For tree sides, make patterns out of cardboard: cut one isosceles triangle 10" wide at base and 12½" high. Cut pieces of cardboard for box sides and lids. For box at right, cut 3" square for sides, top, and bottom. For box at center front, cut cardboard 4" × 2¾" for top, bottom, and two sides, and 2¾" square for two ends. For box at left, cut piece of cardboard 2¾" × 4" for sides and 2¾" square for top and bottom. Cover patterns with aluminum foil.

Make Gingerbread Cookies as follows:

Gingerbread Cookies

 3 cups sifted all-purpose flour
 ½ teaspoon baking soda
 ½ teaspoon salt
2½ teaspoons ginger
 ½ teaspoon nutmeg
 ½ cup soft butter or margarine
 ½ cup light brown sugar, firmly packed
 1 egg
 ½ cup light molasses

Note: To make all of the gingerbread pieces, you will need to double this recipe.

Sift flour with baking soda, salt, ginger, and nutmeg; set aside. In large bowl of electric mixer, at medium speed, beat butter, sugar, and egg until light and fluffy. At low speed, beat in molasses until smooth. Gradually add flour mixture, beating until smooth and well combined. With rubber scraper, form dough into a ball. Wrap in waxed paper or foil; refrigerate overnight.

Divide dough into four parts. Use two parts now and refrigerate two parts until ready to roll out.

Preheat oven to 375° F. Lightly grease cookie sheets. Lightly flour cookie sheets; roll out gingerbread dough to ¼″ thickness. Place tree pattern on dough and cut around it with knife. Repeat twice for a three-sided tree. Roll out more dough as needed. Using pattern, cut six bird wings. Using patterns, cut all the box pieces.

Bake pieces 10 to 12 minutes or until brown. Using spatula, remove carefully to sheet of waxed paper; let cool.

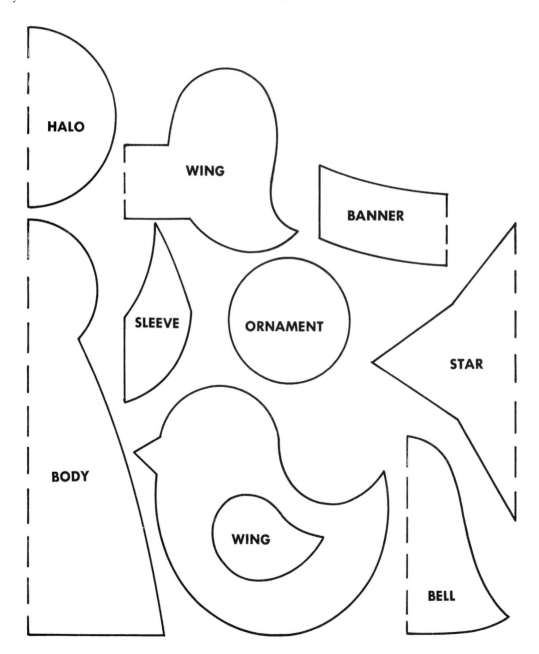

Make Sugar Cookies as follows:

Sugar Cookies

1¾ cups sifted all-purpose flour
½ teaspoon baking powder
½ teaspoon salt
½ teaspoon baking soda
½ cup sugar
½ cup butter or margarine
1 egg
2 tablespoons milk
1 teaspoon vanilla

Sift flour with baking powder, salt, baking soda, and sugar into large bowl. With pastry blender or two knives, cut butter into flour mixture until it has the consistency of coarse corn meal.

With fork, stir in egg, milk, and vanilla. Mix well with hands. Form into ball. Wrap in waxed paper and refrigerate at least two hours.

Preheat oven to 350° F. Lightly grease cookie sheets.

Divide dough into three balls and roll out one at a time to ⅛″ thickness. Place patterns on dough. Using sharp knife, cut out each piece. For each side of tree, cut out angel body, one wing piece, two sleeves (reverse sleeve pattern for second sleeve), halo, two birds, one banner, two ornaments, one bell, and two stars for top of tree; cut one star in half.

Bake 7 minutes, until lightly golden. Using spatula, remove pieces to waxed paper; let cool.

For tree trunk, roll the strong cardboard into a 4″ diameter tube 2½″ high; tape to secure. Cover tube with brown paper and tape. For base of tree, cut a 10″ equilateral triangle out of cardboard. Set the base on tree trunk.

Attach cookie pieces as follows:

Make a sugar glue: Put sugar in saucepan and melt over low heat. Using pastry brush, brush edges to be adhered with sugar glue and, very quickly, put pieces together.

Attach the three tree triangle sides with sugar glue. Sugar-glue bottom edges to cardboard base. With sugar glue, put the angel cookie parts together. Following photograph, sugar-glue angel and all other sugar cookie pieces in place. Glue gingerbread wing on each bird. Make sure you use enough sugar glue to hold pieces securely. Glue on mint candy leaves.

Make Decorating Icing as follows:

Decorating Icing

2½ cups confectioner's sugar
¼ teaspoon cream of tartar
2 egg whites
½ teaspoon vanilla

Sift sugar and cream of tartar into large bowl. Add egg whites and vanilla. Beat until very stiff. Cover with damp cloth until ready to use.

Complete decoration as follows:

Place about one-half of the icing in separate bowl; add green food coloring until you get desired shade of green. Using white icing in tube and writing tip, make all lines of white icing on each side as shown; imbed dragées in icing for bird eyes, wing, and halo decorations. Using rosette tip, make white rosettes along side and bottom edges as shown. Glue star pieces together with sugar glue; glue in place on top of tree and trim with white icing rosettes. Imbed candle cups into icing, adding more icing to secure. To make candle in angel's hands, cut tiny slice of mint leaf or green gumdrop and secure with icing. Mix yellow coloring in small amount of icing and put in tube with writing tip; use to make angel hair, trim on dress and sleeves, and candle flame.

Put green icing in tube and with writing tip finish decorating as shown. Add red hots and dragées as shown, securing with dabs of icing.

Assemble boxes with sugar glue. Decorate boxes as shown. To cover box with icing, use knife to spread icing over surface smoothly. To get wavy line, use serrated tip in one continuous line.

RIBBON CRAFTS

Ribbons descend layer upon layer for crisp Christmas decor. Cut strips, glue to florist's wire, then insert in styrofoam shapes. Table-topper has matching bands stitched around the edges.

RIBBON WREATH

EQUIPMENT: Scissors. Ruler.

MATERIALS: Styrofoam wreath, 11½" diameter, 1⅜" wide. Two packages white florist's wire. Polka-dot grosgrain ribbon, 1½" wide in the following colors and yardage: red, 3½; rust, yellow, and gold, 2½ each. White craft glue.

DIRECTIONS: Cut ribbon into 3½" lengths. Trim one end of each length into a V and the other end to a point. Cut florist's wire into 3" lengths. Glue a length to the back of each piece of ribbon, allowing about 1" of wire to extend beyond the pointed end.

Working in counterclockwise direction and varying ribbon colors, insert extending ends of wire into styrofoam wreath, with "V" ends of ribbon slanting outward. Overlap ribbons just enough so styrofoam and the pointed ends of ribbons are covered.

When wreath is completely covered with inserted ribbons, bend ribbons into a nicely rounded shape so that none protrudes awkwardly.

RIBBON TABLECLOTH

EQUIPMENT: Scissors. Tape measure. Straight pins. Sewing machine.

MATERIALS: White tablecloth, 49" square or white linen or cotton fabric pieced to make cloth to fit your table. Polka-dot grosgrain ribbon, 1½" wide; 3⅓ yards each of red, rust, yellow, and gold (more for larger size). White sewing thread.

DIRECTIONS: **Note:** If you are making tablecloth a different size, cut ribbons the size of one edge of cloth plus 11" for the extensions. To make 90" cloth of fabric 45" wide, you will need 180" (5 yards) of fabric cut into two 90" lengths and seamed together.

Cut ribbons into 60" lengths so you have two lengths of each color. Pin red grosgrain ribbon to tablecloth on two parallel sides, 4½" in from edge of tablecloth, with ends extending 5½" over edges of tablecloth. Pin rust grosgrain ribbon in same manner, leaving ½" space between rust and red ribbons.

Pin yellow grosgrain ribbon to tablecloth on the other two parallel sides, 4½" in from the sides of tablecloth, then pin on gold

grosgrain ribbon, leaving ½″ space between the gold and yellow.

At each of the four corners weave ends of ribbons over and under each other and pin in woven position. Machine stitch all ribbons in place on tablecloth along both edges of each ribbon. Cut extending ends of all ribbons into points.

RIBBON TREE

EQUIPMENT: Ruler. Scissors.

MATERIALS: Dowel, ½″ diameter, 12″ long. Styrofoam cone, 18″ high. Piece of 1″ thick styrofoam, at least 4″ square. Two packages white florist's wire. White craft glue. Polka-dot grosgrain ribbon 1½″ wide, in the following yardage: yellow, 4; gold, 3; red, 6; rust, 4. White decorative flowerpot, about 4″ in diameter. Small amount of red sewing thread.

DIRECTIONS: Reserving one yard of red ribbon to make bows to trim tree top, cut and assemble ribbons as for wreath.

Working from the bottom up, insert extending ends of wire into the styrofoam cone with "V" ends of ribbon pointing down. Vary the different colors and overlap ribbons just enough so that the ends of all ribbons show.

Cut remaining yard of red ribbon in half. Fold each piece into a bow shape but do not tie in a knot; hold each together by twisting red thread around center of bow and securing. Clip each end of each bow into V shape. Loop a 3″ length of wire through thread at back of each bow and fold wire into hairpin shape. Insert these ends into very top of styrofoam cone.

Push about 6″ of dowel into the center of the cone base. Cut 1″ thick styrofoam to fit securely inside the top rim of flowerpot. Place in flowerpot and insert end of dowel so that tree base sits on flowerpot rim (trim dowel if necessary).

PATCHWORK SQUARES

Make a wall hanging in which patchwork squares revolve around a diamond-patch star, then repeat the pattern in a matching tablecloth. Both pieces honor Christmas tradition with joyous red and green.

STAR HANGING

SIZE: 26¾″ square.

EQUIPMENT: Pencil. Ruler. Paper for patterns (preferably graph paper). Glue. Thin, stiff cardboard. Scissors. Sewing needle. Sewing machine.

MATERIALS: Closely woven cotton or cotton-blend fabric, 36″ wide: green, 2½ yards; solid red, large red print, and small red print, ⅛ yard each. (**Note:** We used polished cotton for the solid red and green.) Batting. Sewing thread, red and green.

GENERAL DIRECTIONS: Make patterns, following directions below and Diagrams A, B, and C. Draw patterns on paper as accurately as possible, using a ruler and sharp pencil; graph paper will help in drawing corners square. Glue paper to cardboard, then cut out pattern on lines drawn.

Cut patch pieces, marking patterns on wrong side of fabric and leaving at least ½″ between pieces; place as many straight edges as possible on the straight of goods, across width of fabric. Cut out pieces ¼″ away from marked lines, which will be stitching lines.

To join patch pieces, place them together, right sides facing, and sew on marked lines, making ¼″ seam allowance.

A Pieces: For pattern, draw a rectangle 9⅝″ × 4″. Mark midpoint of each side. Connect midpoints as shown in Diagram A, making a diamond shape with sides 5¼″ long; cut out diamond. Before cutting patch pieces, test your pattern by drawing around it eight times to make an eight-pointed star as shown in center of diagram for Assembling Wall Hanging; the diamonds drawn should fit neatly side by side, with no gaps or overlaps. Using pattern, cut eight diamond pieces (A) from green fabric, following General Directions above.

B Pieces: Make a pattern 1¹⁵⁄₁₆″ square. Using pattern and following General Directions, cut 32 square pieces each from solid red fabric and from small-print red fabric; cut 64 square pieces from large-print red fabric. Assemble 16 squares to make a block as shown in Diagram B, following Color Key; sew squares together in rows, then sew rows together, following General Directions. Block should measure 5¾″ square (5¼″ plus ¼″ around outside edges for seam allowance). Make seven more blocks in same manner for eight B pieces.

C Pieces: For pattern, draw a rectangle 12⅝" × 3¾". On one long side, mark a point 3¹¹⁄₁₆" from each corner. Connect points marked with opposite corners for pattern C, as shown in Diagram C. Using pattern and following General Directions, cut eight C pieces from green fabric.

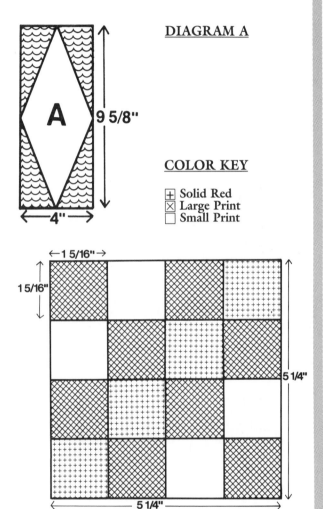

DIAGRAM A

9 5/8"

4"

COLOR KEY

⊞ Solid Red
⊠ Large Print
☐ Small Print

1 5/16"

15/16"

5 1/4"

5 1/4"

DIAGRAM B

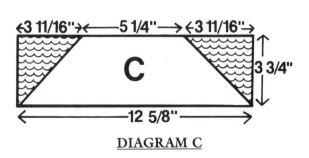

3 11/16" 5 1/4" 3 11/16"

C

3 3/4"

12 5/8"

DIAGRAM C

Assembling Wall Hanging: See diagram. Begin in center by joining A pieces to each other to make an eight-pointed star; when joining two pieces, stitch from wide angles to center point of star. Stitch B pieces between the star points, placing each block so that solid red squares are at tips of star points; see photograph. Stitch C pieces in place around the B pieces. The design made should now measure 25¾" square (25¼" plus ¼" around outside edges for seam allowance). **Note:** If your design has a different measurement, adjust following measurements accordingly.

From green fabric, cut piece 26¾" square for lining (or 1" longer and wider than your piece). Cut a layer of batting same size. Place lining, wrong side up, on a flat surface. Place batting on lining. Place pieced design on batting, centered and right side up; there should be ½" margin of batting and lining all around pieced design. Baste layers together securely, lengthwise, crosswise, diagonally, and around perimeter.

Quilting: Thread bobbin and needle on sewing machine with red thread. Stitch through all thicknesses of wall hanging at the following places: over seams joining A pieces; around perimeter of star, ¼" in from edges of points; around three inner sides of C pieces, ¼" in from edges.

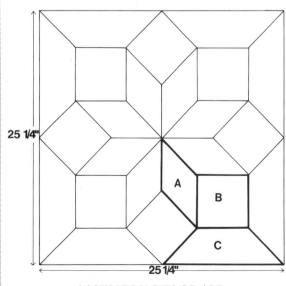

25 1/4"

A

B

C

25 1/4"

ASSEMBLY DIAGRAM

Finishing: To bind edges, cut four strips from green fabric 2¾″ wide, two 26¾″ long and two 27¾″ long. Sew a shorter strip to one side of hanging as follows: Pin strip to hanging, right sides facing and matching raw edge of strip to raw edge of pieced design. Stitch ¼″ from these raw edges, through all thicknesses. Turn strip to right side, then fold it over to back of hanging, enclosing raw edges of batting and lining. Turn long raw edge of strip under ½″ and baste in place to lining. Turn hanging back to right side and topstitch with red thread, around design, close to stitched edge of binding. Attach second shorter strip to opposite side in same manner. Repeat to attach longer strips to remaining sides, but centering each one and turning in extra ½″ at each end before basting to lining.

PATCHWORK TABLE SKIRT

SIZE: 89¾″ in diameter.

EQUIPMENT: See Star Hanging. **Additional:** String. Yardstick. Thumbtack. Tape.

MATERIALS: Closely woven cotton or cotton-blend fabric, 36″ wide: green, 3½ yards; solid red and small red print, ¾ yard each; medium red print, 1 yard; large red print, ½ yard. (**Note:** We used polished cotton for the solid red and green.) Sewing thread, red and green.

DIRECTIONS: See Star Hanging for General Directions: to make patterns, follow directions below and Diagrams A and B for Table Skirt.

A Pieces: To make pattern, draw a rectangle 14″ × 33″. Mark midpoint of each side. Connect midpoints as shown in Diagram A, making a diamond shape with sides 18″ long. Before cutting patches, test accuracy of your pattern by drawing around it eight times on a

piece of paper to make an eight-pointed star as shown in center of diagram for Assembling Table Skirt; the diamonds drawn should fit neatly side by side, with no gaps or overlaps. Using pattern, cut eight diamond pieces (A) from green fabric, following General Directions given for Star Hanging.

B Pieces: Make a pattern 4½″ square. Using pattern and following General Directions, cut 32 square pieces each from solid red fabric and from small print fabric; cut 16 square pieces from large print fabric; cut 48 square pieces from medium print fabric. Assemble 16 squares to make a block as shown in Diagram B, following Color Key; sew squares together in rows, then sew rows together, following General Directions. Block should measure 18½″ square (18″ plus ¼″ around outside edges for seam allowance). Make seven more blocks in same manner for eight B pieces.

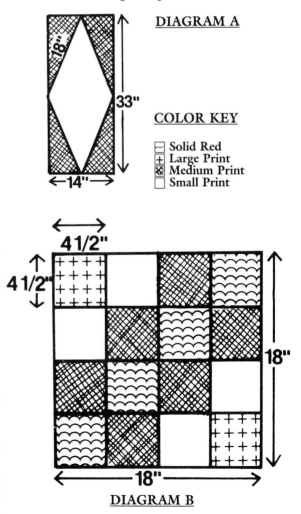

DIAGRAM A

COLOR KEY

- ⊟ Solid Red
- ⊞ Large Print
- ⊠ Medium Print
- ☐ Small Print

DIAGRAM B

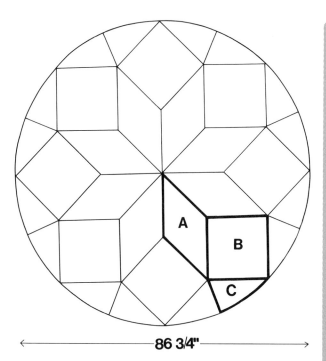

←———— 86 3/4" ————→

<u>ASSEMBLY DIAGRAM</u>

Assembling Table Skirt (A-B piece): See diagram. Begin in center by joining A pieces to each other to make an eight-pointed star; when joining two pieces, stitch from wide angles to center of star. Stitch B pieces between the star points, placing each block so that solid red squares are at tips of star points; see photograph.

C Pieces: On two adjacent B pieces, turn remaining ¼″ seam allowance around outside edges to front, folding on marked lines; temporarily pin in place and press folded edges.

Spread your A-B piece on a flat working surface, smoothing it out all around as evenly as possible. Slip a piece of paper (about 18″ × 36″) under edges of two prepared B pieces, leaving most of paper exposed. Tape A-B piece and paper securely to working surface.

Make compass as follows: Cut string about 50″ long. Tie a knot at one end. Thumbtack knot to center of A-B piece. Measure distance between knot and outside corner of a prepared B piece; tie a pencil to other end of string, keeping this measurement. Holding pencil upright, mark an arc on paper between the outside corners of the two prepared B pieces. Remove compass. Position yardstick from center of A-B piece through center of arc drawn, going through acute angles of the A piece; mark short line of C piece on paper as shown in diagram. Mark along outer edge of B piece on paper as shown, completing shape of pattern C. Untape A-B piece and paper, unpin seam allowance. Cut pattern C.

Using pattern, cut 16 C pieces from green fabric, following General Directions and placing short straight edge of pattern on straight of goods.

Sew C pieces to each other in pairs, joining on short straight edges, for eight double-C pieces. Sew double-C pieces between B pieces as shown in diagram. Table skirt should now measure about 87¼″ in diameter (86¾″ plus ¼″ seam allowance all around).

Edging: Cut bias strips 3½″ wide; place together to make strip long enough to go around perimeter of table skirt. Fold strip in half lengthwise, wrong side inward, and press carefully without stretching. Place folded strip around tableskirt, right sides facing and matching raw edges. Stitch all around, ¼″ from raw edges. Press seam allowance toward center of skirt on wrong side.

HOLIDAY TABLE SETTING

Deck your holiday table with holly! Festive cutwork place mats are stitched on the machine—the quick and easy way. Ribbon "bouquets" for the candles are a charming addition.

PLACE MATS AND RUNNER

See General Directions for enlarging a pattern.

SIZES: Table Runner, 34½″ × 14½″. Place Mat, 17″ × 14½″.

EQUIPMENT: Pencil. Ruler. Paper for patterns. Sharp-pointed and regular scissors. Compass. Dressmaker's tracing (carbon) paper. Tracing wheel or dry ball-point pen. Embroidery hoop, 8″ × 10″. Straight pins. Sewing needle. Sewing machine with zigzag attachment. Iron.

MATERIALS (makes two place mats or one table runner): Off-white medium-weight coarsely woven linen fabric, 44″ wide, ½ yd. Scraps of red heavy-weight satin fabric. Sewing thread, red and green. Appliqué or embroidery support backing, at least 36″ × 24″.

DIRECTIONS: Draw lines across desired pattern, connecting grid lines. Enlarge pattern by copying on paper ruled in 1″ squares.

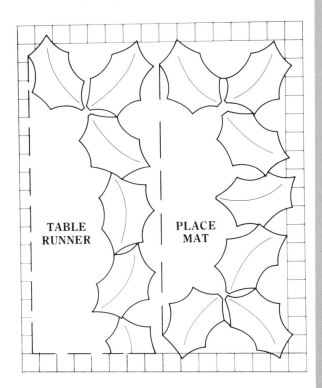

Complete half- or quarter-pattern indicated by dash lines. Use dressmaker's carbon and tracing wheel or dry ball-point pen to mark two place mats or one table runner on right side of linen fabric, placing pieces 1″ from fabric edges and 1″ apart. On red fabric, mark twelve 1″ circles for each place mat or runner; set aside extra fabric for test sample. Do not cut out pieces until directed.

To Embroider: Read all directions, then practice on test sample before beginning work. Cut support backing into pieces about 2″ larger than embroidery hoop. Center fabric area to be embroidered face down over inner ring of hoop. Place support backing on top; close and tighten hoop. Turn hoop so design faces up. Place hoop below sewing machine needle. Using green thread for place mat or runner, zigzag-stitch all heavy lines within hoop (see original pattern) with machine set for ⅛″-wide stitches. Reset machine for ¹⁄₁₆″-wide stitches and zigzag-stitch fine lines. Move hoop as necessary as you stitch; do not remove backing, but add a new piece to hoop each time you move it. Using red thread and ⅛″-wide stitches, outline berries. When all embroidery is complete, remove fabric from hoop. Gently tear away backing from wrong side of fabric; a little of backing will remain under stitches.

To Finish: Use sharp-pointed scissors to carefully cut out embroidered pieces along outlines, making sure not to cut into stitching. Pin a cluster of three berries to each corner of place mat or runner; see photograph for placement. Tack berries in place with invisible stitches. Press completed piece with cool iron.

RIBBON CANDLES

SIZE: About 7″ wide and 12″ tall.

EQUIPMENT: Ruler. Pencil. Scissors. Cardboard, 4″-wide piece and 5¼″-wide piece. Sharp knife. White craft glue.

MATERIALS (FOR TWO): One plastic foam ball, 5″ diameter. Red/green plaid lace-edged ribbon, 1½″ wide, about 35 yards. Thin green wire. Red or green Christmas ornaments, 1″ diameter, 20. Stiff green paper, 3″ × 5″. Two 2½″ clear bobeches. Two tapered 10″ candles.

DIRECTIONS: For Bows: Cut 15 pieces of ribbon 2½ ft. long, 20 pieces 3 ft. long. Cut 35 pieces of wire 8″ long. To make a bow, wrap a ribbon piece, right side out, around cardboard, then cut notches in loops at center of each side (Fig. 1). Slip ribbon off cardboard. Twist and tighten a piece of wire around notched ribbon (Fig. 2). Fan out bow (Fig. 3). Make 15 small bows with 4″ cardboard and 2½ ft. ribbon; make 20 large bows with 5¼″ cardboard and 3 ft. ribbon. Attach Christmas ornaments to wire on large bows. **For Candle Base:** With sharp knife, carefully cut plastic foam ball in half, for two bases. Smooth flat side for base bottom with hand and edge of knife. Placing bases flat side down, draw a circle, slightly smaller than bottom of candle, in

Fig. 1

Fig. 2

Fig. 3

MAKING BOW

center of rounded top. Cut plastic foam, digging out a ¾″-deep hole. Attach 10 large bows evenly around edge of base by dipping wire end in glue and sticking wire into plastic foam. If using more than one color ornament, alternate colors. Add about seven small bows randomly to fill out base and cover plastic foam. Do not cover candle hole.

Cut a 2¼″-diameter circle of stiff green paper. Cut a circle, slightly larger than bottom of green candle, in center of green circle. Put white glue in bottom of hole in plastic foam. Place bottom of candle through bobeche, then through green circle, and push firmly into hole. Let dry.

SNOWFLAKING

With a little gingham and a few simple embroidery stitches, you can sew all sorts of cute kitchen accessories. Towels, pot holder, hot mitt, tea cozy, ornaments, napkin rings, jar covers—all have the snowflake theme.

See General Directions at end of book for embroidery instructions.

EQUIPMENT: Ruler (or yardstick). Pencil (or tailor's chalk). Scissors. Straight pins. Tapestry needle. Sewing machine. Iron. Embroidery hoop (optional). See individual directions for any additional equipment.

MATERIALS: Gingham with 6 checks to the inch, 58½" wide, red/white or green/white; see individual directions for yardage or size of pieces. Matching sewing thread. Six-strand cotton embroidery floss in matching red or green and white, one skein each unless otherwise indicated. See individual directions for any additional materials.

GENERAL DIRECTIONS: To prevent fabric from raveling, bind raw edges with masking tape, whipstitch edges by hand, or machine-stitch ⅛" in from edges. To keep fabric taut, work embroidery in a hoop if desired or where possible; move hoop as needed. Cut floss into 24" lengths; separate strands and use three strands in tapestry needle throughout. Begin and end strands by knotting on back of work. Stitching tends to twist the working strand; now and then let needle and strand hang freely to untwist.

Work embroidery following individual directions, charts, and stitch details; each graph square on charts represents one check on

gingham fabric: Using red or green floss to match fabric, work double cross-stitches shown with heavy lines first. Changing to white floss, work double cross-stitches shown with light lines next. Continuing with white floss, work straight stitches where indicated by long horizontal and vertical lines. Connect straight stitches with Threaded Squares, following detail: Bring needle to front of work at A. Slide needle under each straight stitch in turn as shown for one round; continue for second round, then take needle to back of work at A; rounds will look square, as shown on charts.

When all embroidery is completed, press piece gently, face down, on a padded surface.

KITCHEN TOWELS

SIZE: 14½" × 19½", plus fringe.

EQUIPMENT: See above.

MATERIALS: See above. Gingham, 15" × 20" piece red or green for each towel.

DIRECTIONS: See General Directions above. To bind edges, straight- or zigzag-stitch a line all around piece, counting three rows of checks from one short edge (bottom) of towel and two rows from side and top edges; stitching lines will be fringing guides later. Fold piece in half vertically to find center row of white checks; mark with pin. Unfold and reposition pin for first stitch, counting seven or five white checks up from bottom stitching along center row, for wide or narrow margin; see photograph. Work design following chart, beginning at stitch indicated by arrow: Working across toward right edge, work A-B 5 times. Work in reverse toward left edge, omitting center column. When all embroidery is completed, press piece. To finish, fringe each edge of towel by pulling crosswise threads to stitching line.

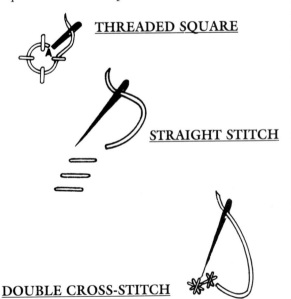

THREADED SQUARE

STRAIGHT STITCH

DOUBLE CROSS-STITCH

POT HOLDER

SIZE: 7″ square, plus trim.

EQUIPMENT: See above. Plus: Sewing needle. Knitting needle.

MATERIALS: See above. Gingham, 8″ × 16″ piece red. Plus: White pre-ruffled cotton eyelet trim, ⅞″ wide, ⅞ yard. Polyester ribbon, ⁵⁄₁₆″ wide, 3″ piece red.

DIRECTIONS: See General Directions above. Cut gingham in half to form two 8″ squares. Cut 2 same-size pieces of batting; set aside. Prepare one gingham piece (front) for embroidery.

To Embroider: Fold piece in half twice to locate centermost white check; mark with straight pin. Count three white checks up from center and mark, for first stitch. Beginning at arrow, work entire chart for left half of design, omitting Threaded Squares in center (starred) column. Reverse chart to work right half, omitting starred column, then work Threaded Squares down center as shown. When embroidery is completed, press piece.

To Assemble: Baste one piece of batting to wrong side of each gingham piece. Fold ribbon in half widthwise for hanging loop. Baste loop to right side of back piece at one corner (top) with raw edges even. Cut eyelet to fit around embroidered front, plus 1″. Fold eyelet in half widthwise, wrong side out, and stitch ends together with ½″ seam; press seam open. Pin eyelet around front piece wrong side out and with raw edges even; baste. Pin pot holder back to front, wrong sides out, and enclosing hanging loop and eyelet; stitch ½″ from edges,

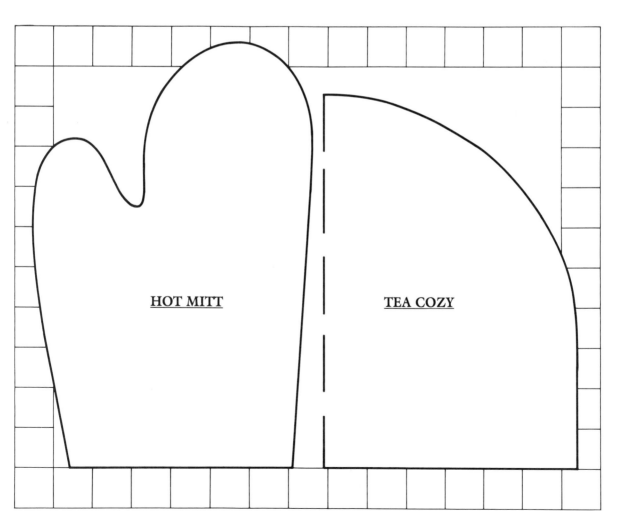

HOT MITT

TEA COZY

leaving an opening in one edge for turning. Clip across seam allowance at corners; turn to right side, poking out corners with knitting needle. Fold raw edges ½" to inside; slip-stitch opening closed.

HOT MITT

SIZE: 10½" long, plus trim.

EQUIPMENT: See above. Plus: Paper for pattern.

MATERIALS: See above. Gingham, 12" × 18 piece green. Plus: White pre-ruffled cotton eyelet trim, ⅞" wide, ⅜ yard. Closely woven cotton fabric, 12" × 18" piece white, for lining.

DIRECTIONS: See General Directions above. Draw lines across pattern, connecting grid lines. Enlarge pattern by copying on paper ruled in 1" squares; cut out. Mark 2 mitts on gingham, placing them ½" from fabric edges and 1" apart and lining up wrist edge with a row of checks. Cut out, adding ½" seam allowance all around each. Cut 2 same-size pieces each from lining fabric and batting; set aside. Prepare one gingham mitt (front) for embroidery. (For right-handed mitt, thumb should be at left.)

To Embroider: Measure along marked wrist edge to find centermost white check; mark with straight pin. Measure about 2" up from pin to nearest white check and mark, for first stitch. Following chart, beginning at stitch indicated by arrow, work A-B twice to right; end with C. Repeat in reverse to left, omitting first (center) row worked. When embroidery is completed, press piece.

To Assemble: Baste one piece of batting to wrong side of each gingham mitt. Cut 2 lengths of eyelet to fit wrist edges. Pin one length to each mitt, right sides facing and with raw edges even; baste. Cut 1½" × 4½" bias strip from lining fabric. Press long edges ¼" to wrong side; press in half lengthwise right side out;

stitch close to folds. Fold strip in half widthwise for hanging loop. Baste to right side of plain gingham mitt at one end of wrist with raw edges even. Pin gingham mitts together, wrong sides out. Stitch around hand, making ½" seam; do not stitch wrist. Clip into seam allowance at curves; turn to right side. Stitch linings together in same manner, leaving 4" opening in longer side edge; clip curves; do not turn. Slip lining over mitt with wrist edges even. Stitch around wrist ½" from edges through all thicknesses. Pull mitt through lining. Turn raw edges ½" to inside; slip-stitch opening closed. Insert lining into mitt.

TEA COZY

SIZE: About 9" × 13".

EQUIPMENT: See above. Plus: Paper for pattern. Sewing needle.

MATERIALS: See above. Gingham, ⅓ yard green. Plus: Muslin, 36" wide, ⅓ yard. Jumbo rickrack, ¾ yard white. Batting.

DIRECTIONS: See General Directions above. Draw lines across pattern, connecting grid lines. Enlarge pattern by copying on paper ruled in 1" squares. Complete half-pattern, indicated by dash line. Cut out pattern. Mark two cozy shapes on gingham, placing them 1" from fabric edges and 1" apart and lining up straight (bottom) edge with a row of checks. Cut out, adding ½" seam allowance all around each. Cut two same-size pieces from muslin and four from batting; set aside. Prepare one gingham cozy (front) for embroidery.

Fold gingham front piece in half, matching curved edges, to locate centermost white check on bottom line; mark with straight pin. Measure up 6½" from bottom white check to nearest white check for first stitch; mark. Work design, following chart for Tree Ornament and beginning at stitch indicated by arrow. Work entire chart for left half of design, omitting Threaded Squares in center (starred) column. Reverse chart to work right half, omitting starred column, then work Threaded Squares down center as shown. When all embroidery is completed, press piece. Work design on cozy back in same manner.

Baste 2 pieces of batting to wrong side of each gingham cozy. Cut rickrack the length of side and top edge of cozy front. Pin rickrack on right side with center ½″ from edge; baste through all layers. Pin gingham cozies together with batting on outside. Stitch around sides and top, following line of basting and leaving bottom edge open. Clip into seam allowance at curves; turn to right side. Press bottom edges ½″ to inside; baste. Stitch muslin pieces (linings) together in same manner; clip into curves; do not turn. Press bottom edges of lining ½″ to outside. Insert lining into cozy, matching seams and folds. Whipstitch folded edges together all around. Tack lining to cozy through seam at center top.

ORNAMENTS

SIZE: Both, about 5″ high.

EQUIPMENT: See above. Plus: Sewing needle. Knitting needle.

MATERIALS **(for each):** See above. Gingham, 8″ × 16″ piece red. Plus: Polyester ribbon, 5/16″ wide, 3″ piece red. Polyester fiberfill or cotton balls, for stuffing.

DIRECTIONS **(for each):** See General Directions above. Cut fabric in half to form two 8″ squares. Prepare one fabric square (front) for embroidery. Fold piece in half twice to locate centermost white check; mark with straight pin. For Star, count 4 white checks up from center check and mark for first stitch; for Tree, count up 6 white checks. Work design, following chart for Star Ornament or Tree Ornament and beginning at stitch indicated by arrow. Work entire chart for left half of each design, omitting Threaded Squares in center

(starred) column. Reverse chart to work right half, omitting starred column, then work Threaded Squares down center as shown. When embroidery is completed, press piece.

Mark Star or Tree shape on wrong side of fabric, counting one check beyond outermost stitches for Star; for Tree, count 2 checks at upper sides, one check at lower sides, and 3 checks at bottom. Cut out beyond marked line for ¼″ seam allowance all around. Cut matching fabric back. Fold ribbon in half widthwise for hanging loop. Baste loop to right side of ornament front at center top with raw edges even. Pin front and back pieces together, right sides facing, matching edges, and sandwiching loop between. Stitch on marked line, leaving an opening in one side for turning and stuffing. Clip into seam allowance at corners; turn to right side. Stuff firmly, using knitting needle to poke stuffing into corners. Fold raw edges ¼″ to inside; slip-stitch opening closed.

NAPKIN RINGS

SIZE: 1⅞″ long, plus trim.

EQUIPMENT: See above.

MATERIALS: See above. Gingham, 6″ × 8″ piece red. Plus: Pre-ruffled eyelet trim, 1″ wide, 14″ piece white. Cardboard tubing 1½″ diameter, 1⅞″ piece. White craft glue.

DIRECTIONS **(for each ring):** See General Directions above. Prepare fabric for embroidery. Fold piece in half twice to locate centermost white check; mark with straight pin. Place piece with long edges at top and bottom; move pin to first white check directly above center white check, for first stitch. Following chart, beginning at stitch indicated by arrow, work pattern across to right, then to left; for 13 red cross-stitches at top or bottom. When embroidery is completed, press piece.

With wrong side facing out, wrap piece around tubing, bringing short edges together;

STAR ORNAMENT

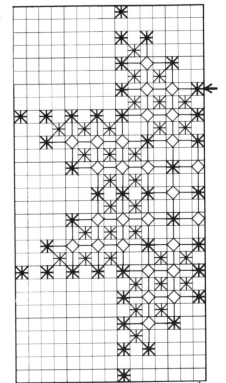

APRON BIB

NAPKIN RING

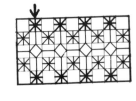

JAR COVER

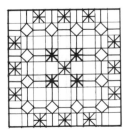

NAPKIN, PLACE MAT

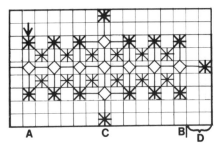

A   C   B| D

TREE ORNAMENT

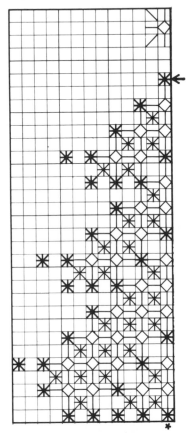

HOT MITT

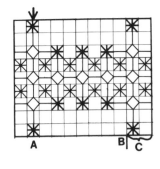

A   B| C

POT HOLDER

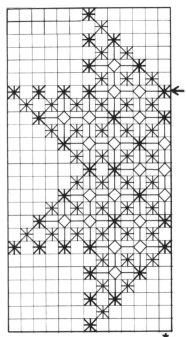

TOWEL

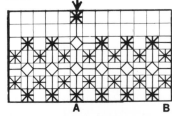

A   B

132

mark seamline. Remove from tubing and stitch on line; press seam open; turn cover to right side. Slip cover over tubing, centering design. Fold fabric edges neatly to inside of tube; glue to secure. Cut eyelet in half for two 7″ lengths. Press one end of each length ½″ to wrong side. Starting with folded end, glue a piece of eyelet inside each edge of ring; overlap ends and glue in place.

JAR COVERS

SIZE: Makes 2 covers (ours, 2¾″ diameter).

EQUIPMENT: See above. Plus: Compass. Pinking shears.

MATERIALS: See above. Gingham, 9″-square piece red or green for each. Plus: Grosgrain ribbon, ⅛″ wide: 1½ yards white, ¾ yard each red and green.

DIRECTIONS: See General Directions above. Prepare fabric for embroidery. Fold piece in half twice to locate centermost solid-color check; mark with straight pin. Following chart, work complete design as shown; begin by working 4 colored cross-stitches on the white checks touching center check. When embroidery is completed, press piece. Set compass for 7½″ circle; place point of compass at centermost check and mark circle. Cut out circle on marked line; pink edges. Center cover on jar lid right side up. Cut ¾-yard length from white ribbon. Place white and colored ribbons together with ends even; tie bow around base of jar lid as shown.

KITCHEN CRAFT IDEAS

Welcome a new neighbor or say "Merry Christmas" to an old friend with harvest home gifts that make the most of your crafts know-how. Beautiful hand-decorated baskets, for example, are gifts in themselves. Fill with your own zucchini pickles, corn relish, or "no cooking" jams.

HARVEST RECIPES

No–Cook Strawberry Jam

- 1 quart fully ripe strawberries
- 1 cup light corn syrup
- 3 cups sugar
- ¾ cup water
- 1 package (1¾ oz.) powdered fruit pectin

Rinse and stem strawberries. In deep bowl, fully crush berries, one layer at a time, to let juice flow freely. Measure and turn 2 cups berries/juice into 4-quart bowl. Add corn syrup; stir well. Gradually add sugar, stirring thoroughly to dissolve sugar. Let stand 10 minutes. In 1-quart saucepan, stir together water and fruit pectin. Stirring constantly, bring to boil over medium heat and boil 1 minute. Stir into fruit mixture. Stir vigorously 3 minutes. Ladle into ½- or 1-pint freezer containers, leaving ½″ headspace (no paraffin needed). Cover with tight lids. Let stand at room temperature until set. (It may take up to 24 hours.) Jam to be eaten within a week or two may be stored in refrigerator. Store remaining containers in freezer and transfer to refrigerator as needed. Makes six ½-pint containers.

No–Cook Raspberry Jam

- 2 pints red raspberries
- ½ cup light corn syrup
- 5 cups sugar
- 1 cup water
- 1 package (1¾ oz.) powdered fruit pectin

Rinse raspberries. In a deep bowl, fully crush berries, one layer at a time, to let juice flow freely. Measure and turn 2½ cups berries/juice into 4-qt. bowl. Add corn syrup; stir well. Gradually add sugar, stirring thoroughly to dissolve sugar. Let stand 10 minutes. In 1-quart saucepan, stir together water and fruit pectin. Stirring constantly, bring to boil over medium heat and boil 1 minute. Stir into fruit mixture. Stir vigorously 3 minutes. Ladle into ½- or 1-pint freezer containers, leaving ½″ headspace (no paraffin needed). Cover with tight lids. Let stand at room temperature until set. (It may take up to 24 hours.) Jam to be eaten within a week or two may be stored in refrigerator. Store remaining containers in freezer and transfer to refrigerator as needed. Makes seven ½-pint containers.

No–Cook Peach Jam

2 lbs. fully ripe peaches
2 tbsp. lemon juice
½ cup light corn syrup
4½ cups sugar
¾ cup water
1 package (1¾ oz.) powdered fruit pectin

Peel, pit, and finely chop peaches, using fine blade of food grinder, blender, or food processor. Measure 2¼ cups. In 4-quart bowl, stir together peaches and lemon juice. Add corn syrup, stirring well. Gradually add sugar, stirring thoroughly to dissolve sugar. Let stand 10 minutes. In 1-quart saucepan, stir together water and fruit pectin. Stirring constantly, bring to boil over medium heat and boil 1 minute. Stir into fruit mixture. Stir vigorously 3 minutes. Ladle into ½- or 1-pint freezer containers, leaving ½″ headspace (no paraffin needed). Cover with tight lids. Let stand at room temperature until set. (It may take up to 24 hours.) Jam to be eaten within a week or two may be stored in refrigerator. Store remaining containers in freezer and transfer to refrigerator as needed. Makes six ½-pint containers.

Corn Relish

5 packages (10 oz.) frozen corn, thawed and drained
2 cups chopped onions
1 bottle (16 oz.) light corn syrup
2 cups white vinegar
1 cup sugar
1 cup water
2 tbsp. mustard seeds
1 tbsp. uniodized salt
2 tsp. celery seeds
2 cups chopped green peppers
2 cups chopped sweet red peppers

In 8-quart stainless steel or enamel saucepan, place corn, onions, corn syrup, vinegar, sugar, water, mustard seeds, salt, and celery seeds. Stirring occasionally, bring to boil over high heat and boil rapidly 10 minutes. Stir in peppers. Return to boil. Immediately ladle into clean, hot 1-pint jars, leaving ¼″ headspace. With handle of wooden spoon or other nonmetallic utensil, release air bubbles. Wipe top edge with damp towel. Seal according to manufacturer's directions. Process in boiling water bath 15 minutes. Cool on wire rack or folded towel. Makes about six 1-pint jars.

Note: Substitute 12–16 ears fresh corn for frozen corn. To prepare corn, remove husks and silks. Cut enough corn from cobs to measure 8 cups. In stainless steel or enamel saucepan, place corn and enough water to cover. Bring to boil over high heat; reduce heat and simmer 5 minutes. Drain; immediately plunge into cold water; drain.

Zucchini Freezer Pickles

1¾ lbs. small zucchini
¾ lb. yellow or white onions, thinly sliced, separated into rings (2¾ cups)
2 tbsp. uniodized salt, divided
1 large sweet red pepper, cut into matchstick strips (about 1¼ cups)
1 medium green pepper, cut into matchstick strips (about ¾ cup)
2 tbsp. dried dillweed
¼ tsp. pepper
1¾ cups white vinegar
1 cup light corn syrup
½ cup sugar

Cut off ends and thinly slice zucchini. Measure 6 cups. Place zucchini and onions in large stainless steel or enamel saucepan. Sprinkle with 1½ tbsp. of the salt; toss together well. Cover with plate or bowl placed directly on vegetables; let stand 2 hours. Place red and green pepper in another large bowl. Sprinkle with remaining ½ tbsp. salt. Cover as directed for zucchini; let stand 2 hours. Drain all vegetables, pressing out as much water as possible with the back of a spoon; do not rinse. In large stainless steel or enamel saucepan, toss together the vegetables, dillweed, and pepper. In small saucepan, stir together vinegar, corn syrup, and sugar. Stirring constantly, bring to boil over medium heat until sugar is dissolved. Pour over vegetables. Stirring and turning vegetables constantly, cook over medium heat 2 minutes. Remove from heat. With slotted spoon,

loosely pack vegetables in ½- or 1-pint freezer containers. Pour hot liquid over vegetables, completely covering vegetables and leaving ½″ headspace. Cover. Cool to room temperature. Store in freezer up to 6 months and at least 1 week before using. Thaw pickles in refrigerator. Store in refrigerator up to 2 weeks after thawing. Makes six ½-pint containers.

Ginger-Carrot Bread

1¾ cups unsifted flour
  1 tsp. baking powder
 ½ tsp. ground ginger
 ½ cup margarine, softened
 ⅓ cup firmly packed brown sugar
 ⅓ cup dark corn syrup
  2 eggs
  1 cup coarsely shredded carrots

¾ cup coarsely chopped nuts
½ cup raisins

Grease two 5½″ × 3″ × 2″ loaf pans. In small bowl, stir together flour, baking powder, and ginger. In large bowl with mixer at medium speed, beat together margarine and sugar until smooth. Beat in corn syrup. Add eggs; beat until well mixed. Add carrots.

With wooden spoon, stir in flour mixture, nuts, and raisins. Divide batter evenly between prepared pans. Bake in 350°F oven 55 minutes, or until cake tester inserted in center comes out clean. Cool in pans 10 minutes. Remove from pans. Cool completely on wire rack. Wrap in plastic wrap. Makes two small loaves.

Note: Bread slices best on second day.

Pear-Coconut Bread

- 2 cups unsifted flour
- 1 cup flaked coconut, toasted
- 1 cup coarsely chopped nuts
- 1½ tsp. baking powder
- ¼ tsp. salt
- 1 cup chopped peeled pears
- 2 tsp. grated lemon rind
- 1 tbsp. lemon juice
- ⅓ cup margarine, softened
- ⅔ cup light corn syrup
- 2 eggs
- 2 tbsp. milk
- ½ tsp. vanilla

Grease 9″ × 5″ × 3″ loaf pan. In medium bowl, stir together flour, coconut, nuts, baking powder, and salt. In small bowl, stir together pears, lemon rind, and juice. In large bowl with mixer at medium speed, beat together margarine and corn syrup until smooth. Beat in eggs until well mixed. Beat in milk and vanilla. With wooden spoon, stir in flour mixture just until moistened. Stir in pear mixture. Turn into prepared pan. Bake in 350°F oven 60 minutes, or until cake tester inserted in center comes out clean. Cool in pan 10 minutes. Remove from pan. Cool completely on wire rack. Wrap in plastic wrap. Makes one large loaf.

Note: Bread slices best on second day.

PUNCHED LOAF PAN

SIZE: About 9″ × 5″ × 2½″.

EQUIPMENT: Heavy tracing paper. Pencil. Tapestry needle. Freezer. Tape. Black permanent felt-tip pen. Towels. Awl. Hammer. Nail polish remover.

MATERIALS: Aluminum loaf pan, 9″ × 5″ × 2½″. For fabric liner, follow Yellow Basket directions.

DIRECTIONS: Trace actual-size star pattern. Pierce pattern dots with tapestry needle; set pattern aside. Fill loaf pan with water; place in freezer overnight. Cover work surface with towels to protect it from ice chips. Center and tape pattern on one long side of pan. Trace star onto pan through dots with felt-tip pen. Leaving ½″ between stars, trace a star on either side of center star. Repeat three stars on other long side of pan.

Punch holes at dots: Holding awl in one hand and hammer in the other, hit awl handle with hammer so that point pierces pan and ice. Establish a rhythm to your punching so that the holes will be of uniform size. Remove ice from pan; remove pen markings with nail polish remover.

LOAF PAN

GIFT WRAPPINGS FOR FOOD

EQUIPMENT: Pencil. Tracing paper. Ruler. Masking tape. Newspapers. Paintbrushes, 1"-wide and fine. Glue. Cardboard. Scissors. Dressmaker's tracing (carbon) paper. Tracing wheel or dry ball-point pen. Pinking shears. Sewing machine. Straight pins. Iron. Compass. Sewing and tapestry needles. Tape measure.

For Stenciling: Graph paper, 8 squares-to-the-inch. White paper. Stencil paper or mylar. Glass with filed or masked edges. X-acto knife with extra blades. Stencil brushes. Paper towels. Small plastic bags. Fine-grade sandpaper.

MATERIALS: (See photograph and individual directions for colors and amounts.) Acrylic paints: red, green, blue, brown, tan, rust, white, yellow. Satin-finish spray varnish. Light oak wood stain. Spray paints: white and assorted pastels. Paint markers: green, red and yellow (available at art supply stores). Black very fine felt-tip permanent marker. White self-adhesive labels at least 1¼" × 2¼" (available at office supply stores). Wooden breadboard, 7" × 14" × ⅝". Aluminum loaf pan, 9" × 5" × 2½". Plaited wooden baskets with handles, 9" × 5" × 3". Wicker basket with handle, 8½" × 5" × 2⅜". Assorted scraps of cotton fabrics such as calico, gingham, and broadcloth in various prints and solids. Matching sewing threads.

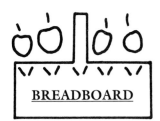

BREADBOARD

Green felt. Batting. Lace trims, ⅜"–¾" wide. Fiberfill. Embroidery floss: red, green, olive, peach, brown, dark rust, light rust, blue, and yellow. Scraps of natural color 14-count Aida cloth and perforated paper. Rubber bands.

Rings to fit canning jars used. Sisal cord, ⅛". Assorted ribbons, ⅛"–½" wide. Pearl cotton No. 3. Heavy paper or office file folder. Balsa wood heart ornament about 2½" across.

GENERAL DIRECTIONS:

Stenciling: Place stencil paper over actual-size pattern as directed and trace design. To cut stencil, place white paper, then tracing on glass; tape in place. Holding X-acto knife like a pencil, carefully cut out marked areas; cut toward you, turning the glass as you cut and not lifting blade until an entire area has been cut out; change knife blades often. If knife should slip, mend cut area on both sides of stencil with masking tape and trim with knife.

To stencil, tape stencil in position on object. Work with acrylic paints, undiluted. Dip tip of dry brush into paint, then pounce on paper towel to remove excess. Holding brush like a pencil, brush over cut-out areas with a circular motion, working over edges of stencil for a clean line. Let paint dry before removing stencil and adding details in other colors. Use a separate brush for each color, keeping each used brush in a separate plastic bag until design is finished, then wash brushes in soap and let dry overnight between colors.

Sewing: Trace patterns as directed. Following individual directions below, use dressmaker's carbon and tracing wheel or dry ball-point pen to transfer patterns to wrong sides of fabrics, placing patterns ½" from fabric edges and ½" apart. Cut out pieces ¼" beyond marked line for seam allowance. When cutting additional pieces without patterns, do not add seam allowance. To assemble items, pin pieces together with right sides facing and raw edges even; stitch with ¼" seams, leaving an opening for turning. Trim seam allowances; clip curves and turn piece to right side. Turn in raw edges and slipstitch opening closed; press well.

Pinked Items, Fabric "Ribbons": Use pinking shears to cut strips of fabric ⅝"–1" wide, to length specified.

Jar Bonnets: Mark 6″ squares or circles on fabric; cut out on marked lines with pinking shears. Topstitch lace trim to edges if desired. Cut two circles of batting the same size as canning jar lid; glue to top of lid. Center pinked fabric piece over batting and secure to lid with rubber band. Tie ribbon, fabric "ribbon," or braided sisal cord over rubber band; or screw on a painted jar ring. Add additional trims as shown or as desired.

BREADBOARD

Read General Directions above and prepare stencil for basket with apples. For border pattern, draw a ⅜″ × 5⅝″ rectangle on graph paper. Draw lines between long edges to divide rectangle into fifteen ⅜″ squares. With pencil, darken outlines of first and last squares, then every other square. Prepare stencil for eight squares.

Sand breadboard smooth; then apply one coat varnish. Place board with handle at top. With pencil, lightly mark guidelines: Mark horizontal lines across board ⅞″ and 8″ above lower end; mark vertical line down center of board. Tape over one square of border stencil, leaving seven squares exposed. Place stencil on board horizontally, with lower edge of squares centered on ⅞″ guideline, and tape down; stencil squares blue. Repeat at other end of board, with upper edge of squares on 8″ line. When dry, tape over one more square of stencil, leaving six squares exposed; use to stencil inner row of upper and lower borders as shown. Remove all tape from stencil and, continuing in established pattern, stencil side borders as shown. Stencil six tan baskets with red apples, spacing them evenly within the center area. Add green stems to apples and brown detailing on baskets. Erase guidelines. Paint edges of board red. When paint is thoroughly dry, apply two coats varnish. Trim with red ribbon, if desired.

BREAD PAN

Read General Directions above and prepare stencil for apple. Sand outer sides of pan lightly; wash and dry thoroughly. Mark center of each side of pan. Tape stencil at center mark. Stencil, making apple rust and leaves and stem green. Stencil five apples in all on each side of pan, then one on each end. Apply varnish when paint is dry. Make two fabric "ribbons" 1″ × 15″; tie into bows through holes in rim of pan as shown.

Bread Pan

TAN BASKET

Read General Directions above and prepare three stencils as follows: heart with two pairs of leaves, heart with one pair of leaves, and heart and leaf border; omit stems from first two stencils. Following package directions, apply oak stain to basket; dry thoroughly. Use rust and green paints to stencil border design on handle and hearts with leaves on slats as shown in photograph. Paint green stems with a fine brush. Cut a fabric "ribbon" the circumference of the basket rim plus 14″. Glue around basket rim, starting at handle and leaving 7″ of ribbon at beginning and end free. Tie ends into a bow as shown.

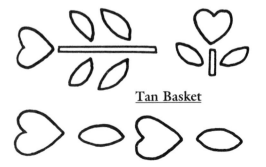

Tan Basket

YELLOW BASKET

Read General Directions above and prepare stencil for flower. For border pattern, draw a ¼″ × 3¾″ rectangle on graph paper. Draw lines between long edges to divide rectangle into fifteen ¼″ squares. With pencil, darken outlines of first and last squares, then every other square. Prepare stencil for eight squares. Mix one part yellow acrylic paint with 3 parts water; using paintbrush, stain basket yellow; dry thoroughly. Using border stencil, paint checkerboard in blue around rim of basket, completing lower row all around before shifting stencil for upper row. Stencil basket slats, making flowers rust and leaves green as shown in photograph.

LINER: Cut two pieces calico, each 12½″ × 15¼″. Join pieces, following General Directions.

Yellow Basket

WHITE BASKET

Paint basket with two coats white paint; let dry. Referring to photograph and actual-size detail, draw red berries and green leaves on basket with paint markers. When paint is dry, add seeds with black very fine marker.

LINER: Cut two pieces calico 9″ × 11½″. Join pieces, following General Directions above.

White Basket

CROSS-STITCH LABELS

PICKLES AND PEACH JAM: See General Directions for embroidery at end of book. Fold Aida cloth in half twice to locate center; mark with pin. Unfold cloth and measure up 1⅜″ for pickles, 1⅛″ for peach jam; mark with a second pin for first stitch. Separate floss and use two strands in needle to stitch design, beginning at second pin with stitch marked by arrow on chart. Each symbol on chart represents one cross-stitch worked over one "square" of fabric; different symbols represent different colors. Work "PICKLES" in dark rust backstitches.

Trim cloth ⅜″ from outermost stitching; cut a piece of calico the same size for back. Stitch together, following General Directions above. Cut pieces ribbon long enough to go around jar and tie; tack the center of each ribbon across back of label, one at top and one at bottom. Tie to jars.

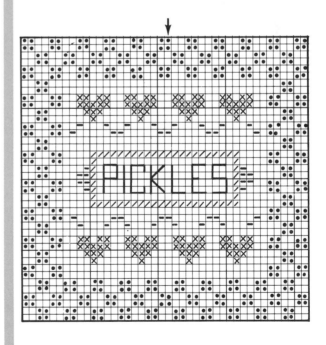

⬤ **Blue**
☒ **Light Rust**
⊟ **Green**
⧄ **Yellow**

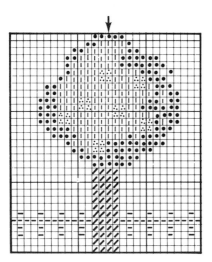

- ● Green
- Olive
- ∴ Peach
- Dark Rust
- ∕ Brown

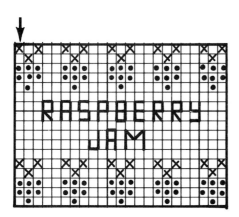

- ☒ Green
- ● Red

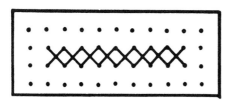

Stitch Detail

RASPBERRY JAM: Cut a piece of perforated paper 2″ × 1½″. Count 2 holes down and 2 holes in from upper left corner for first stitch, marked by arrow on chart. Separate floss and use two strands in needle to stitch design, following chart and stitch detail. Work lettering in backstitch, using two strands brown floss. After embroidering, trim piece along right and bottom edges to center design. Glue two pieces calico together, having right sides out. With pinking shears, trim to measure 2⅜″ × 2″. Center and glue wrong side of embroidered paper to fabric. Make a hanging loop of pearl cotton at corner of tag.

HEART TAGS

WOODEN: Apply oak stain to wood heart; let dry. With black marker, write "homemade for you" in center of heart. Referring to photograph and actual-size detail, draw ears of corn with yellow and green paint markers; add dots with red. When paint is dry, outline ears and draw kernels with black very fine marker. Apply one coat varnish. Thread a strand of pearl cotton through hanging hole; knot ends together.

PAPER TAG

PAPER: Trace half-pattern; complete along dash line. Use pattern to cut heart from heavy paper or file folder. Write message in center with black very fine marker; draw border design with green paint marker. Punch a hole at center top and thread through a piece of pearl cotton for hanging loop.

OVAL LABELS

Trace actual-size label outline; glue to cardboard. When glue is dry, cut along traced line to create an oval template. Place template on self-adhesive label and trace around it with a pencil; do not cut out. Use black marker to write product name within oval. Use paint markers to draw tiny red ovals with green leaves for jam or yellow ovals with V-shaped husks for relish. Trim labels along pencil line; apply to jars.

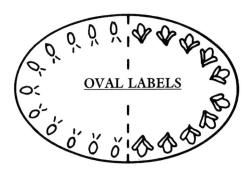

OVAL LABELS

STUFFED ORNAMENTS

HEARTS: Trace actual-size patterns. Mark two of each size on fabric; cut out and assemble, following General Directions above, stuffing with fiberfill before closing opening. String hearts on a length of pearl cotton and tie around jar.

BERRIES: Following General Directions above, make two berries of solid red fabric, stuffing with fiberfill before closing opening. Cut leaves of green felt, omitting seam allowance, and tack to berry tops. String berries on a length of pearl cotton and tack to fabric jar bonnet.

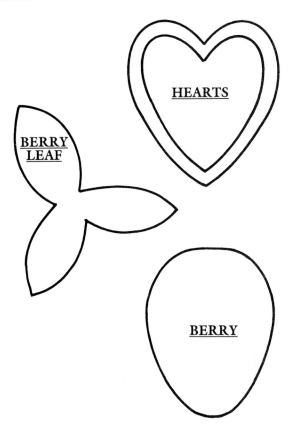

HEARTS

BERRY LEAF

BERRY

MISCELLANEOUS DECORATIONS

SISAL BRAIDS: Braid three strands sisal cord; secure ends of braid with overhand knots. Tie around jars instead of ribbon.

COLORED RINGS: Spray canning jar rings with various pastel paints. Use rings of ribbon or sisal to secure fabric jar bonnets.

Bedroom

On Christmas Eve, you might stay awake watching for Santa, but you'll be warm and comfy in your cozy Christmas bedroom. Spirited red and green quilt is so pretty you'll leave it on the bed year-round!

CHAINED STAR QUILT

See General Directions for quilting stitch detail.

SIZE: Approx. 75″ × 102″.

EQUIPMENT: Pencil. Tracing paper. Ruler. Thin, stiff cardboard. Glue. Scissors. Sewing and quilting needles. Paper for pattern. Yardstick. Tailor's chalk. Optional:

Dressmaker's tracing (carbon) paper. Tracing wheel or dry ball-point pen. Quilting frame.

MATERIALS: For patchwork—closely woven cotton fabric, 44″ wide: bright red print, 2½ yards; dark red print, 1¾ yards; dark green print, 3 yards; white, 4¼ yards (use bleached muslin if desired). For background—bleached muslin 80″ wide, 3 yards. For lining—fabric 44″ wide, 6 yards. Batting. White sewing thread. For pillow—red piping, 1⅛ yard. Fiberfill.

DIRECTIONS

Patterns: Using ruler and sharp pencil, carefully trace patterns A and B; do not cut out. Glue tracing paper to thin, stiff cardboard; let dry. Cut on marked lines for patch patterns. Patterns A and B are used for all patch pieces of quilt; see outlined center of Block 1 for basic design.

Before cutting any patch pieces, test accuracy of your patterns: Holding pencil at an outward angle so point rests against cardboard, draw around patterns on a sheet of paper to recreate the entire basic design, drawing around A 12 times and B 18 times; there should be no gaps or overlaps in your drawn design. Adjust patterns if necessary; if they don't fit together properly, your patch pieces won't either. Reserve test design drawn to use later as a quilting pattern.

Patch pieces: To cut patch pieces for blocks, place pattern on wrong side of fabric, at least ½″ from edges and with arrow following grain. Mark around pattern with sharp pencil held at an outward angle. Mark as many pieces at one time as needed on each fabric, leaving at least ½″ between pieces. When all are marked, cut out pieces ¼″ outside pencil lines, for seam allowance. Pencil line will be stitching line.
From dark green print fabric, cut 282 of piece A. From bright red print, cut 258 of piece A. From dark red print, cut 318 of piece B. From white, cut 96 of piece A and 648 of piece B.

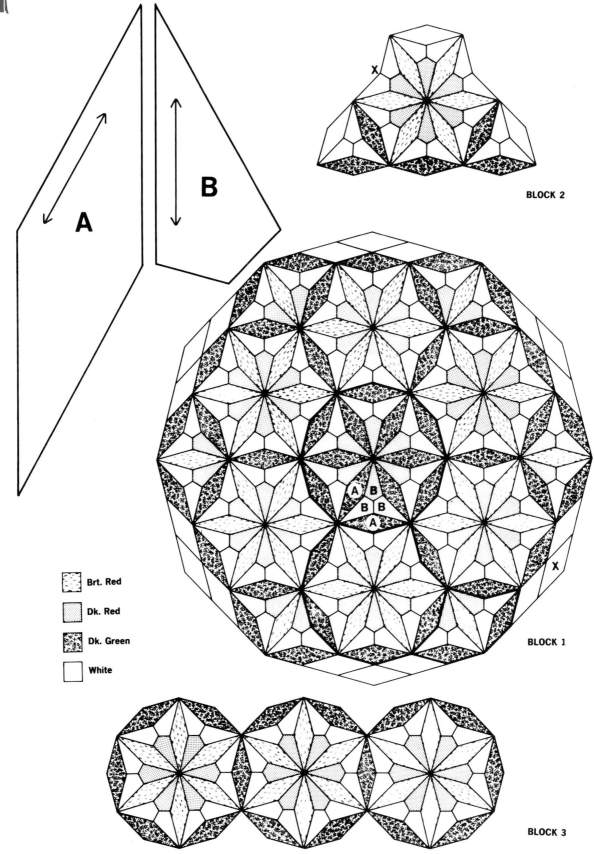

A

B

BLOCK 2

X

Brt. Red

Dk. Red

Dk. Green

White

A B
B B
A

X

BLOCK 1

BLOCK 3

Blocks: See diagrams and color key for Blocks 1, 2, and 3. To join pieces, place them with right sides facing, matching one edge; try to match a straight edge to a bias edge as much as possible. Stitch together on marked line with small, even running stitches; press seam to one side, under darker color. Continue adding pieces as directed until block is completed.

For Block 1, make several smaller sections and join: To begin, join 2 green A's, one dark red B, and 2 white B's, following labeled section within outlined center of Block 1. Make 5 more sections in same manner and join the 6 sections for the 12-sided center (or basic) design. Next, make design outlined directly below center design, joining 4 green A's, 6 bright red A's, 6 dark red B's, and 12 white B's, as shown. Make 5 more of second design and join all 6 to center design all around. For third design (small outlined area at bottom right of Block 1), join 2 green A's, one bright red A, 2 dark red B's, and 4 white B's, as shown. Make 5 more of third design and join all 6 to second designs all around. Add 18 white A's in groups of 3 around edges of piece, to complete the 12-sided Block 1. Make 4 more of Block 1.

Following diagrams, make two each of Block 2 and Block 3.

Join a Block 2, to a Block 1, matching indentation of Block 2 marked X to white A of Block 1 marked X. Join another Block 1 to other side of Block 2 in same manner; see 1-2-1 end pieces in Quilt Diagram. Make another end piece in same manner. Finish the end pieces, the remaining Block 1, and both Block 3's by turning in outer raw edges ¼″ to wrong side; press in place, then topstitch ⅛″ from folded edges all around. **Quilt Top:** Lay out bleached muslin on a flat surface; pin or weight edges to prevent shifting. Following Quilt Diagram, arrange the 5 pieces on muslin (dash line) as desired, leaving about 2″-3″ between each corner block and adjacent side or center block; there will be excess muslin on all four sides of patchwork grouping. When satisfied with arrangement, pin blocks in place.

See General Directions for quilting stitch detail at end of book. Plan quilting pattern:

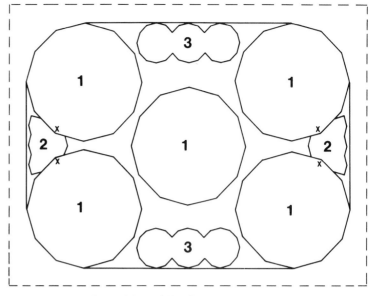

QUILT DIAGRAM

You may wish to quilt around the patchwork only, leaving the muslin background unquilted. Or, you may wish to quilt the patchwork and background both, using elements of the patchwork pattern for your design. To do so, make several tracings of the basic design you drew when testing patch patterns. Place tracings on muslin, centering over large background areas; the edges of traced design will overlap the patchwork. Adjust tracings until satisfied with arrangement; you may want to adjust position of patchwork blocks as well. Pin adjacent tracings together to make one pattern, then remove from muslin. Slip-stitch blocks in place, then replace tracings and transfer designs to muslin, using dressmaker's carbon and tracing wheel or dry ball-point pen. If desired, add small quilting designs around edges of piece, using A and B patterns; do not add quilting at corners.

Using yardstick and tailor's chalk, draw a line at each end of quilt top, connecting outermost points of each Block 1; draw a line at each side in same manner; see heavy lines of Quilt Diagram. Trim away excess muslin all around edges, cutting 1″ outside drawn chalk lines and corners, for quilt top.

Lining: Cut lining fabric in half crosswise, for 2 pieces, 3 yards long. Join together at one long edge with ½″ seam. Trim lining to match quilt top. Cut batting same size.

Quilting: Place lining flat, wrong side up. Place batting on top. Anchor batting to lining by crossing 2 long stitches in center. Place quilt top over batting. Pin and baste through all layers, lengthwise, crosswise, and diagonally in both directions.

Starting in center and working outward in all directions, quilt around each pair of white B's in all blocks, close to outer seam; quilt around each Block 1, 2, and 3; quilt on any lines marked on muslin. Use white thread. Stitch all around edge of quilt on marked chalk line and around corner blocks.

Finishing: Trim margins of quilt to ⅜″. From dark green fabric, cut long strips 1½″ wide (bias or straight, as preferred). Piece strips to make one strip long enough to fit around edge of quilt, or join strips to quilt separately. Turn under one long edge of strip(s) ⅜″ and press. With right side of quilt facing up, place strip(s) face down, matching other long edge to raw edge of quilt. Stitch in place with ⅜″ seams. Fold strip to back and slip-stitch folded edge to lining.

Pillow: For pillow front, make one basic design (outlined center of Block 1); see directions above. If desired, use bright red print instead of green for the six center A pieces. Using pillow front as pattern, cut pillow back from green print. Pin red piping all around right side of pillow front, matching raw edges; stitch in place. Place pillow front and back together, right sides facing and piping enclosed. Stitch around with ¼″ seam, leaving 2 adjacent sides open. Turn pillow to right side, stuff, and slip-stitch closed.

RAG RUG

SIZE: 24″ × 38″.

EQUIPMENT: Warping device such as clamped pegs, board, or mill. Yardstick. Scissors. Rigid heddle or harness loom with at least a 25″ weaving width and a 10-dent reed. Stick shuttle or other yarn holder. Plastic laundry bags cut into strips.

MATERIALS: For warp, 8/4 (4-ply) cotton, 250 yards white, 240 yards brown. For weft, tightly woven preshrunk cotton or cotton-blend fabric, 36″ wide, 7½ yards red, 3¾ yards white.

DIRECTIONS: Following manufacturer's directions for warping device and loom, warp and weave rug as follows: Wind a continuous warp, taking one strand white and one strand brown together; wind warp to a 2-yard length for 120 double ends (actually 120 white ends, 120 brown ends). * Thread 10-single ends, taking strands in this order: white, brown, white, brown, etc., finishing with brown. Thread next ten strands, beginning with brown, alternating colors, and ending with white. Repeat from * until all ends are threaded. (Note: This warp will produce 5 white, 5 brown, 5 white, etc. threads for one row, alternating with 5 brown, 5 white, 5 brown, etc. threads for the next row on the face of the weaving.)

All weaving is tabby, or plain weave. Weave a "filler" of plastic strips for 3″, to be removed later. For heading, wind 4 yards of same white cotton used for warp onto yarn holder, and weave 5 rows, beating succeeding rows hard against preceding ones.

To prepare weft, cut red fabric in half crosswise, then cut both red and white fabrics into 1½″-wide strips, cutting parallel to selvages for full length of fabric. Combine 2 red strips and one white strip together with short ends even; wind onto shuttle. Insert shuttle into shed, leaving even ends of strips protruding ¼″ from one side. Continue weaving, aiming for even selvages and beating hard so rows are tightly packed, about 3 rows to an inch. When nearing end of first set of strips, trim 6″ from end of one red, 12″ from end of white, cutting at an angle so ends taper off gradually. Wind succeeding strips onto shuttle as follows: Cut all ends at same angle. Wind a white strip on for 6″, then add a red strip. Wind for another 6″ before adding second red strip, then wind remainder of all strips together. In this way, ends will always be staggered; in weaving, overlap tapered edges of same color strips that end and begin each group. Also try to encase cut edges between other 2 strips.

After 38″ (approximately 114 rows of weaving), cut weft strips ¼″ past end of row. Weave in heading and filler same as for beginning of weaving. Remove rug from loom. Slide out all plastic strips but the 2 rows closest to each heading. Starting from one end, slide 6 warp ends at a time out from filler and tie together in an overhand knot, close to heading. Repeat at other end of rug. Trim fringe evenly to 3″.

CALICO DOLL

See General Directions for enlarging a pattern.

SIZE: 17″ tall.

EQUIPMENT: Sharp colored pencil. Pencil. Ruler. Scissors. Tracing paper. Paper for patterns. Dressmaker's tracing (carbon) paper. Tracing wheel or dry ball-point pen. Straight pins. Iron. Sewing machine. Sewing needle.

MATERIALS: Cotton fabric: red/white calico, 45″ wide, ¾ yard; scrap small red print. White pre-gathered lace trim, ½″ wide, ⅓ yard. White sewing thread. Polyester fiberfill for stuffing.

DIRECTIONS: Using sharp colored pencil, draw lines across patterns, connecting grid lines. Enlarge patterns by copying on paper ruled in 1″ squares. Heavy lines indicate seam lines; dash lines indicate darts. Trace patterns,

including all markings and dash lines. Use patterns to mark the following pieces on wrong side of fabric, placing them at least ½″ apart and reversing patterns for all second and fourth pieces; cut out each, adding ¼″ for seam allowance: From calico, cut 2 body fronts, 2 body leg-backs, 4 leg fronts and one face; from red print, cut 2 bonnets. Using dressmaker's carbon and tracing wheel or dry ball-point pen, transfer all dart lines and markings to wrong side of fabric pieces.

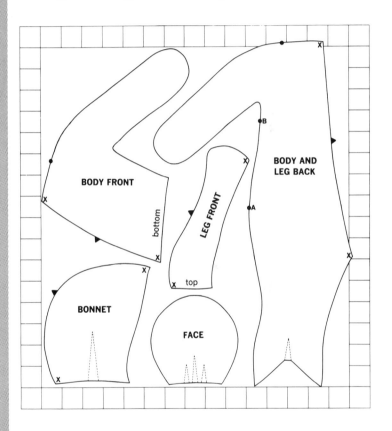

Make darts on body/leg back, bonnet, and face pieces as follows: Pinch fabric from wrong side until dash lines meet; stitch along dash lines. Clip fold to within ⅛″ of stitching line; press seam open.

Make one pleat on each body back as follows: With wrong side of fabric facing you, fold "A" up to meet "B"; baste along seam-line, through all three thicknesses. For each "heel," stitch leg/back together from bottom of dart to point.

Stitch all pieces together as indicated below, with right sides facing and raw edges even, making ¼" seams. When stitching like pieces together, stitch along seamline between X's, matching notches.

Pin and stitch body/leg backs together, leaving 5" opening in center for turning after doll is completed. For each leg front, pin and stitch two leg front pieces together. Then pin and stitch top edge of leg fronts to bottom edge of body front, one at each side. Pin and stitch complete body front to complete body back, leaving neck edge open between dots.

Stitch bonnet pieces together along long curved edge. Pin face to front opening of bonnet, with lace between so that gathered edge of lace is even with raw edges of fabric; stitch in place. Pin bottom of head to neck opening, matching raw edges and lining up center dart of face with center seam of body front; stitch in place. Turn doll to right side; stuff firmly with fiberfill, using eraser end of pencil to reach into arms and legs. Turn raw edges of back opening to inside and slipstitch closed.

POINSETTIA CENTERPIECE

See General Directions for enlarging a pattern.

SIZE: Approximately 12" wide, 7" high.

EQUIPMENT: Colored pencil. Ruler. Pencil. Paper for patterns. Lightweight cardboard. Compass. Scissors. Dark-colored tailor's chalk. Sewing machine. Sewing needle. Iron. Ironing board. Knitting needle.

MATERIALS: Closely woven white cotton fabric, 36" wide, ¼ yard. Calico print fabric, 45" wide: red print #1, ⅓ yard; red print #2, ¼ yard; green, ⅓ yard; yellow, ⅛ yard. Sewing thread to match fabric. Polyester quilt batting. Polyester fiberfill.

DIRECTIONS: **Patterns:** Using sharp colored pencil, draw lines across patterns, connecting grid lines. Enlarge patterns by copying on paper ruled in ½" squares; complete each half pattern by reversing it for the other side. Glue patterns to cardboard and cut out when dry. Make cardboard patterns for 2" and 4" circles, using compass.

Flower Pot: Cut two 7" × 23" strips and two 4" circles from white fabric; cut one each from a single layer of batting. Set circles aside. Stack strips together, right sides facing, with batting layer on top and raw edges even; machine-stitch ¼" in from one long edge through all thicknesses. Turn piece so batting layer is between strips and seam is inside; press; topstitch ¼" from finished edge to form top edge of pot.

Lay piece on flat surface, top edge up. Using a ruler and dark-colored tailor's chalk, and starting 1½" in from one short (side) edge, draw 21 lines across the width of the strip, 1" apart and parallel to side edges; end each line at topstitching and mark with a dot. Machine-baste along each line through all thicknesses. Working on wrong (marked) side, fold piece along each line of basting and stitch a dart ¼" wide from bottom raw edge, narrowing it to vanishing point at dot; make 21 darts. Fold piece in half widthwise, wrong side out and raw edges even. Stitch side edges together, making a ¼" seam; turn. Fold bottom edge ¼" to inside and press.

Place fabric circles together with raw edges even and batting sandwiched between; topstitch ¼" from raw edge through all thicknesses. Clip seam allowance and fold at seam, so excess fabric lies flat against one side of the circle; press. Fit circle into bottom edge of pot made, with seam allowances inside; whipstitch in place all around. Fill pot with fiberfill.

Leaves and Petals: Using pattern A for both, make six large petals from red #1 and six leaves from green calico. Using pattern B, make six small petals from red #2. Cut and assemble pieces as follows: Fold fabric in half, with wrong side out. Using pattern, mark designated number of pieces on doubled fabric, spacing them ½" apart; cut out ¼" beyond marked outlines (seamline). Stitch pairs together with right sides facing and raw edges even, making ¼" seams and leaving bottom straight edge open; clip into seam allowance at curves; turn to right side; press. Stuff lightly and evenly, poking fiberfill into points with knitting needle. Referring to pattern, machine-stitch veins along dotted lines through all thicknesses, using white thread. Fold each leaf or petal lengthwise down center and tack at dots to form pleat. Smooth pleat flat and machine-baste across base ¼" from raw edge.

To Assemble Poinsettia: Arrange each matching set of leaves or petals in a ring with sides touching at bases and tips pointed out; tack bases to each other where they touch.

With inside raw edges even, stack the 3 rings with the leaves on the bottom; place the large petals second, so that one petal lies between each leaf; position the small petals last, aligning them over the leaves. Tack rings together at points along inside raw edge.

Place poinsettia in pot and push down as shown in photograph; tack flower in place along pot edge.

Using pattern, cut twenty 2" circles from yellow calico for stamens and join in a chain as follows: fold each circle in half with right side out. Using a double thread knotted at one end, hand-baste each half circle ¼" from raw edge; push piece off needle onto thread and add another half circle; repeat until all stamens are strung. Curl chain into a spiral with all raw edges down and sides of stamens touching; tack edges where needed to form a solid piece. Position piece in center of poinsettia as shown and tack at edges to flower petals.

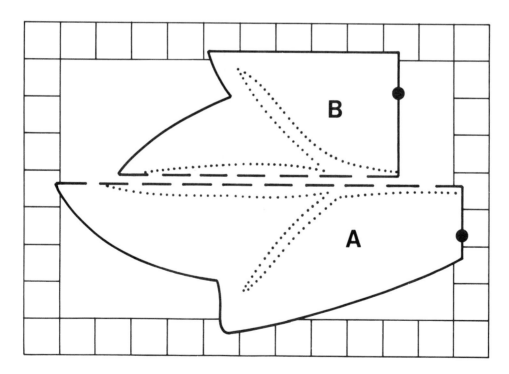

TAFFETA PLAIDS

Taffeta fabric—a plain-woven silk, rayon, or nylon— can turn a homey gift into something elegant. All the projects shown here are quick and easy.

EQUIPMENT: Pencil. Ruler. Scissors. Additional equipment given in individual directions.

MATERIALS: Taffeta fabric 45" wide, amounts and additional materials given in individual directions.

COVERED BASKET

Additional Equipment: Iron. Sewing needle. Paper for pattern. Sewing machine.

Materials: Rectangular wicker basket, desired size. Taffeta fabric, 1 yard red plaid for basket shown, which is 11" long and 3½" deep; adjustments should be made for smaller or larger basket. Red satin ribbon, 1½" wide, 1 yard. Sewing thread to match fabric.

Directions: To cut fabric for sides, measure outside depth of basket; measure outer perimeter of basket along top edge. Using a line of plaid pattern as a guide, cut fabric piece 3" wider than depth measurement and two times the perimeter, piecing, if necessary, for length. Turn long raw edges under ¼"; slip-stitch in place. Fold piece in half widthwise with wrong side out; stitch short edges together, making ¼" seam. Baste piece ¼" in from each long edge. Fit around basket sides, pulling top basting thread to fit top edge and bottom basting thread to gather fabric under bottom of basket; secure threads.

To cut fabric for handle, measure width and length of handle. Double these measurements and add ½" to each; cut strip of fabric this size, using line of plaid pattern as a guide. Press long edges under ¼". Beginning at one side, fold strip around handle and slip-stitch in place, centering seam underneath and shirring fabric as you stitch.

To cut fabric for lining, measure length and width of floor and each wall of basket. Draw exact size of floor on paper; add a wall to each edge of floor; add ¾" to outside edge of each wall; pattern will have shape of a cross. Cut out pattern. Mark outline of pattern on wrong side of fabric, using line of plaid pattern as a guide. Cut out lining, ¼" beyond marked lines all around. To assemble lining, stitch adjacent walls together on marked lines. Turn top raw edges under ¼"; slip-stitch in place. Lower lining into basket and whipstitch top edges to top of gathered side piece, enclosing ends of handle covering.

Cut 22" length of ribbon; cut ends on the diagonal. Tie ribbon into bow; tack to one side of basket at handle.

WINE BOTTLE TOTE

Additional Equipment: Compass. Sewing machine. Iron. Pinking shears. Small safety pin.

Materials: Taffeta fabric: ¼ yard red plaid; ⅜ yard solid red, or large scraps of each (see dimensions below). Thin, stiff cardboard. Grosgrain ribbon ⅜" wide, 1 yard white. Sewing thread to match fabrics.

Directions: From red taffeta, cut rectangle 15½″ × 9½″; use compass to cut two circles, each 5¼″ in diameter. From plaid taffeta, cut rectangle 15½″ × 6½″, using line of plaid pattern as a guide. Stitch rectangles together along one long edge, making flat fell seam as follows : With right sides facing and raw edges even, stitch pieces together ½″ from edges; trim seam allowance of plaid taffeta to ⅛″. Press seam open. Press edge of red seam allowance ⅛″ to wrong side and lap over trimmed seam allowance as shown; topstitch in place. Press carefully. Fold piece in half with wrong side out, forming a cylinder, as shown in photograph; stitch side edges together, making ½″ seam. Pink seam edges. Press seam open. Using compass, mark 4¼″-diameter circle on cardboard; cut out. Sandwich cardboard circle between two taffeta circles, right sides out; stitch all around, close to cardboard edges, enclosing cardboard. With raw edges even and making ½″ seam, stitch bottom circle to plaid taffeta. Pink seam edges. At top, turn red edge down ¼″, then 1¾″; topstitch in place along bottom fold. Turn tote to right side. Make buttonhole through outside layer of taffeta only, ½″ down from upper edge and opposite center "back" seam. Cut 24″ length of ribbon; trim ends on the diagonal. Using safety pin, lace ribbon through buttonhole for drawstring.

WREATH

Additional Equipment: Compass. Sewing needle. Straight pins. White craft glue.

Materials: Plastic foam wreath, about 9″ in diameter. Taffeta fabric, ⅜ yard red plaid or 12″-square piece. Red felt, piece 9″ × 12″. Satin ribbon 1½″ wide, 1 yard white. Sewing thread to match fabric.

Directions: Use plastic foam ring as pattern to cut three layers of batting and one ring of felt. Using compass, mark 12″-diameter circle on fabric, with 3″-diameter circle in center; cut out along both marked lines, leaving ring. Baste a line ¼″ from outer edge of fabric. Center three layers of batting and plastic foam ring over wrong side of fabric ring. Pull basting thread to tighten fabric over batting and plastic foam; secure basting thread. Clip into curves along inner edge of fabric; pull fabric to back of plastic foam; pin in place. Glue felt ring to back of wreath, covering all raw edges. Cut and notch ends of 22″ length of ribbon. Tie into bow and tack to top of wreath as shown.

PICTURE FRAME

Additional Equipment: X-acto knife.

Materials: Heavyweight cardboard. Batting. Taffeta fabric, ¼ yard each red and red plaid or 10″ × 18″ piece red and 10″-square piece plaid. White craft glue.

Directions: Mark a 6⅜″ × 7⅝″ rectangle on cardboard; mark a second rectangle 3⅜″ × 4⅝″ centered inside first. Carefully cut on marked lines with X-acto knife, leaving frame; use as pattern to cut matching piece from batting. Also use cardboard frame as pattern to mark matching piece on plaid fabric, placing straight edges of cardboard on bias of fabric; cut out piece, ½″ beyond marked lines on inside and outside edges. Glue batting to cardboard. Center cardboard frame, batting side down, over wrong side of plaid piece; fold ½″ margins over edges and glue in place; mitering corners. For back, mark a 6⅜″ × 7⅝″ rectangle on cardboard; carefully cut out with X-acto knife. Use as pattern to mark a matching rectangle on wrong side of red fabric. Cut out rectangle, ½″ beyond marked edges. Center board over wrong side of piece; fold ½″ margins over edges and glue in place, mitering corners.

From cardboard, cut three 1″-wide spacer strips, two 7″ long for sides and one 3″ long for bottom. Glue strips to wrong side of frame front; let dry. Spread glue on strips; press front and back frame pieces together, matching edges.

Cut 3″ × 6″ easel stand from cardboard. Using X-acto knife, score (do not cut through) stand across width, 1″ below top short edge. From red fabric, cut pieces 5″ × 8″ and 2½″ × 5½″. Cover stand with larger piece, gluing excess to wrong side. Glue smaller piece to center of wrong side. Spread glue on wrong side of stand between top and scoring. Position stand on frame back so that bottom edge of stand is flush with center bottom edge of frame; let dry.

BASKET OF ROSEBUDS

Materials: Small wicker basket. Green plastic foam piece, to fit bottom of basket. Red plaid taffeta, 3″ × 9″ scrap for each rosebud or ⅛ yard for five as shown. Florist's wire. Green florist's tape. Baby's breath. Small artificial greenery. Red satin ribbon ½″ wide, ⅜ yard. Glue.

Directions: To make bud, wrap 6″ length of florist's wire with green florist's tape. Cut 3″ × 9″ rectangle of fabric, using line of plaid pattern as a guide. Fold in half lengthwise, right side out. Wrap 1½″ × 9″ piece around one end of wire stem as follows: With folded edge at top, wrap one short end of piece around stem, covering about ½″; secure with florist's tape. Continue to wrap piece around stem, spiraling downward slightly. As you wrap, hold piece tight at bottom, letting top flare a bit. (You may need to practice this technique somewhat before you are satisfied.) When you reach the opposite short end of piece, pull entire short raw edge to bottom of bud, for

hip. Wrap hip with florist's tape to secure, enclosing all raw edges. Make five buds. Place plastic foam in basket. Arrange rosebuds, baby's breath and greenery in plastic foam. Cut 10″ length of satin ribbon; trim ends on the diagonal. Tie ribbon into bow; glue to side of basket at handle, or tie bow around handle.

GUEST TOWELS

Additional Equipment: Straight pins. Sewing machine. Iron.

Materials: For Each: White guest towel. Red plaid ribbon 1″ wide, about 1 yard. Sewing thread to match ribbon.

Directions: Soak ribbon in cold salt water to set colors; let dry and press. Measure width of towel; cut length of ribbon twice that measurement. Place towel right side up on work surface, with short edges at top and bottom. Following photograph and directions below, pin ribbon in a zigzag pattern, across width of towel: Holding ribbon horizontally, fold right end of ribbon diagonally down to back, with upper corner meeting lower edge. Pin folded edge of ribbon flush with right edge of towel, with "point" of ribbon 3″ up from bottom of towel. Fold ribbon down over itself at a 90° angle, so top folded edge is parallel to top and bottom edges of towel; pin in place. Lay 1½″ of ribbon onto towel, then fold ribbon up over itself at 90° angle, so that second fold is also parallel to top and bottom edges of towel; pin in place. Working to the left, continue to fold and pin ribbon up and down over itself every 1½″ until you reach left edge of towel (about 10 folds). Trim excess ribbon, leaving ½″ to turn under. Fold excess ribbon under, so that folded edge is flush with edge of towel; tuck in any raw edges; pin in place. With matching thread, topstitch ribbon in place along top, bottom, and sides.

COVERED HANGERS

Additional Equipment: Iron. Sewing needle.

Materials: For Each: Wooden hanger. Green electrical or heavy-duty plastic tape. Red plaid taffeta, ½ yard to make up to five hangers, or one **bias** strip. 17¾″ × 3½″. Sewing thread to match fabric. Batting. Satin ribbon ½″ wide, ⅜ yard white. Glue. Crushed potpourri or essential oil, if desired.

Directions (for each): Wrap hook of hanger with green tape. From plaid taffeta, cut a bias strip 17¾″ × 3½″. Cut a layer of batting, 17″ × 3″. Fold batting around hanger; glue in place. If desired, sprinkle batting with essential oil, or add some crushed potpourri at this time. Press raw edges of strip under ¼″. Holding one long edge of strip at top of hanger, pull opposite long edge tightly around hanger, overlapping edges at top; bias strip will stretch to fit curve. Slip-stitch top edges in place, working around base of hook. Slip-stitch short ends in place, making small tucks at corners to fit fabric to curves. Cut 10″ length of satin ribbon; cut ends on the diagonal. Tie ribbon in bow around base of hanger hook.

HEARTS AND FLOWERS

An old-fashioned, sentimental motif decorates these practical projects, appropriate for a cozy bedroom.

STENCILED WOODEN ITEMS

See General Directions below for enlarging a pattern.

EQUIPMENT: Sandpaper. Tack cloth. Paintbrushes. Pencil. Ruler. Paper for patterns. Black fine-tip felt pen. Masking tape. Stencil paper. Scissors. Glass, 12″ square with filed or masked edges. White paper. X-acto knife and extra blades. Paper towels. Stencil brushes, at least 4. Liner brush., Natural sponge. Small plastic bags.

MATERIALS: Unfinished wooden items and acrylic paints in muted colors: Turtle stool, 8″ × 14″ × 8½″; 2 ounces holly green, 1 ounce each brick red and peach. Wastebasket, 9½″ × 8¼″ × 11″; 2 ounces holly green, 1 ounce each brick red, off white, peach. **For All:** Acrylic sealer. Quick-drying acrylic varnish.

GENERAL DIRECTIONS

To Prepare Surface: Sand unfinished wooden items smooth. Wipe with tack cloth. Seal with acrylic sealer. Let dry, then sand again; wipe with tack cloth. Apply base color if directed; let dry. To add a mottled effect where directed, dip natural sponge in water, then squeeze out excess. Dip damp sponge into paint, pounce on towel to remove excess, then pat on object gently.

To Stencil: Using pencil and ruler, draw lines across patterns, connecting grid lines. Enlarge patterns by copying on paper ruled in 1″ squares. Complete half and quarter-patterns indicated by long dash lines. Strengthen heavy lines with felt-tip pen. (Lighter lines are painting details.) Using enlarged patterns, trace designs for each project on stencil paper, making one or several stencil(s) for each design, as directed. To cut stencils, place white paper, then stencil paper on glass; tape in place. Holding X-acto knife like a pencil, carefully cut out marked areas; cut

toward you, turning the glass as you cut and not lifting blade until an entire area has been cut out; change knife blades often. If knife should slip, mend cut area on both sides of stencil with masking tape and trim with X-acto knife.

Place stencil on prepared wooden surface and tape securely in place. Do not dilute paints. To stencil, dip tip of dry brush into paint, pounce on towel to remove excess. Holding brush like a pencil, perpendicular to surface, brush over cut-out area with a circular motion, working over stencil edges for a clean line. For a soft, antique effect, use paint sparingly so that background will show through in some areas. Clean stencil between colors and before reversing it.

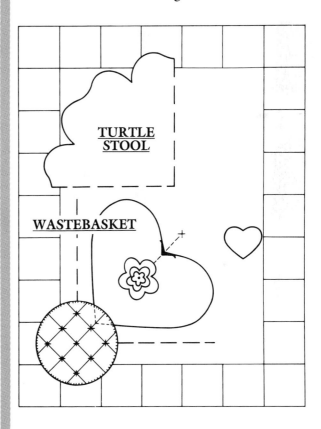

If adding details in other colors, let first color dry thoroughly before overpainting. To add small dots, use liner brush. For larger dots, use tip of wooden brush handle dipped in paint. Use a separate brush for each color, keeping each used brush in a separate plastic bag until design is completed; then wash brushes in soap and water. (If you have only one brush, wash and let dry thoroughly between colors.) Let paint dry before removing stencil. To protect finish, seal with quick-drying acrylic varnish.

TURTLE STOOL: Read General Directions above. Make five stencils: large flower, smallest heart, large heart and the two largest flowers from wastebasket motif. Prepare stool as directed and paint with holly green. Center large flower on stool seat; stencil lightly with peach. Stencil two medium flowers on seat near turtle's neck in same color. Center and stencil large heart over large flower, using brick red. Stencil two tiny flowers near turtle's neck in brick red. With an almost dry brush, spot brick onto peach flowers nearby. Stencil three small hearts around arch of each pair of legs, using brick red. Stencil two small flowers in peach between hearts as shown. Stencil a small flower of peach around each eye. Outline large heart with small holly green dots. If desired, write name inside heart, using peach. Outline eye flowers with small brick dots. Apply dots of brick to end of tail. Outline small hearts in peach dots and apply dots to end of tail. Lightly outline edges of turtle in peach.

WASTEBASKET: Read General Directions above. Make six stencils: four large hearts; circle; small, medium, and large flowers; small heart. Prepare wastebasket as directed and paint inside with holly green. Lightly mottle rim of basket with holly green. Center hearts on wastebasket front and stencil, using brick red. Stencil circle in center of hearts in holly green. Lightly stencil two opposite hearts with large peach flowers, then tiny off white ones. Make a dot for flower center of peach. Repeat for remaining hearts, reversing colors. Stencil large holly green flowers at either side of hearts; stencil medium brick flowers nearby. Stencil small brick hearts around rim. Outline hearts in small off white dots. Make off white and peach dots for centers of green flowers. Outline large hearts with small holly

green dots; draw dotted lines and X's as on pattern. Make small holly green dots for brick red flower centers. Make large holly green dots about 1″ apart around bottom of basket as shown. Make lines inside green circle in peach; make X's of brick red.

BEDSIDE CADDY

SIZE: 14″ × 17½″.

EQUIPMENT: Pencil. Ruler. Scissors. Dressmaker's tracing (carbon) paper. Tracing wheel or dry ball-point pen. Water-erasable marking pen. Embroidery hoop. Straight pins. Sewing and embroidery needles. Sewing machine. Iron.

MATERIALS: Unbleached muslin 36″ wide, ¾ yard. Closely woven cotton fabric, at least 36″ wide, ⅛ yard green calico. Welting cord, ½ yard. Pre-gathered cluny lace trim, 1″ wide, 1 yard ecru. Three-strand Persian wool yarn, one skein each blue-green, peach, light brick, and dark brick. Batting. Sewing thread to match fabrics.

DIRECTIONS: Draw lines across pattern for embroidery, connecting grid lines. Enlarge pattern by copying on paper ruled in 1″ squares; complete quarter-pattern indicated by dash lines.

On muslin, mark four rectangles, two 11½″ × 15½″ for caddy front and lining, and two 11½″ × 5½″ for outer pocket and lining, leaving ½″ between pieces and ½″ at fabric edges. For inner pocket, mark a 11½″ × 7¾″ rectangle; mark a point on each short side, 2″ from one long side; draw a line from each side point to the center of the closest long side, forming a pentagon; mark a lining in same manner. Do not cut out muslin pieces yet.

Using water-erasable pen, mark a center line on outer pocket between 5½″ edges, forming two halves; also mark a line across width of caddy front, 7¾″ from one short edge (top).

Use dressmaker's carbon and tracing wheel or dry ball-point pen to transfer embroidery pattern to center of both halves of outer pocket. Transfer a single heart to caddy front, placing bottom point of heart on marked line. Transfer two more hearts at each side of center heart, 1½″ and 3¾″ away.

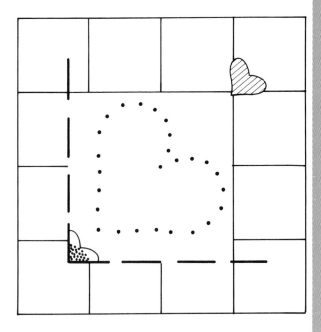

Place fabric in hoop. Separate yarn to work embroidery with one strand in needle, following pattern and stitch details (see General Directions at end of book for embroidery). Dots indicate French knots, toned areas satin stitch. Work a row of hearts on caddy front, alternating peach and light brick; work a single blue-green French knot between hearts and at each end. Work large hearts on pockets in dark brick, small hearts in light brick, and center in peach and light brick. After all embroidery is completed, remove fabric from hoop; steam-press gently on wrong side. Cut out all pieces ¼″ outside marked lines. Cut one same-size layer of batting each for caddy front and inner pocket. Set batting and lining pieces aside.

For cording, cut 12″ × 2″ bias strip from calico fabric. Center welting cord along wrong side of bias strip; fold strip over cord so that edges are aligned. Using zipper foot attachment, machine-stitch along strip with needle as close to cord as possible. Baste cording to one long (top) edge of embroidered pocket on right side with all raw edges even. Stitch matching lining to pocket along top edge with cording between, making ¼″ seam; turn and press.

With ¼″ seam, stitch inner pocket and lining together along two shortest edges (top) with batting on top; turn and press. Place caddy front, inner pocket, then outer pocket together, all right side up and with bottom raw edges even. Beginning at center bottom, top-stitch along center marked line; continue in straight line to top point of inner pocket. Cut 32½″ length of cluny trim. Beginning 1¼″ up from row of embroidered hearts, pin lace around sides and bottom of caddy front, with raw edges even; baste in place. To make ruffle, cut a 1¾″ × 67″ bias strip from calico fabric, piecing for length. Press short ends under ¼″. Press strip in half lengthwise, right side out. Gather raw edges to 32½″. Place ruffle over lace with raw edges even; baste. Place caddy lining, then batting on top, with ruffle and lace between. Stitch all around with ¼″ seam, leaving 4″ opening at top for turning. Turn to right side; turn raw edges under ¼″; slip-stitched closed.

Around the Tree

Christmas morning arrives with special gifts for everyone—adults, children, even baby!

NEEDLEWORK GIFT IDEAS

Sharpen your needlework skills. To make these four festive gifts, you'll need to appliqué, quilt, sew, cross-stitch, and embroider—but they're all easy!

DRESDEN PLATE HANGING

See General Directions for enlarging a pattern and for quilting stitch detail.

SIZE: 17" square.

EQUIPMENT: Ruler. Pencil. Tailor's chalk. Sewing needle. Tracing paper. Acetate film (or thin, stiff cardboard). Scissors. Compass. Sewing machine. Iron.

MATERIALS: Unbleached muslin, two pieces 17" square. Red white-dotted cotton fabric 36" wide, ¼ yard. Scraps of several green print fabrics. Batting, piece 17" square. Off-white and light-colored sewing threads.

DIRECTIONS

Quilting: Place one muslin piece flat. Mark pattern for quilting: Using ruler and tailor's chalk, mark diagonal center line from one corner to opposite corner. Mark parallel lines on both sides of center line, 1⅛" apart, to cover piece. Starting again in center, mark diagonal lines in opposite direction, for diamond grid pattern. Turn piece over, so marked side faces down. Place batting on top, then other muslin piece, right side up. Keeping edges even, pin and baste around four sides, using light-colored thread. Take two long stitches crossing in center, to keep batting from shifting. Turn to marked side. Starting in center and working out toward edges, baste on all marked lines. Turn piece over to other (right) side; check basting to see that all lines are straight and fabric is not puckered. Using off-white thread, quilt on all lines of basting, starting in center; see General Directions at end of book for quilting stitch detail. Remove basting.

Cutting Patches: Trace pattern for wedge shape; complete half pattern indicated by dash line. Make template from pattern, using acetate film (or thin, stiff cardboard). For patch pieces, place template on wrong side of fabric with one long edge on straight of goods; mark around with sharp pencil held at an outward angle, so point rests against template. Cut out piece ¼" beyond marked line all around for seam allowance. Cut 16 pieces from several green prints (we used eight prints, cutting two of each).

Appliquéing Patches: Using compass and tailor's chalk, mark two concentric circles—one 3¼" and one 10¾" in diameter—on right side of quilted muslin, placing point of compass in center of piece where diagonal lines cross. To prepare each patch, press

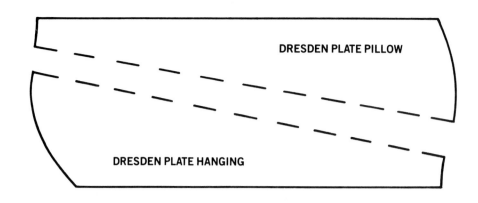

DRESDEN PLATE PILLOW

DRESDEN PLATE HANGING

curved edges ¼″ to wrong side, clipping if necessary to make piece lie flat. To appliqué first piece, fold one in half lengthwise, matching edges; finger-press fold. Pin piece right side up on muslin, aligning fold line with a diagonal center line of quilting, and inner (small) curve with inner circle. Pin a second piece over first piece, right sides facing and matching all edges. Stitch along right edge, on marked line. Turn top piece over so it lies adjacent to first piece, and press seam, checking to see that inner curve aligns with inner marked circle and "shoulders" of two pieces align with outer circle. Add third piece to second piece in same manner. Continue around in same direction until all pieces are in place and wreath is complete; on final piece, turn under right edge ¼″ and slip-stitch in place, covering left edge of first piece. Slip-stitch inner and outer curved edges of wreath.

Bow: Using sharp pencil, draw lines across large bow pattern, connecting grid lines. Enlarge pattern by copying on paper ruled in 1″ squares; complete half pattern indicated by dash lines. Cut five outer pieces of bow from right side of dotted red fabric; cut two inner (shaded) pieces from wrong side of same fabric. Prepare pieces and hand-appliqué in place; see color illustration.

Finishing: Quilt close to all seams of wreath and bow.

From dotted red fabric, cut four edging strips 1½″ wide, two 17″ long and two 17½″ long. On all pieces, press under one long edge ¼″. At each side of hanging, place a 17″ strip on top, right sides facing and matching raw edges; stitch in place with ¼″ seam. Fold strips to back of hanging and slip-stitch folded edge in place, for ½″ edging front and back. At top and bottom of hanging, sew 17½″ strips in place in same manner, but centering strips so ¼″ extends at each end; fold in ends and slip-stitch closed.

HOSTESS DOLLS

See General Directions for enlarging a pattern and for embroidery.

SIZE: Each 12″ tall.

EQUIPMENT: Colored pencil. Pencil. Ruler. Paper for patterns. Scissors. Straight pins. Sewing and embroidery needles. Embroidery hoop. Stiff cardboard, 3″ × 7″. T-pin. Sewing machine. Iron.

MATERIALS

For Rebecca (blond doll at left): Cotton or cotton-blend fabrics; Christmas motif print on white, 36″ wide, ¼ yard; pale peach or other flesh tone, large scrap. Flat white lace 1″ wide, 2½ yards. Green satin ribbon, ⅜″ wide, ½ yard. Narrow gold metallic tinsel trim, 1 yard. Red and green felt, one 9″ × 12″ sheet each. Four yellow pipe cleaners (or chenille stems). Fingering yarn, small skein yellow. Six-strand cotton embroidery floss, small amounts of peach, red, blue, brown, and black. Red-orange crayon. Sewing thread, white and to match yarn. Dacron polyester fiberfill.

For Rachel (brown-haired doll at right): Red polished cotton, 36″ wide, ¼ yard. Christmas motif print cotton, 9″ × 18″ piece for apron. Pale peach or other flesh-tone cotton, large scrap. White lace trim, ⅜″ wide, 1¼ yards. Gold, yellow-green, and dark green felt, one 9″ × 12″ sheet each. Green satin ribbon, ⅜″ wide, ½ yard. Fingering yarn, small skein brown. White seed beads, 18. Six-strand cotton embroidery floss, small amounts gold, peach, red, and brown. Sewing thread, white, red, and brown.

DIRECTIONS **(for either doll):** Note variations for **Rebecca** (blond hair) and **Rachel** (brown hair). Using sharp colored pencil, draw lines across patterns, connecting grid lines. Enlarge patterns by copying on paper ruled in ½″ squares; you'll need gown, sleeve, hand and one head for either doll, plus trims: poinsettia patterns for Rebecca; mistletoe, bib, basket for Rachel. Complete half patterns where indicated by long dash lines. Solid lines are stitching lines, fine dash lines are placement lines, and fine lines indicate embroidery. Transfer patterns to fabric as directed below, using dressmaker's carbon and dry ball-point pen; mark pieces to be cut from same fabric at least ½″ apart. Cut out all fabric pieces ¼″ beyond outlines for seam allowance. Stitch pieces together as directed with right sides facing and raw edges even, making ¼″ seams.

For Body: Transfer two gown pieces and four sleeves to wrong side of print fabric for Rebecca or solid red fabric for Rachel; reverse pattern for second and fourth sleeves; cut out. Stitch gown pieces together, leaving 3″ opening on one side; turn to right side and stuff. Turn raw edges to inside and slip-stitch opening closed. Stitch pairs of sleeves together, leaving lower (wrist) edges open. Press raw edges ⅛″ to wrong side twice; slip-stitch. Turn each sleeve to right side and lightly stuff to within 1″ of hemmed open edge. Set sleeves aside.

For Head: Transfer face for Rebecca or Rachel to right side of peach fabric; do not cut out. Insert fabric in embroidery hoop. Embroider as follows, using single strand of floss in needle for outline stitch and two strands for satin and straight stitch. **For Rebecca:** Work eyebrows, nose, and lids in brown outline stitch. Work eyes in blue satin stitch with black straight-stitch pupils. Work mouth in red satin stitch with upturned straight-stitch corners. **For Rachel:** Work brown brows and nose and red mouth in outline stitch. Work eyes in brown satin stitch.

Cut out face; use as pattern to cut head back from same fabric. Stitch face and head together, leaving opening at top for turning. Clip into seam allowance about every ½″; turn head to right side; stuff firmly. Turn raw edges ¼″ to inside; slip-stitch opening closed. "Rouge" cheeks with crayon.

For Hands: Transfer 4 hands to wrong side of peach fabric; reverse pattern for second and fourth hands. Cut out and stitch pairs of hands together, leaving top straight edges open; turn to right side. Mark dots, then stuff. Topstitch straight edge closed. Use two strands of peach floss in needle, knotted together at one end, to "quilt" fingers on each hand as follows: Pass needle through hand at one outside dot; tug floss slightly to embed knot in stuffing. Take a straight stitch down to end of hand; take a tiny backstitch at seam and a straight stitch up on other side, back to first dot. Insert needle at dot and bring it out at middle dot on one side. Repeat, "quilting" next two fingers; end with tiny backstitch and knot at third dot.

Assembly: Place head over neck of gown, with "chin" at top dash line on pattern. Pin in place and turn body over. Slip-stitch "neck" to back of head between dots. **For hands and sleeves: For Rebecca:** Insert a hand ⅜″ into each sleeve opening between dots; topstitch across sleeve opening, just behind slip-stitched hem, securing hand. Cut two 8″ lengths of lace trim. For each, stitch short edges together; baste one long edge and pull basting to

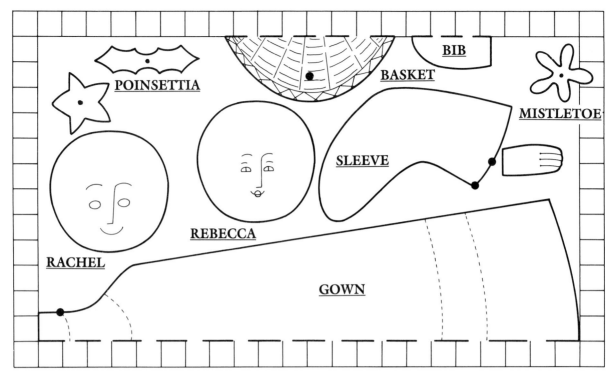

POINSETTIA

BASKET

BIB

MISTLETOE

SLEEVE

RACHEL

REBECCA

GOWN

gather lace to fit around sleeve; tie off. Slip lace over sleeve and pin in place, so that ungathered edge is even with hemmed sleeve edge; slip-stitch gathered edge in place. **For Rachel:** Baste around each sleeve ½″ from hemmed edge. Center a hand ⅜″ into sleeve opening; pull basting to gather sleeve around hand; tie off. Secure hand with backstitches taken over basting. **For each doll:** Pin sleeves to matching gown at shoulders so that elbows point backward and hands touch. Tack sleeve to body, just below shoulder, on inside.

Finishing—For Rebecca: Cut an 11″ length of 1″-wide lace. Stitch short edges together. Baste ¼″ in from one (lower) long edge. Slip over doll's head with seam at back and upper long edge touching chin. Pull basting to gather lace to fit neck; tack in place all around. Cut a 15″ length from same lace; stitch short edges together. Baste all around close to one (upper) long edge; pull basting to gather. Slip over head with seam at back and pin to gown where indicated by second dash line; slip-stitch in place. Cut two 20″ lengths of lace; gather and stitch to gown skirt in same manner, where indicated by dash lines.

For hair, wrap yarn, lengthwise, around 3″ × 7″ cardboard to cover. Cut through yarn at one end. Working with ¼″-wide bundles of cut yarn and matching thread, stitch center of bundles to center of head, starting ⅜″ above eyebrows and working up toward head seam and down to top of neck. Lay a length of metallic trim over crown and tie ends at back of head under hair; tack in place. "Comb" hair with fingers and trim ends even. Tie green satin ribbon tightly around waist with bow at back.

Using patterns for poinsettias, mark eight flowers on red felt and eight leaves on green felt; cut out on marked lines and snip center hole in each with point of scissors. Cut four 4″ lengths from yellow pipe cleaners. Onto each, thread two leaves, then two flowers; bend upper end of pipe cleaner for flower center. Tie "stems" together with remaining metallic trim. Place bouquet in hands as shown in color illustration; curl fingertips around "stem" and tack in place. Trim "stem" ends even.

For Rachel: Cut one 3½″ and one 10″ piece from ⅜″-wide lace. Baste one long edge of longer piece and pull basting, gathering edge to fit one long edge of shorter piece; slip-stitch edges together for collar. Place collar around doll's neck, ruffled edge up against chin; lap short ends at back and slip-stitch in place. Sew 3 seed bead "buttons" to center front of gown under collar, as shown.

For apron, cut skirt piece 11" × 6" and strip 1" × 18" for waistband/ties. Using pattern, cut 2 bib pieces. Press bottom straight edge of each 1/8" to wrong side. Stitch bib pieces together, leaving bottom open; turn, then slip-stitch opening closed. Cut 10" of 3/8"-wide lace; gather one long edge to fit curved bib edge. Slip-stitch gathered edge to one (wrong) side of bib close to seam, so that lace extends beyond edge. Press short side edges of skirt piece 1/8" to wrong side twice; slip-stitch. Press one (bottom) long edge 1/8", then 1/2" to wrong side from hem; slip-stitch in place. Cut 20" length from same lace; gather one long edge to measure 11". Pin gathered edge across skirt 1 1/2" up from hem, folding ends to wrong side; slip-stitch. Gather raw edge of skirt to measure 3 1/2". Press raw edges of waistband strip 1/8" to wrong side; press strip in half lengthwise, right side out. Leaving a 3 1/2" opening at center of strip, slip-stitch folded edges together. Insert gathered skirt edge into strip opening and slip-stitch in place on both sides. With wrong sides facing up, pin bib to center of waistband, so that slip-stitched folded edges are even; stitch in place on both sides. Tie apron tightly around doll; tack bib to center front of gown.

Make hair as follows: Push T-pin halfway into forehead 3/8" up from eyebrows. Work with groups of ten 24"-long strands of brown yarn at a time: Beginning at lower back of head, 1/4" below top of gown, wrap a group across head and around to front, above pin, and back around to beginning; overlap strand ends and continue wrapping turban-style, ending at back. Stitch hair in place with matching thread at center back and at center front, for a center part, maintaining inverted "V" shape caused by pin; also stitch at sides to keep shape. Continue in this manner until head is covered. Wind a final group around fingers to make chignon; tack to head top, concealing ends.

Using patterns, mark one basket on gold felt, ten mistletoe leaves on dark green, and five on yellow-green felt. Cut out pieces on marked lines. Also cut a 3/4" × 7" gold felt strip for handle. Using two strands of gold floss in needle, embroider basket as follows: Work straight-stitch spokes first, radiating out toward rim, then work straight stitches between. Work cross-stitches for rim over felt edge all around. Fold basket in half, embroidered side out, as shown in pattern. Fold long edges of strip to center of one side; work row of cross-stitches on other side through both thicknesses. Stitch handle ends to outside of basket at dots. Stitch one seed bead "berry" to center of each leaf. Fill basket with leaves, tacking them to each other and to basket. Tack basket closed. Tie green ribbon into bow around handle; place over right arm and tack to secure.

QUILTED EVENING BAG

See General Directions for quilting stitch detail and embroidery.

SIZE: About 6 1/2" × 8 1/4".

EQUIPMENT: Scissors. Ruler. Yardstick. Tailor's chalk or very hard, sharp pencil. Straight pins. Quilting, sewing and embroidery needles. Iron.

MATERIALS: Off-white, pongee-type polyester fabric 36"–45" wide, 1/2 yard. Red velveteen, piece 8 1/4" × 17 3/4". Polyester batting, two pieces 8 1/4" × 17 3/4". Red velvet ribbon, 1/4" wide, 1 yard. Red sequins, 5/16" wide, 96. Gold seed beads, 96. Green six-strand embroidery floss, 1 skein. Off-white quilting thread. Red and light-colored sewing thread.

DIRECTIONS: From polyester fabric cut piece 8 1/4" × 35 1/2"; cut in half widthwise for two 8 1/4" × 17 3/4" pieces.

Quilting: Using ruler and yardstick and tailor's chalk (or sharp pencil), mark lines on one piece as follows: Starting from one long edge and working toward other long edge, mark six parallel lines at these intervals: 2", ¼", 1¾", ¼", 1¾", ¼", 2". Starting from one short edge, and working toward other short edge, mark 16 parallel lines at these intervals: 1¾", ¼", 1¾", ¼", etc. Piece is now marked with a double-line grid for quilting.

Place piece on flat surface, marked side down. Place 2 pieces of batting on top, then second polyester piece, right side up. Keeping edges even, pin and baste around all 4 sides, using light-colored sewing thread. Take 2 long stitches crossing in center, to keep batting from shifting. Starting in center and working out toward edges, baste on all marked lines. Turn piece over to other (right) side; check basting to see that all lines are straight and fabric is not puckered. Using off-white quilting thread, quilt on all lines of basting, starting in center. Remove basting.

Embroidery: Using ruler and sharp, very hard pencil, mark a dot in center of each ¼" square formed by quilting lines. At each square, lightly mark two 2¼" diagonal lines in an X, each line going through dot and opposing corners and measuring 1⅛" from dot. Using two strands of green embroidery floss in needle, embroider over lines, through top fabric only and following Embroidery Diagram. Work lines in stem stitch, then add

lazy daisies as shown, leaving space for sequin (dash lines); add a single straight stitch to center of lazy daisy. For sequin, bring thread through fabric, through hole in sequin, through bead and back through sequin and fabric; finish off thread on underside of piece.

Finishing: To line bag, baste red velveteen piece to underside of quilted piece, around edges. Cut 5" × 35" strip of polyester for strap; set aside. From remaining polyester, cut two 1¼" × 17¾" strips; press under one long edge of each strip ¼". With right sides facing and raw edges even, sew other long edge to bag on velveteen side, taking small running stitches and making ¼" seam. Fold strips to front of bag for ½"-wide binding; topstitch near folded edge. Cut two 17¾" pieces from red ribbon. Sew ribbons to front of bag, butting one long edge of each against binding and going through top fabric only. Cut two 1¼" × 9½" strips of polyester. Turn ends under ½"; press. Bind short edges of bag as for long edges; slip-stitch ends of strips together.

Embroidered side out, fold up bag 5¾" from one short edge; slip-stitch sides together. Fold strip for strap in half lengthwise and press. Fold again, not quite in half, bringing raw edges almost to folded edge; press. Fold in half again; press. Stitch along both long edges close to folds. Turn ends under slightly; press. Sew ends inside bag opening at side seams. Fold down flap.

EMBROIDERY DIAGRAM

CROSS-STITCH NAPKIN HOLDERS

See General Directions.

SIZE: 2½" square.

EQUIPMENT: Pencil. Ruler. Scissors. Masking tape. Small embroidery hoop. Embroidery and sewing needles. Straight pin.

MATERIALS (for 4 holders shown):
Hardanger cloth, 22 threads-to-the-inch, green, two 9″ square pieces. DMC pearl cotton No. 8, one ball white. Thin, stiff cardboard. Grosgrain ribbon, ⅜″ wide, 4 yards green. Green sewing thread.

DIRECTIONS: Divide each fabric square into quarters (four 4½″ squares) as follows: With pencil, draw a line from center of one edge to center of opposite edge, using thread of fabric as a guide; draw a second line from center of third edge to center of fourth edge. Place one square aside to be used for backings. Use remaining square for designs: For each design, locate position of first stitch (in upper right corner of chart) by measuring

1¼″ in and down from upper right corner of a 4½″ square; mark mesh with a pin. Insert fabric in hoop. Follow charts to work all designs in cross-stitch, using white.

After all embroidery is completed, cut out all squares along marked lines.

To finish each napkin holder: Place one back over right side of one front, matching edges; stitch together, making 1″ seams and leaving one edge open for turning. Trim seam allowance to ¼″; clip corners. Turn to right side; slip 2½″ square of cardboard inside. Turn raw edges ¼″ to inside and slip-stitch opening closed. Cut 24″ length of ribbon; cut ends on the diagonal. Working diagonally from one corner of napkin holder to opposite corner, slip-stitch edges of ribbon across back of napkin holder.

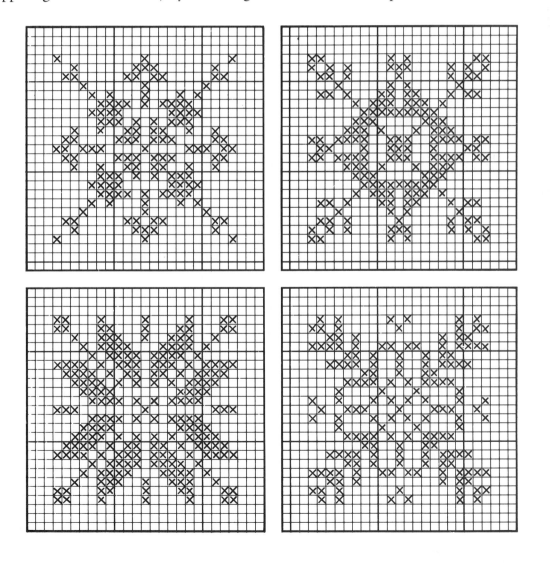

METALLIC STENCILING

Here is the simplest stenciling technique ever! Cut desired shape from stencil paper, then add the inside design with a paper doily.

See General Directions for enlarging a pattern.

EQUIPMENT: Sandpaper. Tack cloth. Paintbrushes. Pencil. Ruler. Paper for patterns. Compass. Black fine felt-tip pen. Masking tape. Sheets of acetate or stencil paper. Scissors. Glass 12″ square with filed or masked edges. White paper. X-acto knife and extra blades. Paper doilies in various shapes and designs. Chalk. Spray adhesive. Small glass jar with lid. Cotton swabs. Liner brush. Small plastic bag. Newspapers to cover working area.

MATERIALS: Acrylic water-base paint (bronze): One jar green or red for each item.

Acrylic sealer. Quick-drying acrylic varnish. One jar gold, wax metallic finish. Turpentine. Unfinished wooden and metal items (see photograph—smallest item is approximately 3″ × 3″ × 3″; largest, 16″ × 11″ × 2″).

DIRECTIONS

To Prepare Surfaces: Sand objects smooth; wipe with tack cloth. Seal with acrylic sealer. Let dry, then sand again, wipe with tack cloth. Paint with base color of red or green as desired; let dry. (We left lid of large box and outer rim of tray unpainted.) Apply a second coat of paint and let dry overnight. Finish with sealer.

To Stencil: Using pencil and ruler, draw lines across patterns for ornament stencils, connecting grid lines. Enlarge patterns by copying on paper ruled in ½″ squares; complete half-patterns indicated by dash lines. Make additional patterns for ball ornaments by drawing circles with compass; we made two patterns 2⅛″ and 2¾″ in diameter. Strengthen pattern outlines with felt-tip pen. Plan stenciling design for each object, combining ornaments as shown in photograph (those designs with solid outlines) or as desired. Trace design(s) on acetate or stencil paper, making one or several stencil(s) for each item as needed.

To cut each stencil, place white paper, then stencil paper on glass; tape in place. Holding X-acto knife like a pencil, carefully cut out marked area; cut toward you, turning the glass as you cut and not lifting blade until an entire area has been cut out; change knife blades often. If knife should slip, mend cut area on both sides of stencil with masking tape and trim with X-acto knife.

Mark desired position of ornaments with chalk on surface of object. Spray back of stencil(s) lightly with adhesive; allow to dry five minutes. Place stencil on surface and press in place. Choose a doily for stenciling each ornament. Spray both sides of doily with acrylic sealer; let dry. Apply spray adhesive to back of doily and press in place over stencil.

In small jar, dilute gold with turpentine to a brushable consistency. Keep jar closed when not using gold. Dip cotton swab into diluted gold and brush over holes of doily, working over stencil edges for a clean line. "Erase" mistakes with a swab dampened with turpentine. Allow gold to dry thoroughly—at least one hour—before removing doily and stencil. To prevent smearing, dust excess gold off doily and stencil, then remove them gently so as not to mar painted surface.

Using liner brush, outline stenciled ornament with gold and paint hangers and other details as shown. Paint edges of object with gold. Store brush in plastic bag until design is completed: then clean with turpentine.

Variations: On some objects, we used the border of a large doily as our stencil design, omitting ornament; see green scalloped box and large red oval box. On others, we stenciled ornament design(s) in center, then added small motifs from doilies around edge (green lazy Susan) or at sides (red card holder). On unpainted lid of oval box, we stenciled a red ornament, then added gold designs with doily.

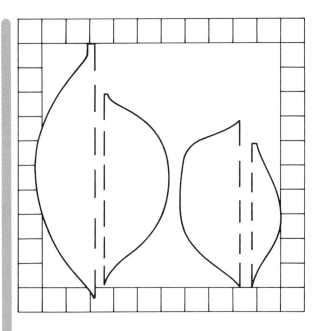

ORNAMENT STENCILS

Finishing: When gold is thoroughly dry, brush off chalk lines and seal with acrylic sealer. To further protect finish, apply several coats of quick-drying acrylic varnish, allowing each coat to dry thoroughly before applying another.

PARTY PINAFORES

If you're an apron person, one of these is for you. Most of the embroidery on the poinsettia apron is worked with a punch needle, making quick work. The organdy angels are machine-appliquéd.

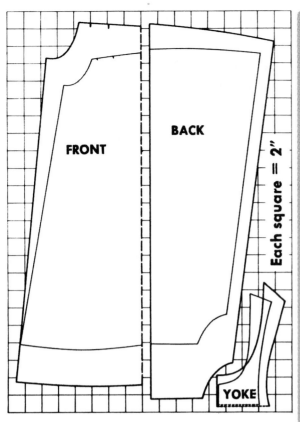

PATTERNS FOR APRON

Each square = 2″

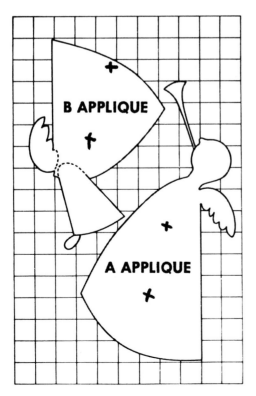

ANGELIC APRONS

See General Directions for enlarging a pattern.

SIZES: Directions are for child's apron (one size fits all). Changes for adult's apron (one size fits all) are in parentheses.

EQUIPMENT: Pencil. Colored pencil. Ruler. Scissors. Paper for patterns. Tape measure. Straight pins. Sewing needle. Sewing machine with zigzag attachment.

MATERIALS: Sheer white fabric, such as organdy or voile, 45″ wide, $2\frac{3}{8}$ ($2\frac{5}{8}$) yards. Heavy white lace trims: small daisy, $7\frac{1}{3}$ ($8\frac{1}{4}$) yards; large daisy, $\frac{5}{8}$ yard; eyelet-edged scallops, $\frac{7}{8}$ yard; flowers-and-leaves, $\frac{3}{8}$ yard. White sewing thread. Hook and eye.

DIRECTIONS: Using sharp colored pencil, draw lines across patterns by connecting grid lines. Enlarge patterns by copying on paper ruled in 2″ squares; complete half-patterns indicated by long dash lines. Using patterns for apron, cut one yoke, one front and 2 back sections on bias of fabric, adding $\frac{1}{4}$″ seam allowance around each piece.

To assemble apron, with right sides facing, pin pieces together and stitch $\frac{1}{4}$″ from raw edges as follows: Join each back section to front at side seam; join long edge of yoke to top edge of front, easing front section as indicated on pattern; join yoke straps to back at armhole edge. Finish seam allowances with zig-zag stitch; press side seams toward back and yoke seams toward bottom. Finish remaining raw edges with close, narrow zigzag stitch. Pin and baste row of small-daisy trim on right side of front over yoke seam, and on right side of each back section over yoke seam and extended raw edges. Pin and baste trim, on right side of apron, over armhole, neck, center back and bottom edges. Secure trim to fabric with regular zig-zag stitch.

For appliqué, cut A and B angel pieces from white fabric, adding $\frac{1}{4}$″ seam allowance around edges. With white thread, mark two center X's on each piece where indicated on pattern; mark stitching lines on B where indicated by short dash lines. Pin and baste A appliqué on front of apron, centered between side seams and with lower point of angel's gown 5″ above bottom of apron; do not turn under excess fabric. Straight-stitch around appliqué on marked lines. Trim away excess fabric to ⅛″ from straight stitching. Set sewing machine for close zigzag stitch as directed (¼″ wide or less). Zigzag around appliqué, covering straight stitching and excess fabric. Place B over A, matching marked X's. Baste and appliqué same as for A, zigzag-stitching over marked lines for top of arm and edge of wing.

Arrange trim for angel appliqué as follows: Turn apron so that angel appears standing up. Pin row of small-daisy trim over lower edge of A; pin scalloped trim over lower edge of B, about 2″ above lower edge of B, and over edge of sleeve; pin flowers-and-leaves trim between two rows of scalloped trim at lower edge of B. Zigzag-stitch rows of trim in place. Cut 50 flowers from remaining piece of small-daisy trim and arrange around angel's head to simulate hair; sew each flower in place. Cut large-daisy trim into separate flowers and arrange in four rows above scalloped trim on B as shown in photograph; sew in place. Sew hook and eye to edge of back sections at neck.

POINSETTIA PINAFORE

SIZES: Directions for small size (4–6). Changes for medium size (8–10) and large size (12–14) are in parentheses.

EQUIPMENT: Pencil. Colored pencil. Ruler. Scissors. Paper for patterns. Tape measure. Straight pins. Dressmaker's tracing (carbon) paper. Tracing wheel or dry ball-point pen. Punch embroidery needle (little loop size). Embroidery hoop, 8″. Sewing needle. Sewing machine.

MATERIALS: Mercerized knitting and crochet cotton, one ball each; red, dark red, yellow, dark green, light green. White cotton or cotton blend fabric, 45″ wide, 1⅔ (2¼, 2¾) yards. Two eyelet strips, each 39″ × 3½″ (40½″ × 4½″, 43″ × 5½″). White thread. Red buttonhole twist thread.

DIRECTIONS: On paper, draw pattern pieces for pinafore as follows: bib, 6″ × 6″ (6¾″ × 7¾″, 7½″ × 9½″); strap, 1½″ × 17½″ (1¾″ × 22½″, 1¾″ × 27½″); waistband, 18″ × 1½″ (20″ × 1¾″, 22½″ × 2¼″); tie, 33″ × 3¼″ (38″ × 4″, 44½″ × 4¾″); skirt, 58½″ × 19½″ (62″ × 26″, 66½″ × 31¼″).

COLOR KEY

1 Red
2 Dark Red
3 Yellow
4 Light Green
5 Dark Green

Each square = 1″

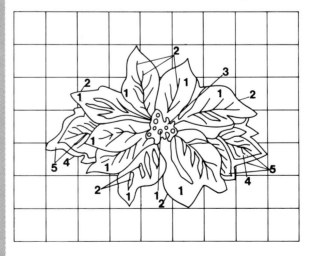

POINSETTIA PATTERN

Use patterns to cut one bib, 4 straps, 2 waistbands, 2 ties, and one skirt from white fabric, adding ½″ seam allowance around all edges. Mark another bib on wrong side of fabric, leaving wide margins all around; do not cut out.

Using sharp colored pencil, draw lines across pattern for poinsettia by connecting grid lines. Enlarge design by copying on paper ruled in ¾″ (1″, 1″) squares. Using dressmaker's carbon and hard lead pencil, transfer poinsettia to wrong side of second bib piece, centering design between all edges.

Stretch fabric tightly over embroidery hoop. Following manufacturer's directions punch-embroider poinsettia design; see color key with pattern. Cut out embroidered bib, adding ½″ seam allowance all around. With right sides together, stitch plain bib piece to embroidered bib piece at top, ½″ from raw edges. Turn to right side and press top edge. Pin remaining three sides together and machine-baste ¼″ from raw edges.

To make ruffle, mark center point on raw edge of one eyelet strip. At one short end of strip, mark point 1¼″ away from finished

**DIAGRAM
FOR RUFFLE**

edge; connect center and end points in a gently curving line; see diagram. Fold strip in half, marked side out; use dressmaker's carbon and tracing wheel to transfer curving line to other half of strip. Cut strip along marked lines. Use strip as pattern to cut second ruffle strip. Starting and ending 3″ (5½″, 8″) from each end, machine-baste ½″ and again ¼″ from raw edge of each strip. Pull bobbin threads to gather strip to a total length of 17½″ (22½″, 27½″). With raw edges even, pin gathered edge of strip to one long edge of a strap, right sides together. Adjust gathers evenly; stitch together ½″ from raw edges. Turn raw edges to wrong side of strap and press toward center of strap. With right sides together and matching raw edges, pin bib to other long edge of strap, with bottom edge of bib even with one short end of strap. Baste ½″ from long raw edges. To face strap, pin a second strap piece to ruffled strap piece with right sides facing and raw edges flush; bib should be enclosed between straps. Stitch ½″ from long raw edges through all layers. Turn straps to right side, exposing bib. Press long, unstitched edge of facing strap ½″ to wrong side; slip-stitch folded edge of strap over stitching line on wrong side of eyelet strip; press. Topstitch strap ¼″ from both long edges with red thread. Repeat.

To make ties, fold two long edges and one short edge of each tie ¼″ to wrong side and press; turn under again, enclosing raw edges, and topstitch in place, using red thread. Make

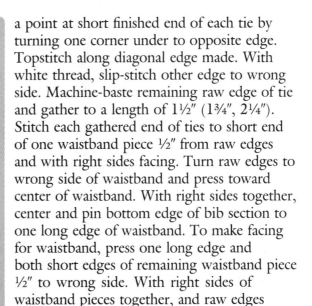

a point at short finished end of each tie by turning one corner under to opposite edge. Topstitch along diagonal edge made. With white thread, slip-stitch other edge to wrong side. Machine-baste remaining raw edge of tie and gather to a length of 1½″ (1¾″, 2¼″). Stitch each gathered end of ties to short end of one waistband piece ½″ from raw edges and with right sides facing. Turn raw edges to wrong side of waistband and press toward center of waistband. With right sides together, center and pin bottom edge of bib section to one long edge of waistband. To make facing for waistband, press one long edge and both short edges of remaining waistband piece ½″ to wrong side. With right sides of waistband pieces together, and raw edges flush, pin waistbands together with bib section between. Stitch ½″ from raw edges through all layers. Turn waistbands to right side exposing bib; press.

To make skirt, fold one long edge and two short edges of skirt ½″ to wrong side and press; turn under again, enclosing raw edges, and topstitch ¼″ from folded edge using red thread (topstitch the long edge ½″ and again ¼″ from fold). Using white thread, machine-baste ½″ and again ¼″ from remaining raw edge. Pull bobbin threads to gather fabric same size as waistband. With right sides together and raw edges flush, pin gathered edge of skirt to bottom edge of waistband, keeping facing free; adjust gathers and stitch ½″ from raw edges. Turn raw edges to wrong side of waistband and press toward center of waistband. Pin folded edge of waistband facing over gathered edge of skirt; slip-stitch together over stitching lines of skirt and ties. Press; topstitch ¼″ from all four edges of waistband, using red thread. Pin free ends of straps to each end of waistband, placing right side of strap against wrong side of waistband. Slip-stitch in place, then topstitch again over previous topstitching lines to secure.

WINTER WARMERS

Delight someone special on Christmas morning with hand-knitted accessories that will let her know all winter long how much you love her!

See General Directions for knitting.

ARGYLE SOCKS

SIZE: Adjustable.

MATERIALS: Chat Botté Petrouchka, 1 50-gram (1¾-oz.) ball each Anthracite #518 (A), Cedre #530 (C), Marine #553 (D), Myrtille #589 (E), Jacinthe #538 (F); 2 balls Blanc #501 (B). Knitting needles Nos. 3 and 4 (3¼ and 3½ mm).

GAUGE: 6 sts = 1"; 9 rows = 1".

Pattern Notes: Always change colors on wrong side, pick up new color from under dropped strand. Wind colors onto separate bobbins. Cut and join colors when necessary.

SOCK: Beg at cuff, with A and No. 3 needles, cast on 48 sts. Work in ribbing of k 2, p 2 for 4 rows. Change to B.

* Next Row: Knit. Continue in ribbing of k 2, p 2 for 3 rows. Change to A.

Next Row: Knit. Continue in ribbing of k 2, p 2 for 3 rows. Change to B. * Repeat from * to * once, inc 2 sts on last row—50 sts. Change to No. 4 needles.

Shape Leg: Row 1 (right side): Following chart, k 24 B, 1 E, 24 B, 1 C.

Row 2: P 2 C, 22 B, 3 E, 22 B, 1 C. Continue to follow chart in stockinette st (k 1 row, p 1 row) until row 75 has been completed.

Shape Heel: Next Row: K 10 B, turn, place remaining 40 sts on a holder.

Next Row: P 10, turn. Continue on these 10 sts for 1½", end wrong side.

Next Row (right side): K 3, k 2 tog, turn.

Next Row: P 4, turn.

Next Row: K 4, k 2 tog, turn.

Next Row: P 5, turn.

Next Row: K 5, k 2 tog, turn.

Next Row: P 6, turn. Sl sts on a holder.

Return to last long row, leave 30 center sts on holder, place last 10 sts on No. 4 needle. Join B. Work in stockinette st for 1½", end right side.

Next Row: P 3, p 2 tog, turn.

Next Row: K 4, turn.

Next Row: P 4, p 2 tog, turn.

Next Row: K 5, turn.

Next Row: P 5, p 2 tog, turn. Sl remaining 7 sts on a holder.

Gusset and Foot: Next Row (right side): With B and No. 4 needles, k 7 sts from first holder, pick up and k 10 sts along side of

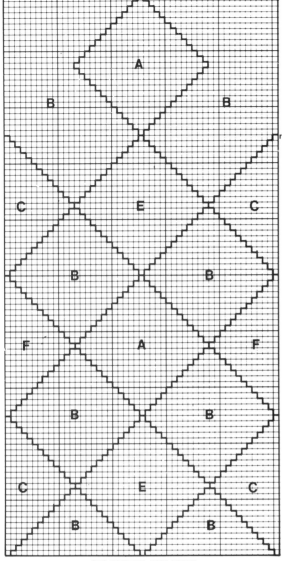

ARGYLE SOCKS

heel, work 30 instep sts following chart, with B, pick up and k 10 sts along other side of heel, k 7 sts from second holder—64 sts.

Next Row: Purl.

Next Row: K 15, k 2 tog, k 30, sl 1, k 1, psso, k 15—62 sts.

Next Row: Purl.

Next Row: K 14, k 2 tog, k 30, sl 1, k 1, psso, k 14—60 sts.

Next Row: Purl. Continue in this manner, dec 1 st each side of center 30 sts every right side row 4 times—52 sts. Continue until

foot measures 6½″ or 2½″ less than desired length, working with B only after center diamond has been completed.

Shape Toe: Next Row (right side): K 10, sl 1, k 1, psso, k 2 tog, k 22, sl 1, k 1, psso, k 2, k 2 tog, k 10—48 sts.

Next Row: Purl. Continue in this manner, working decs over previous decs every right side row 10 times—8 sts.

Next Row (right side): K 2 tog across row.

Next Row: Purl. Cut yarn, leaving a 12″ end. Draw end through remaining 4 sts, draw sts tog and fasten; sew seam.

DIAMOND PATTERN MITTENS

MATERIALS: Chat Botté Petrouchka, 1 50-gram (1¾-oz.) ball each Anthracite #518 (A), Blanc #501 (B), Cedre #530 (C), Marine #553 (D), Myrtille #589 (E), Jacinthe #538 (F). One pair straight and one set dp needles No. 4 (3½ mm).

GAUGE: 6 sts = 1″; 9 rows = 1″.

Pattern Notes: Always change colors on wrong side, pick up new color from under dropped strand. Wind colors onto separate bobbins. Cut and join colors when necessary.

MITTENS: **Right Hand:** With dp needles No. 4 and A, cast on 42 sts. Divide sts on 3 dp needles. Mark end of rnd. Join. Work Chart 1 until piece measures 1½″ from start, inc 2 sts on last row—44 sts. Work to top of Chart 2, working back and forth in stockinette st (k 1 row, p 1 row).

Thumb: Next Row (right side): K 11, sl last 9 sts of these 11 onto holder, finish row following chart.

Next Row: P to holder, cast on 4 F, 3 C, 2 F, work last 2 sts. Continue in pat following chart until 44 rows have been completed.

CHART 1

☑	A
⊘	B
☒	C
◉	D
⊟	E
☐	F

CHART 2

DIAMOND PATTERN MITTENS

Shape Top: Next Row: K 11 F, 11 D, 11 F, 11 D.

Next Row: P 11 D, 11 F, 11 D, 11 F. Repeat these 2 rows for 1″.

Next Row (right side): Keeping to established colors, k 1, k 2 tog, k 16, sl 1, k 1, psso, k 2, k 2 tog, k 16, sl 1, k 1, psso, k 1.

Next Row: P in established colors. Repeat last 2 rows 4 times having decs above previous decs—24 sts.

Next Row (right side): K 2 tog across row— 12 sts. Cut yarn, leaving a 12″ end. Draw end through remaining 12 sts, draw sts tog and fasten; sew seam.

Shape Thumb: From right side, with dp needles and F, pick up and k 11 sts along cast on edge of thumb, k sts from holder—20 sts. Divide sts on 3 dp needles. Work in

stockinette st (k each rnd) until thumb measures 2½″.

Next Rnd: K 2 tog around—10 sts.

Next Rnd: K 2 tog around—5 sts. Cut yarn, leaving an 8″ end. Draw end through remaining 5 sts, draw sts tog and fasten.

Work second mitten to correspond to first, reversing pat and placement of thumb.

STRIPED SCARF

SIZE: 12″ × 48″.

MATERIALS: Chat Botté Petrouchka, 2 50-gram (1¾-oz.) balls each Anthracite #518 (A) and Blanc #501 (B), 1 ball each Cedre #530 (C), Marine #553 (D), Myrtille #589 (E), Jacinthe #538 (F). Knitting needles Nos. 2 and 4 (2¾ and 3½ mm). Circular needle No. 2 (2¾ mm).

GAUGE: 6 sts = 1″; 9 rows = 1″.

Pattern Notes: Always change colors on wrong side, pick up new color from under dropped strand. Cut and join colors when necessary.

SCARF: With No. 4 needles, cast on 12 B, 12 A, 12 B, 12 A, 12 B—60 sts.

Row 1 (right side): K 12 B, 12 A, 12 B, 12 A, 12 B

Row 2: P 12 B, 12 A, 12 B, 12 A, 12 B.

Row 3: K 1 A, 12 B, 12 A, 12 B, 12 A, 11 B.

Row 4: P 11 B, 12 A, 12 B, 12 A, 12 B, 1 A.

Row 5: K 2 A, 12 B, 12 A, 12 B, 12 A, 10 B.

Row 6: P 10 B, 12 A, 12 B, 12 A, 12 B, 2 A. Continue in this manner, inc the color at beg of row by 1 st, and dec the color at end of row by 1 st on right side rows until scarf measures 46″ or desired length. Bind off.

Border: From right side, with No. 2 needles and E, pick up and k 60 sts along bottom edge of scarf. Work in garter st (k each row), inc 1 st each side every right side row 4 times. Bind off. Work same edging with F along other bottom edge of scarf. With circular needle No. 2 and C, pick up and k 1 st in each row along side edge of scarf. Do not join. Work back and forth in garter st, inc 1 st each side every right side row 4 times. Bind off. Work same edging with D along other side edge of scarf. Sew mitered corners tog.

PATTERNED CUFF HAT

MATERIALS: Scheepjeswol Zermatt, 1 50-gram (1¾-oz.) ball each Green #4821 (A), Burgundy #4824 (B), Red #4803 (C), Gray #4802 (D), 2 balls Cream #4826 (E). Knitting needles No. 5 (3¾ mm). Crochet hook size F 3¾ mm).

GAUGE: 6 sts = 1″; 7 rows = 1″.

Pattern Notes: Always change colors on wrong side, pick up new strand from under dropped strand. Carry unused color across loosely, twisting every 3rd st. Cut and join colors when necessary.

PATTERN: **Fancy St** (multiple of 4 sts):

Rows 1 and 5: * K 3, p 1, repeat from * across.

Rows 2 and 4: * K 1, p 1, k 1, p 1, repeat from * across.

Row 3: * K 1, p 1, k 2, repeat from * across.

Row 6: Purl. Repeat rows 1–6 for fancy st.

HAT: With A, cast on 120 sts. Work in stockinette st (k 1 row, p 1 row) for 2 rows.

Work to top of chart. With A, continue in stockinette st for 23 rows. Change to E. Work in ribbing of k 1, p 1 for 5½″, end wrong side.

Dec Row (right side): Rib 4, * k 2 tog, rib 4, repeat from * to last 8 sts, k 2 tog, rib 6—101 sts.

Next Row: Rib.

Dec Row: Rib 3, * k 2 tog, rib 3, repeat from * to last 3 sts, k 2 tog, rib 1—81 sts.

Next Row: Rib.

Dec Row: Rib 2, * k 2 tog, rib 2, repeat from * to last 3 sts, k 2 tog, rib 1—61 sts.

Next Row: Rib.

Dec Row: Work 2 tog across row—31 sts.

Next Row: Rib.

Dec Row: Work 2 tog across row—16 sts. Cut yarn, leaving a 12″ end. Draw end through remaining 16 sts, draw sts tog and fasten; sew seam.

FINISHING: Turn cuff in half to inside and sew cast-on row to first E rib row. Turn cuff back so border pat is on outside.

EARFLAPS (make 2): With E, cast on 20 sts. Work in fancy st for 25 rows. Dec 1 st each side of next 6 rows. Bind off remaining 8 sts.

Ties: From right side, with size F hook and E, work 1 row sc evenly alongside of earflap to the 4th bound-off st; ch 40 for tie, turn. Sc in 2nd ch from hook and in bottom lp of each ch across, then sc evenly along opposite side of earflap. End off.

Top Knot: With size F hook and E, ch 10.

Next Row: Dc in 4th ch from hook and in each ch across. End off. Make 2nd piece to correspond. Place wrong sides of chs tog and fasten with 1 row sc around edges.

Sew earflaps to inside of hat along first row of ribbing. Sew top knot to top of hat.

PATTERNED CUFF MITTENS

MATERIALS: Scheepjeswol Zermatt, 1 50-gram (1¾-oz.) ball each Green #4821 (A), Burgundy #4824 (B), Red #4803 (C), Gray #4802 (D), 2 balls Cream #4826 (E). Set dp needles No. 5 (3¾ mm). Crochet hook size F/5 (3¾ mm).

GAUGE: 6 sts = 1"; 7 rows = 1".

Pattern Notes: Always change colors on wrong side, pick up new strand from under dropped strand. Carry unused color across loosely, twisting every 3rd st. Cut and join colors when necessary.

PATTERN ST (multiple of 22 sts): **Rnd 1:** P 1, k 2, p 3, k 2, p 1, k 5, p 1, k 2, p 3, k 2.

Rnd 2: (P 1, k 1) 4 times, p 2, k 3, p 2, (k 1, p 1) 3 times, k 1.

Rnd 3: P 2, k 2, p 1, k 2, p 2, (k 1, p 1) twice, k 1, p 2, k 2, p 1, k 2, p 1.

Rnd 4: P 1, k 2, p 3, (k 2, p 1) 3 times, k 2, p 3, k 2.

Rnd 5: (P 1, k 1) across.

Rnd 6: P 2, k 2, p 1, k 2, p 3, k 3, p 3, k 2, p 1, k 2, p 1. Repeat rnds 1–6 for pattern st.

To Inc 1 St: Pick up horizontal strand between st just knitted and next st, place on left-hand needle and k through back lp.

MITTENS: With dp needles No. 5 and A, cast on 48 sts. Divide sts on 3 dp needles. Mark end of rnd; join. Working in stockinette st (k each rnd), work to top of chart, dec 4 sts evenly spaced across last row. Change to E. Work in pat st for 1½".

Shape Thumb: Next Rnd: Place marker on needle, inc 1 st, k 1, inc 1 st, place marker on needle, finish rnd in pat st.

Next Rnd: Inc 1 st after first marker, k to second marker, inc 1 st, sl marker, finish rnd in pat st. Repeat last rnd until there are 15 thumb sts between markers. Work thumb sts in stockinette st (k each rnd) and remaining sts in pat st.

Next Rnd. Sl 15 thumb sts on a safety pin, cast on 3 sts, finish rnd in pat st—46 sts. Continue in pat st on all sts until piece measures 6" above cuff.

Shape Top: Next Rnd: Keeping to pat, k 1, k 2 tog, work 19, sl 1, k 1, psso, k 2, k 2 tog, work 19, sl 1, k 1, psso, k 1. Repeat last rnd 6 times working decs above previous decs—22 sts.

Next Rnd: K 2 tog around—11 sts. Cut yarn, leaving a 12" end. Draw end through remaining 11 sts, draw sts tog and fasten.

Thumb: Next Rnd: Sl 15 sts from pin to needle, pick up and k 3 sts along cast-on edge; join. K around until thumb measures 3¼". K 2 tog around—9 sts.

Next Rnd: K 2 tog around—5 sts. Cut yarn leaving an 8" end. Draw end through remaining 5 sts, draw sts tog and fasten.

FINISHING: With crochet hook and A, work 1 rnd sc along bottom edge.

Work second mitten to correspond to first, reversing pat and placement of thumb.

PATTERNED CUFF SOCKS

SIZE: Adjustable.

MATERIALS: Scheepjeswol Zermatt, 1 50-gram (1¾-oz.) ball each Green #4821 (A), Burgundy #4824 (B), Red #4803 (C), Gray #4802 (D), 3 balls Cream #4826 (E). Set dp needles No. 5 (3¾ mm).

GAUGE: 6 sts = 1"; 7 rows = 1".

Pattern Notes: Always change colors on wrong side, pick up new strand from under dropped strand. Carry unused colors loosely across twisting every 3rd st. Cut and join colors when necessary.

PATTERN: Fancy St **(multiple of 4 sts):**

Rnds 1 and 5: * K 3, p 1, repeat from * around.

Rnds 2 and 4: * P 1, k 1, p 1, k 1, repeat from * around.

Rnd 3: K 1, p 1, k 2, repeat from * around.

Rnd 6: K around. Repeat rnds 1–6 for fancy st.

SOCKS: **Cuff:** With A and No. 5 dp needles, cast on 48 sts. Divide sts on 3 dp needles. Join and work around in ribbing of k 1, p 1 for 2 rnds. Work to top of chart. With A, k 2 rnds. Cuff is completed; turn cuff to wrong side.

Leg: Change to E. Work in ribbing of k 1, p 1 for 2″. Work in fancy st for 4½″.

Shape Heel: With beg of rnd as center of heel, place 12 sts from third needle onto spare needle, k across 12 sts of first needle, place remaining 24 sts onto spare needle for instep— 24 heel sts.

Double Heel: Row 1: * Sl 1, k 1, repeat from * across.

Row 2: Sl 1, p across row. Repeat last 2 rows for 2″, end p row.

To Turn Heel: Rnd 1: Sl 1, k 13, k 2 tog, k 1; turn.

Row 2: Sl 1, p 5, p 2 tog, p 1, turn.

Row 3: Sl 1, k 6, k 2 tog, k 1, turn.

Row 4: Sl 1, p 7, p 2 tog, p 1, turn. Continue in this manner always having 1 more st before each dec on every row until 14 sts remain on needle, end p row. K 7 and leave on spare needle.

Gusset and Foot: With first needle, k 7, pick up and k 14 sts along side of heel; with

☐ A   ☒ B   ◹ C   ◉ D   ☐ E

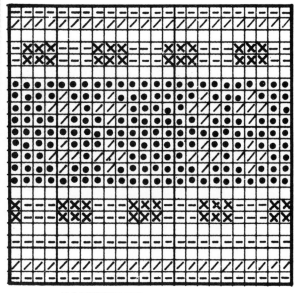

PATTERNED CUFF SOCKS

second needle, work in pat across 24 sts; with third needle, pick up and k 14 sts along other side of heel, k 7 from spare needle.

Shape Instep: Rnd 1: With first needle, k to last 3 sts, k 2 tog, k 1; with second needle, work across in pat; with third needle, k 1, sl 1, k 1, psso, k to end.

Rnd 2: With first needle, knit; with second needle, work across in pat; with third needle, knit. Repeat these 2 rnds until 48 sts remain. Continue working first and third needles in knit and 2nd needle in fancy st until sock is 2″ shorter than desired length.

Shape Toe: Rnd 1: With first needle, k to last 3 sts, k 2 tog, k 1; with 2nd needle, k 1, sl 1, k 1, psso, k to last 3 sts, k 2 tog, k 1; with third needle k 1, sl 1, k 1, psso, k to end.

Rnd 2: Knit. Repeat last 2 rnds until 10 sts remain on second needle.

Next Rnd: K across 5 sts of first needle and place on third needle. Weave sts tog.

MORE WINTER WARMERS

Heavy yarn and large needles make fast work of these delightful sets for teens. Hats are knitted in the round, so there's no seam. Make the matching scarves extra long so they can be wrapped several times for extra warmth.

See General Directions for knitting and embroidery.

RED WARM-UP SET

SIZE: Hat and mittens, medium. Scarf, 65″ long, plus fringe.

MATERIALS: Reynolds Lopi, 100-gram skeins: For hat, 1 skein each red 103, white 51 and green 102. For scarf, 3 skeins red 103, 1 skein green 102, small amount of white 51. For mittens, 1 skein red 103, small amount of white 51 and green 102. Knitting needles: For hat, set of dp needles Nos. 8 (5 mm) and 10½ (6½ mm). For scarf, knitting needles No. 10½ (6½ mm). For mittens, set of dp needles Nos. 8 (5 mm) and 10½ (6½ mm). Tapestry needle.

GAUGE: 10 sts = 3″ (No. 10½ needles).

HAT: With red and No. 8 dp needles, cast on 70 sts. Divide sts on 3 needles. Join and work around in stockinette st (k each rnd) for 2″. Change to No. 10½ needles. Following Chart 1, repeat from A to B around. When top of tree is reached, cut green; work even for 3 rnds.

First Dec Rnd: * K 2 tog, k5, k2 tog, k1 repeat from * around—56 sts. K 4 rnds.

Second Dec Rnd: * K 1, k 2 tog, k 3, k 2 tog, repeat from * around—42 sts. K 4 rnds.

Third Dec Rnd: *K 2 tog, k 1, repeat from * around—28 sts. K 7 rnds. Cut yarn, leaving 10″ end. Pull through remaining sts, gather sts tog tightly and secure end.

EMBROIDERY: With white, following Chart 2, embroider snowflakes in duplicate st. Embroider one line of snowflakes 3 rows apart directly over top of each tree, one line of snowflakes, 3 rows apart between trees as shown. After each dec rnd, snowflakes will be 1 st closer tog.

FINISHING: With white, make a 4″ pompon. Sew to top of hat.

SCARF: With red and No. 10½ needles, cast on 30 sts.

Row 1 (right side): P 10, k 10, p 10.

Row 2: K 10, p 10, k 10. Repeat these 2 rows until piece is 65″ long. Bind off.

FINISHING: Press scarf lightly using thick damp cloth and warm iron. Holding bound-off edge towards you, following Chart 1,

CHART 3

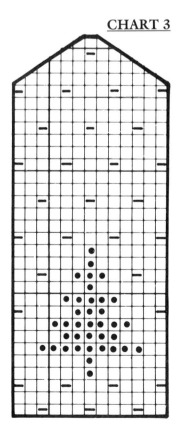

CHART 2

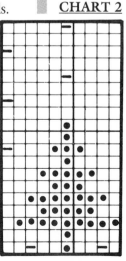

CHART 1

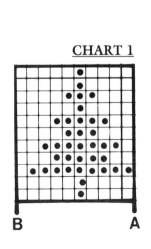

■ Green
□ White

B   A

embroider tree in duplicate st on center knit panel of scarf near end. Cut green and white yarn in 10″ lengths. Holding 4 strands tog for each fringe, knot 5 green fringes on each side panel, 6 white fringes on center panel.

MITTENS: With red and No. 8 dp needles, cast on 24 sts. Divide sts on 3 needles. Join and work around in stockinette st (k each rnd) for 3½″. Change to No. 10½ needles. Work even for 3″.

Thumb opening: K 5, place these sts on a holder, finish rnd.

Next Rnd: Cast on 5 sts, finish rnd. Work even for 3¼″.

First Dec Rnd: * K 2 tog, k 2, repeat from * around. K 1 rnd.

Second Dec Rnd: * K 1, k 2 tog, repeat from * around. K 1 rnd.

Third Dec Rnd: * K 2 tog, repeat from * around. Cut yarn, leaving 10″ end. Pull through remaining 6 sts, gather sts tog tightly and secure end.

Thumb: Sl sts from holder to needle. Join yarn; k 4 of these sts to one needle; with 2nd needle, k 1, pick up and k 1 st at side of thumb and 2 sts on cast-on sts; with 3rd needle, pick up and k 3 sts on cast-on sts and 1 st at side of thumb—12 sts. Work even for 2″. K 2 tog around. Cut yarn, leaving 10″ end. Pull through remaining sts, gather sts tog tightly and secure end.

Work second mitten to correspond to first, reversing pat and placement of thumb.

FINISHING: Press mittens through thick damp cloth, having thumb at left of palm for left mitten and at right of palm for right mitten. Following Chart 3, embroider back of each mitten in duplicate st.

BLUE WARM-UP SET

SIZE: Hat and mittens, medium. Scarf, 65″ long, plus fringe.

MATERIALS: Reynolds Lopi, 100-gram skeins: For hat and mittens, 1 skein each blue 98, green 102 and white 51. Few yards of yellow and red yarn. For scarf, 3 skeins blue 98; some green 102 and red 103 for fringe. Few yards of yellow yarn. Knitting needles: For hat and mittens, set of dp needles No. 8 (5 mm) and 10½ (6½ mm). For scarf, knitting needles No. 10½ (6½ mm). Crochet hook size 1 (5½ mm). Tapestry needle.

GAUGE: 10 sts = 3″ (No. 10½ needles).

HAT: With blue and No. 8 dp needles, cast on 70 sts. Divide sts on 3 needles. Join and work around in stockinette st (k each rnd) for 2″. Cut blue. Change to No. 10½ needles. With yellow, work 1 rnd. Cut yellow. With white, work even for 2″. Join blue.

Pattern: Rnd 1: * With blue, k 1; with white, k 6, repeat from * around.

Rnd 2: * With blue, k 2; with white, k 4; with blue, k 1, repeat from * around.

Rnd 3: * With blue, k 3; with white, k 2; with blue, k 2, repeat from * around. Cut white. Work even with blue for 3 rnds.

First Dec Rnd: * K 2 tog, k 1, k 2 tog, k 5, repeat from * around—56 sts. K 1 rnd blue, 3 rnds white. Cut white and blue, join green.

Second Dec. Rnd: * K 3, k 2 tog, k 1, k 2 tog, repeat from * around—42 sts. K 4 rnds green.

Third Dec Rnd: * K 2 tog, k 1, repeat from * around—28 sts. K 7 rnds green. Cut yarn, leaving 10″ end. Pull through remaining sts, gather sts tog tightly and secure end.

FINISHING: With green, make 4″ pompon. Sew to top of hat. With red, embroider a French knot at top of each white point.

MITTENS: With blue and No. 8 dp needles, cast on 24 sts. Divide sts on 3 needles. Join and work around in stockinette st (k each rnd) for 3½." Change to No. 10½ needles. Work even for 3".

Thumb Opening: K 5, place these sts on holder, finish rnd.

Next Rnd: Cast on 5 sts, finish rnd. Work even for 3¼."

First Dec Rnd: K 2 tog, k 2, repeat from * around, K 1 rnd.

Second Dec Rnd: * K 1, k 2 tog, repeat from * around. K 1 rnd.

Third Dec Rnd: K 2 tog. repeat from * around. Cut yarn, leaving 10" end. Pull through remaining 6 sts, gather sts tog tightly and secure end.

Thumb: Sl sts from holder to needle. Join yarn; k 4 of these sts to one needle; with 2nd needle, k 1, pick up and k 1 st at side of thumb and 2 sts on cast-on sts; with 3rd needle, pick up and k 3 sts on cast-on sts and 1 st at side of thumb—12 sts. Work even for 2". K 2 tog around. Cut yarn, leaving 10" end. Pull through remaining sts, gather sts tog tightly and secure end.

Work second mitten to correspond to first, reversing pat and placement of thumb.

FINISHING: Press mittens through thick damp cloth, having thumb at left of palm for left mitten and at right of palm for right mitten. Following chart, embroider snowman design in duplicate st on center back of each mitten. Sew small green pompon to top of snowman's hat. With blue, make 2 French knots for eyes. With yellow, embroider lazy daisy st nose. Cut 3 strands of red yarn

10" long. Tie strands around snowman's neck, tying tog at center front. Braid each 3 ends; tie ends with white yarn.

SCARF: With blue and No. 10½ needles, cast on 30 sts.

Row 1 (right side): K 6, p 6, k 6, p 6, k 6.

Row 2 (wrong side): P 6, K 6, p 6, k 6, p 6. Repeat these 2 rows until piece is 65" long. Bind off.

FINISHING: With yellow, work 1 row sc across each end of scarf. With blue, sc in each sc across. Steam-press scarf, using thick damp cloth and warm iron. Cut blue, green and red yarn in 10" lengths. Using 2 strands tog for each fringe, knot 5 fringes across center k 6 panel on each end of scarf. On one end, knot 5 red fringes, then 4 blue fringes each side of center panel. On other end of scarf, knot 1 red, 4 green and 4 blue fringes each side of center panel.

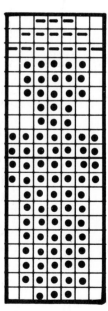

▣ Green
⊟ White

HOLIDAY HOUSE

Stitch this delightful "gingerbread" house on plastic canvas, then fill it with goodies to surprise your little guests. Roof lifts up and door swings open to reveal the treats inside.

See General Directions for embroidery and needlepoint stitch details.

EQUIPMENT: China marking pencil. Ruler. X-Acto knife. Scissors. Tapestry, embroidery, and sewing needles.

MATERIALS: Plastic mesh canvas, three sheets each 10½″ × 13½″. Persian yarns as follows: tan, 3 ozs.; brown, 2 ozs.; red, ½ oz.; green, ½ oz.; white, ¼ oz.; yellow 4 yards: orange, 3 yards; purple, 3 yards. Six-strand embroidery floss, one skein each of bright green, orange, purple, yellow, red and white. Small scraps of light-colored cotton fabric. Plastic "bone" rings: ten ⅝″ diameter, one 1″ diameter. Assorted small beads, 36. One floral design shank button for doorknob. Sewing thread. Small amount of absorbent cotton. Glue.

DIRECTIONS

To Cut Canvas: Follow the charts below for the two sides, front and back. Count the meshes (each graph square) on the graph, then count the meshes (holes) on the canvas. For the roof, count two pieces 35 holes by 70 holes. Use the china marker and ruler to mark off the outline on the canvas. You can fit the two side pieces on one canvas sheet; the front and back on another; the roof on the third. Cut out each piece from canvas. Trim raw edges so all outline edges are smooth except for the gable areas of the sides.

On each house piece, count and mark the window and door areas within the heavy outlines. Use sharp knife to cut out the canvas leaving a smooth edge along the outline. Reserve the two door pieces, trimming the raw edges smooth. Disregard dotted lines on charts until later.

To Needlepoint House: Work house design using continental stitch (Detail 1) throughout. Cut yarn into one yard strands. Thread needle with one 3-ply strand for all needlepoint stitches. To begin, hold yarn end underneath canvas until several stitches have been worked to cover it. Catch yarn ends under stitches on underside to begin and end each successive strand.

Following chart and color key, begin to work design on each piece starting at the upper right corner or at the side gables. Each square on graph represents one stitch on canvas; work each stitch over one canvas thread. Always work from right to left; at the end of each row, turn work upside down to return. Make sides of house the same, following chart, or follow illustration. At edges of door and window openings, make slanted overcast stitches using brown yarn to cover the canvas; make stitches to resemble other needlepoint. For window crossbars, overcast with brown yarn to cover the canvas. Work cellar door following chart. For front door, work piece entirely with red yarn. Use brown yarn to overcast around edges of both door pieces.

To Decorate House: To trim tree next to front door, randomly sew on assorted beads with sewing thread.

To make lollipops (lower dotted line circles) at sides of house trace circles on scraps of fabric as follows, leaving ½″ fabric between each outline; four outlines of a dime, two of a nickel, and two of a quarter (for two sides the same). Using full six strands of embroidery floss in colors shown, satin stitch each circle. When embroidery is complete, cut out each one, leaving ¼″ seam allowance. Turn in seam allowance, pad lightly with absorbent cotton, and appliqué each lollipop in place; see photograph.

To make the peppermint for the gable on one side of house, trace a quarter onto fabric. Divide circle roughly as shown by dotted lines on chart. Make as for lollipops. Use red and white embroidery floss and satin stitch to embroider peppermint, alternating white and red areas.

To make swag at roof line, use long strand of green yarn loosely draped and tacked in the canvas where indicated by dots.

To make each small wreath, wrap a one-yard strand of yarn around one ⅝″ ring; glue loose end. Make three orange, three purple

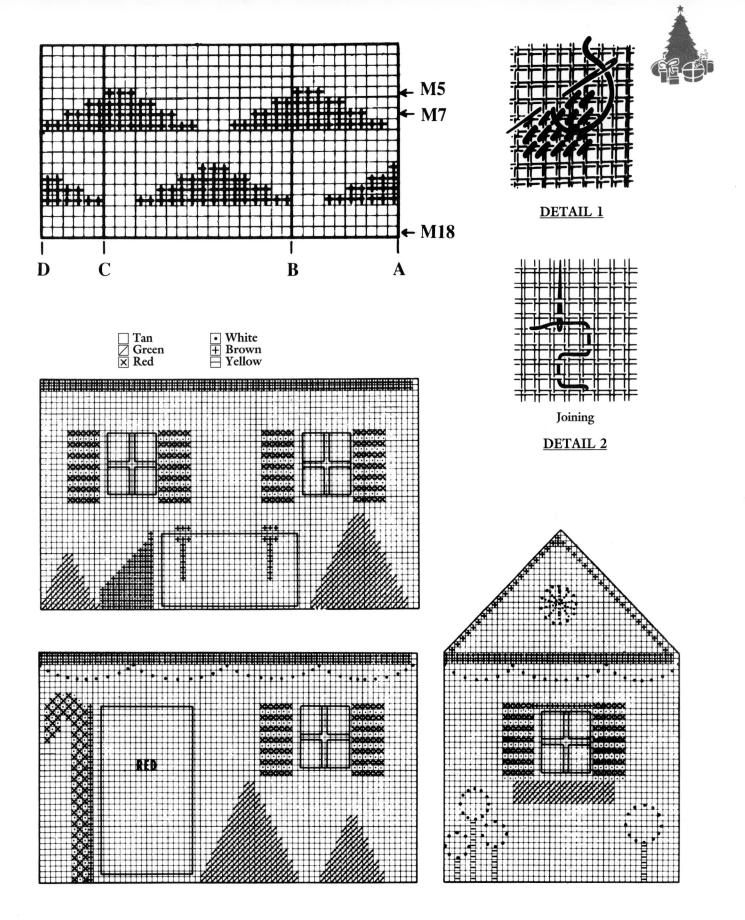

M5

M7

M18

D C B A

DETAIL 1

Joining

DETAIL 2

☐ Tan   ⊡ White
⧄ Green   ⊞ Brown
☒ Red   ⊟ Yellow

RED

and four yellow wreaths. Take in place where swag line is tacked.

To make wreath for front door, use a two-yard strand to wrap around the 1″ ring as directed for small wreaths. Use one ply each of red and white yarn to make bow. Tack wreath and bow onto front door. Sew button onto door for knob.

To Attach Doors. Attach front door along the left side: attach cellar door along the top edge. Use brown yarn to stitch as shown in Joining Detail 2, attaching door to frame.

To Make Roof: Following color key and chart use continental stitch to work charted triangle design on both roof pieces. Work chart from A to B once, from B to C three times, from C to D once. Work down the 18 meshes, then repeat meshes 5–18 once, meshes 5–7 once. Fill areas in between with straight vertical stitches working ends of stitches in same mesh as outside continental stitches. At lower edges, overcast stitches will cover mesh. Use brown yarn to overcast the mesh edges along the sides and top edges. Attach two roof halves together as for the doors.

To Assemble: Use brown yarn to overcast the two sides, front and back together, stitching in each mesh. Then use brown to overcast roof onto the sides of the house at the gables, stitching in every other mesh. Bottom edges of roof will hang over front and back.

GIFTS FOR BABY

Simple techniques create a variety of gifts for your favorite baby—personalized garments, soft rocking horse, dolls, trims, and a bib.

See General Directions at end of book for enlarging a pattern, embroidery stitch details, and appliqué.

SOFT ROCKING HORSE

SIZE: 12″ tall.

EQUIPMENT: Ruler. Pencil. Paper for patterns. Dressmaker's tracing (carbon) paper. Tracing wheel or dry ball-point pen. Straight pins. Scissors. Sewing machine. Sewing needle. Cardboard.

MATERIALS: Sturdy cotton fabrics, 36″ wide; green pin dot, ¼ yd.; solid red, ¼ yd. Matching threads. Polyester fiberfill. White rug yarn, one 70-yard skein. Green satin ribbon, ⅜″ wide, 1⅛ yards. Two ½″ black buttons.

DIRECTIONS: Draw lines across patterns, connecting grid lines. Enlarge patterns by copying on paper ruled in 1″ squares. Complete half-patterns indicated by dash lines. Mark two bodies, one head front, one underbody, and 4 legs on wrong side of green fabric; place pieces ½″ from fabric edges and ½″ apart; reverse body for second piece. On wrong side of red, mark 4 rockers and 2 rails 2½″ × 3¼″. Cut out pieces ¼″ beyond marked lines for seam allowance. To assemble, pin pieces together as directed below, having right sides facing and

raw edges even; stitch on marked lines, making ¼″ seams and easing in fullness where necessary. Clip into seam allowance at curves and across corners.

Body: Stitch head front to bodies between A's. Stitch underbody in place between B's. Stitch remaining body edges together, leaving an opening for turning. Turn to right side; stuff firmly and slip-stitch opening closed.

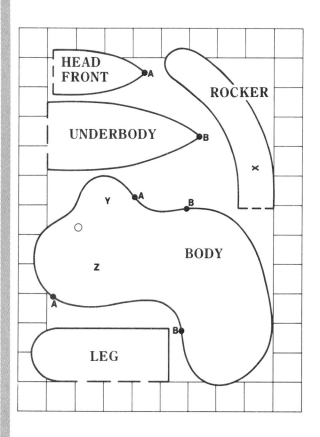

Legs: Fold each leg piece in half, matching raw edges. Stitch around top and side, leaving bottom edge open. Turn to right side and stuff firmly. By hand, sew ¼" from raw edges; pull up stitches to gather tightly and secure thread. Referring to photograph, slip-stitch legs to body, having leg seams toward back.

Tail: Cut 25 9" pieces of rug yarn. Tie pieces together at center with long piece of matching yarn; use tie to tack tail to back of horse. Cut 14" piece of ribbon and tie into bow at top of tail.

Mane: Wind rug yarn 35 times around a 2" strip of cardboard; cut yarn along one edge to make 4" pieces. Tie yarn at center as for tail. Make eight of these yarn bundles. Tack yarn bundles to horse for mane, centering along neck and top of head.

Finishing: Sew buttons at markings for eyes. Cut 33" piece of ribbon and tack each end to horse's nose at Y, so ribbon loops around back of neck for reins. Tack again at Z. Wrap remaining ribbon around nose, covering ends of reins and lapping at underside; stitch in place.

Rockers: Stitch rockers together in pairs, leaving an opening along bottom for turning. Turn to right side and stuff very firmly; turn in raw edges and slip-stitch opening closed. Fold each rail in half lengthwise. Stitch 3¼" edges together, leaving ends open. Turn to right side and stuff very firmly. Sew by hand ¼" from each end; pull up stitches to gather tightly and secure thread. Stitch rails to inside of rockers at X's. Stitch horse's feet to top of rockers over rails.

SANTA BOXES

SIZES: Mrs. Claus, about 5½" × 7"; Santa, about 6" × 4½".

EQUIPMENT: Pencil. Ruler. Paper for patterns. Straight pins. Scissors. Pinking shears. Tape measure. Iron. Sewing and darning needles.

MATERIALS—For Both: Lightweight red knit fabric, 45" wide, ¼ yard. Batting. Nylon from pantyhose. Thread to match hose. Scrap of red felt. Coral crayon. Four ¼" black pompons. White craft glue. One skein white knitting-worsted weight yarn. **Mrs. Claus:** Red satin ribbon, ¾" wide, ⅞ yard. Oval wooden Shaker box, with lid, about 5½" × 7". **Santa:** Oval wooden Shaker box, with lid, about 4½" × 6".

DIRECTIONS

Box: Place box on red knit fabric and trace around bottom. Cut out bottom piece ⅛" inside traced line, using pinking shears. Place lid on box and, using pencil, trace a line on box along lower edge of lid. Remove lid; measure depth of box side from pencil line to bottom and add 1". Measure circumference of box and add ½". Use these measurements to cut fabric strip for box side; press one long edge ½" to wrong side. Glue strip to box side, right side out, with folded edge at pencil line and raw edge extending ½" at bottom. (Box side above line is left bare.) Clip extending edge of fabric and glue clips to box bottom. Glue on bottom piece over clips.

Lid: Place lid on paper and trace around bottom. Cut on traced line and use piece as pattern to cut two pieces batting. Glue batting to lid. When glue is dry, stretch a piece of nylon from pantyhose over lid, and glue to lid side; trim away excess nylon.

Cap: Cut rectangle from red fabric: 10" × 5" for Mrs. Claus, 5" × 7" for Santa. Cut a shallow, concave curve into one 10" edge for Mrs. Claus, one 5" edge for Santa. Press under curved edge ¾". Place piece on lid, making cap as shown; glue down folded edge. Smooth cap over side of lid and glue in place. Trim excess fabric at rim to ½", cutting away front turnunder, and glue to inside. Let dry, then test-fit on box. If lid does not fit easily, cut away excess fabric from inside rim. Make a 2" pompon of white yarn and glue at top of cap.

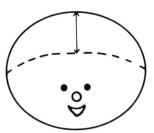

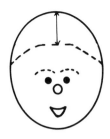

MRS. CLAUS   SANTA

Face: Cut a 1¼″ circle of nylon and gather ⅛″ from edge by hand; pull up stitching slightly. Insert scraps of batting to form a ball about ⅝″ across. Pull stitching tight and secure thread; stitch nose to face, following diagram. Cut mouth of red felt as shown and glue on; glue on black pompon eyes. "Rouge" cheeks with crayon. Using white yarn and starting at edge of cap, work turkey-work loops ¾″ long for band of hair about 1¼″ wide.

Santa: Make ¾″ loops for beard, working to edge of box lid. Glue additional yarn loops to lid sides to cover wood below cap line. Make ½″ loops for eyebrows. Wind yarn ten times around three fingers; remove and tie at center. Glue below nose for mustache.

Mrs. Claus: Cut ribbon 13½″ long; press ends under 1″. Wrap ribbon ¾″ from ends with white yarn to gather; secure yarn. Glue ribbon along chin side of lid with ends on cap. Tie remaining ribbon into a bow; notch ends. Glue bow to lid at center of chin.

APPLIQUED BIB

SIZE: 12¼″ × 16″.

EQUIPMENT: Pencil. Ruler. Scissors. Paper for pattern. Dressmaker's tracing (carbon) paper. Tracing wheel or dry ball-point pen. Zigzag sewing machine. Sewing needle.

MATERIALS: White terry cloth hand towel. Green wide double-fold bias tape. Small amounts of closely woven cotton fabrics: white-dotted green, solid red, white, light blue, gold, dark brown, and light brown. Sewing thread to match fabrics and bias tape.

DIRECTIONS: Enlarge pattern by copying on paper ruled in 1″ squares; complete half-pattern indicated by dash line. Heavy lines indicate bib outline and appliqués; light lines indicate machine embroidery.

Using dressmaker's carbon and tracing wheel or dry ball-point pen, transfer bib to terry cloth; cut out on marked line. Referring to photograph, cut individual pieces for reindeer and wreath. Machine-appliqué antlers, wreath, bow, then reindeer to center of bib front as directed, using matching threads. Machine-embroider "smile" and ear lines with

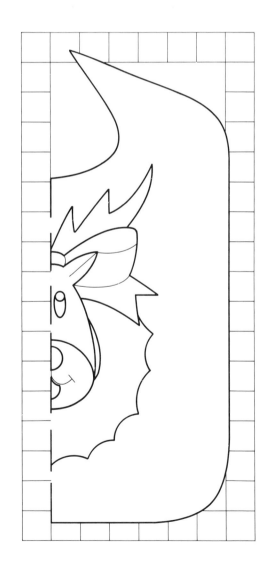

dark brown thread, and lines within bow with green. Bind outer edges of bib with bias tape. With center of a 38" length of bias tape at center of neck edge, bind neck edge, leaving ends free for ties; slip-stitch long edges of ties closed.

ANIMAL HANGERS

EQUIPMENT: Pencil. Ruler. Scissors. Paper for patterns. Dressmaker's tracing (carbon) paper. Tracing wheel or dry ball-point pen. Sewing machine. Sewing needle. Fine-toothed saw. Single-edged razor or seam ripper. For dog only: embroidery hoop and needle.

MATERIALS: White plastic coat hanger. Small amount cotton fabric: green and white print for cat; red and white gingham for dog; brown corduroy for bear. Felt scraps: red and white for cat and dog; red and brown for bear. Sewing thread to match fabric, plus dark green and white for cat, white and black for dog. Buttons: two ⅜" diameter green for cat; two ½" red and one ⅝" black for dog; ½" brown for bear. White ½" pompons, one each for bear and cat. Ribbon, ⅜" wide, 20" length, red for bear and cat, green for dog. Fiberfill for stuffing. For dog only: black embroidery floss.

GENERAL DIRECTIONS: Enlarge patterns by copying on paper ruled in 1" squares; complete half-patterns indicated by dash lines. Heavy lines indicate appliqués and pattern outlines, fine lines and dots indicate embroidery, dotted lines topstitching. Use dressmaker's carbon and tracing wheel or dry ball-point pen to transfer complete pattern to right side of fabric, for hanger front; transfer outline only to wrong side, for pattern back (for Bear, use pattern outline for Dog). Transfer individual patterns to right side of felt, following individual directions. Cut out pieces ¼" outside marked lines; for tongues, cut lower curve on marked line. Appliqué and embroider face following individual directions. Stitch front and back

together with right sides facing, raw edges even, and making ¼" seam; leave bottom straight edge open. Clip into curves and across corners. Turn piece to right side.

Using saw, cut off bottom straight edge of hanger (about 12" length). Cut away upper arms of hanger, leaving about 3" extending at each side of hook. Using single-edged razor or seam ripper, carefully cut a 1½" opening in seam at center top of head. Insert hook through bottom opening; close seam at top around hook. Stuff head with fiberfill, using eraser-end of pencil to reach into ears. Place bottom piece of hanger into bottom opening; surround with fiberfill. Turn raw edges under ¼"; slip-stitch closed. Tie ribbon bow around neck.

CAT: Read General Directions above. Cut hanger front and back from print fabric; from felt, cut two white eyes and red tongue. Machine-appliqué eyes in place, using ⅛"-wide zigzag and green thread; continue stitching to embroider nose and muzzle lines, securing upper curved edges of tongue as shown. With 1/16" zigzag and white thread, embroider whiskers. Tack white pompon nose in place. Sew on green button eyes. Assemble hanger as directed, stuffing ears lightly. Tie ribbon around neck.

DOG: Read General Directions above. Cut hanger front and back from gingham; from felt, cut two white eyes and red tongue. Machine-appliqué eyes in place with matching thread. Using ⅛" zigzag and black thread, machine-embroider muzzle lines, securing upper curved edges of tongue as shown. Using three strands of black embroidery floss, embroider French-knot freckles. Sew on black button nose and red button eyes. Topstitch across ears, following dotted lines on pattern. Assemble hanger as directed, and tie ribbon bow around neck.

BEAR: Read General Directions above. Cut hanger front and back from corduroy, having nap run vertically; from felt, cut two brown eyes, brown muzzle, and red tongue. Machine-appliqué eyes and muzzle in place with matching thread. Using ⅛″ zigzag and brown thread, machine-embroider fine lines on muzzle, securing straight edge of tongue as shown. Tack pompon nose in place. Sew on button eyes. Assemble hanger as directed, and tie ribbon bow around neck.

SANTA, ELF, AND ANGEL

SIZE: Each about 7″ tall.

EQUIPMENT: Pencil. Ruler. Scissors. Paper for pattern (for Santa and Elf only). Sewing machine. Sewing and embroidery needles. Compass. Iron.

MATERIALS: **For Each:** Plain white or pale pink stretch sock, size 1 year. Sewing thread to match sock, fabrics, and yarn. Fiberfill. Pink crayon. **For Santa:** Small amount red cotton fabric. Red and blue six-strand embroidery floss. White-worsted-weight yarn. three white 1″ pompons. Green grosgrain ribbon, ⅜″ wide, 18″ length. **For Elf:** Small amount white-dotted green fabric. White-dotted red trim, 1½″ wide, 18″ length. Black and red six-strand embroidery floss. Orange worsted-weight yarn. Three red ¾″ pompons. Green satin ribbon ⅜″ wide, 18″ length. **For Angel:** Small amount white cotton fabric. White eyelet trim 1½″ wide, 1 yard.

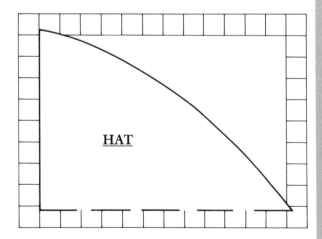

HAT

Brown and red embroidery floss. Yellow fingering-weight yarn. White loopy braid trim ⅜″ wide, 11″ length.

GENERAL DIRECTIONS

To Make Body: From cotton fabric, cut 11½″ × 6″ rectangle. With right side inward and making ¼″ seam, stitch 6″ edges together, forming tube. Fold tube so that seam is centered; stitch one end (bottom) closed with ¼″ seam. Still wrong side out, turn body so that one side edge is facing you. Spread bottom corner to flatten into triangle and stitch across triangle ¾″ above point. Repeat on opposite corner, thus "boxing" bottom of body. Turn raw edges at top ¼″ to wrong side. Baste along fold. Turn body to right side; stuff, then pull basting thread to gather neck, leaving ½″-diameter opening.

To Make Head: Flatten toe of sock; mark a line 5″ from toe seam. Cut on marked line through double thickness. Stuff toe with a firm, apple-sized ball of fiberfill. For Santa's and Elf's noses, place a firm pea-sized ball of fiberfill at center of one side; thread needle with 18″ length of thread. Bring needle through back of head to front at center bottom of nose; pull gently, burying knot in fiberfill. Wind thread around base of nose a few times. Reinsert needle through bottom of nose; bring out at back of head; end off. Gently push face upward to form 2″-long neck. Wrap thread around neck to secure.

Insert neck of head into neck of body; tack in place. For neck ruff, cut 18″ length of trim (for Santa, cut 3″ × 18″ piece of red fabric; fold in half lengthwise, wrong side inward). Press short ends under ¼″. Baste close to long unfinished edge(s). Place ruff around neck. Pull basting to fit neck; secure gathers. Follow individual directions and color illustration to embroider face, inserting needle from back of head. "Rouge" cheeks with crayon. Make hair, following individual directions.

For Santa's and Elf's Hats: Enlarge pattern by copying on paper ruled in ½″

squares. Cut out pattern; use to mark hat on fabric, placing dash line of pattern on fold of fabric. Cut out ¼″ beyond marked lines. With right side in, stitch long curved edges together with ¼″ seam. Press bottom edges ¼″ to wrong side. Turn hat to right side. Tack pompon to tip. Tack hat to head. Finish, following individual directions.

SANTA: Read General Directions above. Make head and body; add red neck ruff. With two strands floss in needle, make blue straight-stitch eyes and red outline-stitch mouth. For hair and beard, thread embroidery needle with two strands white yarn. Work two parallel rows of 1″-long loops around sides and bottom of face as shown, having rows ¼″ apart. Make and attach hat. Tack two pompons to center front of body. Rouge nose with crayon. Tie ribbon in bow around neck.

ELF: Read General Directions above. Make head and body, using green fabric for body; add red neck ruff. With two strands floss in needle, make black straight-stitch eyes and red outline-stitch mouth. For hair, cut 12 6″ lengths of orange yarn. Mark center part on head, 1″ long. Working from front of part to back, tack center of each strand of yarn to part, using matching thread. Finger-comb strands down to cover head; fray ends. Make and attach green hat. Tack two pompons to center front of body. Tie ribbon in bow around neck.

ANGEL: Read General Directions above. Make head and body; add eyelet neck ruff. With two strands floss in needle, make brown outline-stitch eyes with matching straight-stitch lashes; work red backstitch mouth. With one strand floss, work fly-stitch nose. For hair, cut sixty 24″ strands of yarn. Wind a strand of yarn around two extended fingers of one hand; tie together at center with matching thread. Make sixty sets of curls in this manner. Tack curls to head. For wings, cut two 7″ lengths of eyelet; press short ends under ½″. Gather unfinished edges to 2½″. Stitch gathered edge to each side of body back, having center of each wing curve out

slightly so eyelet extends beyond body side. For halo, stitch short ends of braid together, forming loop; tack to hair.

BABY GARMENTS

SIZE: Infants, toddlers.

EQUIPMENT: Pencil. Ruler. Paper for patterns. Dressmaker's tracing (carbon) paper. Tracing wheel or dry ball-point pen. Scissors. Straight pins. Zigzag sewing machine. **For Sacque:** Iron.

MATERIALS—**Sacque:** Purchased infant's sacque. Yellow iron-on fabric, 2″ square. Yellow and red sewing threads. Red grosgrain ribbon, ⅜″ wide, 1 yard. **Pants:** Purchased training pants. Red sewing thread.

DIRECTIONS: Draw lines across patterns, connecting grid lines. Enlarge patterns by copying on paper ruled in 1″ squares. Referring to photograph, transfer designs to garments, using dressmaker's carbon and tracing wheel or dry ball-point pen. Embroider lettering and notes in red thread, using a ¹⁄₁₆″ to ⅛″-wide closely spaced zigzag stitch on machine; fill in shaded notes with stitching. For Sacque, cut star of yellow iron-on fabric and appliqué, following manufacturer's directions. Zigzag around star with matching thread, covering raw edges of fabric. Thread ribbon through casing at bottom and tie ends into a bow.

PANTS

CHRISTMAS BUNTING

Sweet baby will stay toasty warm at the Christmas party, all zipped up in a holiday bunting with matching cap—all in single crochet.

See General Directions for crochet.

SIZE: Infants to one year.

MATERIALS: Worsted-weight yarn, four 3½-oz. skeins white (A), 3 skeins green (B), 1 skein red (C). Crochet hooks sizes H and J, 14″ zipper.

GAUGE: 3 sc = 1″; 7 rows = 2″ (J hook).

Pattern Notes: To Dec 1 Sc—Pull up a lp in each of next 2 sts, yo and through 3 lps on hook.

BUNTING: FRONT: Beg at lower edge, with size J hook and B, ch 49.

Row 1: Sc in 2nd ch from hook and in each ch across—48 sc. Ch 1, turn.

Row 2: Sc in back lp of each sc across. Ch 1, turn each row. Repeat row 2 for sc pat on B sts; on A sts, work sc in both lps of sts. Following chart from row 3 to row 38, dec 1 st each side on row 15, then on row 29—44 sts. Check gauge; piece should measure 15″ wide.

Divide Work: Left Front: Row 39 (right side): Work 21 sts. Ch 1, turn. Continue to follow chart for left front, dec 1 st at side edge on rows 43, 57, 71 and 78 as indicated on chart—17 sts.

Row 78 (wrong side): Work across row; with A, ch 18 for left front sleeve.

Row 79: Sc in 2nd ch from hook and in each sleeve ch, finish row—34 sts. Work until row 86 on chart has been completed.

Shape Neck: Row 87 (right side): Work to last 3 sts. Ch 1, turn. Dec 1 st at neck edge on next 2 rows—29 sts. Work to top of chart. End off.

Right Front: Row 39 (right side): Return to last long row, sk 2 center sts, join yarn, finish row. Continue to follow chart for right front, dec 1 st at side edge on rows 43, 57, 71 and 77 as indicated on chart. Ch 18 with A at end of row 79.

Row 80: Sc in 2nd ch from hook and in each sleeve ch, finish row—34 sts. Complete to correspond to left front, reversing shaping.

BACK: With A only, working in both lps of each sc, work as for front, omitting tree, front opening and neck shaping until row 94 has been completed—70 sts.

Next Row: Sl st across 29 sc, work 12 sc, sl st in next st. End off.

HOOD: With size J hook and B, ch 37.

Row 1: Sc in 2nd ch from hook and in each remaining ch—36 sts. Ch 1, turn. Continue in sc until 24 rows from start. End off. Fold last

row in half to form top seam. From right side, with B, sc edges together.

Hood Edging: Row 1: From wrong side, with size H hook and B, work 1 row sc around face edge. Ch 1, turn.

Row 2: Sc in back lp of each sc across. Ch 1, turn.

Row 3: Repeat row 2. End off.

CUFFS (make 2): With size H hook and A, ch 5.

Row 1: Sc in 2nd ch from hook and in each ch across—4 sc. Ch 1, turn.

Row 2. Sc in back lp of each sc across. Ch 1, turn. Repeat row 2 for 14 more rows. End off. Sew last row to first row to form round cuff.

FINISHING: Sew shoulder, side, sleeve, and bottom seams. Sew cuffs to sleeves, gathering in sleeves evenly. Sew hood in place above neck shaping.

Tie: With size H hook and B, make a 36″ ch.

Next Row: Sl st back across ch. End off. Weave ch through neck and face edge of hood.

Starting at top of left front opening, with size J hook and A, sc until beg of tree, change to B and continue in sc down left front, up right front to end of tree, change to A and complete edging. End off. Sew in zipper.

Pompons: With C, make 14 1″ pompons. Sew 2 pompons to point of hood, 1 on each end of tie, 1 at outside edge of each point of tree.

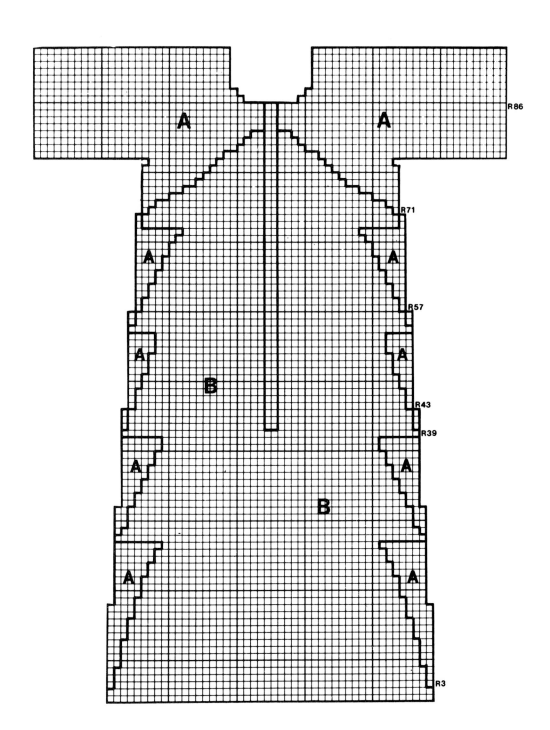

General Directions

Enlarging a Pattern

If the pattern is given on squares, you must enlarge it to its actual size by drawing a grid on a sheet of paper with the same number of squares as in the grid of the pattern, but making each square of your grid the size directed (usually 1"). The grid can be easily drawn on graph paper. Or, if graph paper is not available, on plain paper mark dots around the edges 1" apart (or the size directed) and form a grid by joining the dots across opposite sides of the paper. Then copy the design onto your grid, square by square. Glue to cardboard and cut on lines of design, ignoring the grid lines. An easier procedure is to have the design enlarged by photostat, if such a service is available in your area.

Appliqué

Choose a fabric that is closely woven and firm enough so a clean edge results when the pieces are cut. Press fabric smooth. There are two methods of transferring appliqué patterns to fabric.

TO TRANSFER LARGE DESIGNS: Mark a pattern on paper for each appliqué piece; do not cut out. Place paper on right side of fabric, inserting dressmaker's tracing (carbon) paper between fabric and pattern. Go over lines of pattern with tracing wheel or a dry ball-point pen, to transfer design. Remove pattern and carbon. Mark a second outline ¼" outside design outline. Appliqué as directed below.

TO TRANSFER SMALL DESIGNS: For each motif, make a cardboard pattern. Trace design; do not cut out. Glue tracing paper to thin, stiff cardboard and let dry; cut along traced line. Place cardboard pattern on right side of fabric. Holding sharp, hard pencil at an outward angle (light-colored pencil on dark fabric and dark pencil on light fabric), mark around pattern. When marking several pieces on the same fabric, leave at least ½" between pieces. Mark a second outline ¼" outside design outline. Appliqué as directed below.

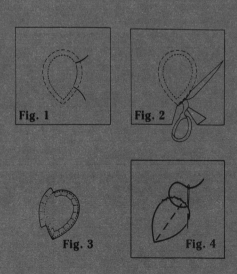

Fig. 1   Fig. 2   Fig. 3   Fig. 4

STITCH DETAILS

 **Straight Stitch**

 **Herringbone Stitch**

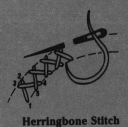 **Lazy Daisy Stitch**

 **Split Stitch**

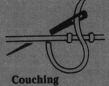 **French Knot**

 **Seed Stitch**

 **Cross-Stitch**

 **Closed Fly Stitch**

Long and Short Stitch

 Couching

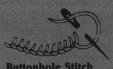 **Blanket Stitch**

Chain Stitch

 **Fly Stitch**

Buttonhole Stitch

 **Running Stitch**

 **Featherstitch**

Laid Filling or Intersected Trellis

Double Cross-Stitch

  **Backstitch**

 **Turkey Work**

Satin Stitch

 **Satin Leaf Stitch**

 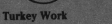 **Outline (Stem) Stitch**

 Padded Satin Stitch

 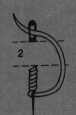 **Bullion Stitch**

 **Woven Spider Web Stitch**

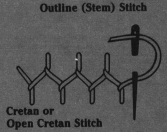 **Cretan or Open Cretan Stitch**

 **Radiating Straight Stitch**

TO APPLIQUE BY HAND: Using matching thread and small stitches, machine-stitch all around design outline, as shown in **Fig. 1**. This makes edge easier to turn and neater in appearance. Cut out appliqué on the outside line, as in **Fig. 2**. For a smooth edge, clip into seam allowance at curved edges and corners, then turn seam allowance to back, just inside stitching as shown in **Fig. 3**, and press. (**Note:** You may prefer to place some pieces so they overlap the extended seam allowance of adjacent pieces; study overall design before turning under all seam allowances.) Pin and baste the appliqués on the background, the underneath pieces first, and slip-stitch in place with tiny stitches. See **Fig. 4**.

TO APPLIQUE BY MACHINE: Cut out appliqués on outside lines. Pin and baste appliqués in place; do not turn under excess fabric. Straight-stitch around appliqués on marked lines. Trim away excess fabric to ⅛″ from straight stitching. Set sewing machine for close zigzag stitch as directed (¼″ wide or less). Zigzag around appliqués, covering straight stitching and excess fabric.

Embroidery

TO PREPARE FABRIC: To prevent fabric from raveling, bind all raw edges with masking tape, whipstitch edges by hand, or machine-stitch ⅛″ in from all edges.

FRAMES/HOOPS: Work embroidery in a frame or hoop. With the material held tautly and evenly, your stitches are more likely to be neat and accurate than if the fabric were held in hand while working.

TO BEGIN AND END A STRAND: Cut floss or yarn into 18″ strands. To begin a strand, leave an end on back and work over it to secure; to end, run needle under four or five stitches on back or take a few tiny backstitches. Do not make knots. Fasten off the thread when ending each motif, rather than carrying it to another motif.

TO REMOVE EMBROIDERY: When a mistake has been made, run a needle, eye first, under the stitches. Pull the embroidery away from the fabric; cut carefully with small scissors pressed hard against the needle. Pick out the cut portion of the embroidery and catch loose ends of the remaining stitches on back by pulling the ends under the stitches with a crochet hook.

FOR COUNTED CROSS-STITCH: For counted cross-stitch on even-weave fabrics, work stitches over a counted number of threads both horizontally and vertically, following a chart. Each symbol on the chart represents one stitch. Different symbols represent different colors.

For fabrics such as Aida cloth or hardanger, follow the mesh of the coarse flat weave (much like needlepoint canvas), where holes are obvious. Each "thread" is actually made up of four or more fine threads in a group and stitches are worked from hole to hole.

For counted cross-stitch on gingham fabric, work stitches over checks, so that one complete cross-stitch covers one check.

When working cross-stitches, work underneath stitches in one direction and top stitches in the opposite direction, making sure all strands lie smooth and flat; allow needle to hang freely from work occasionally, to untwist floss. Make crosses touch by inserting needle in same hole used for adjacent stitch (see Stitch Details).

TO FINISH: When your embroidered piece is completed, finish off the back neatly by running ends into the back of the work and clipping off any excess threads. Place piece face down on a well padded surface and press, using a steam iron, or regular iron and damp pressing cloth. Press lightly from the center outward. For embroidery that is raised from the surface of the background, use extra thick, soft padding, such as a thick blanket.

Needlepoint

TO PREPARE CANVAS: Bind all raw edges of canvas with masking tape to prevent raveling. Find center of canvas by basting a line from center of one edge to center of opposite edge, being careful to follow one row of mesh across. Then baste another line from center of third edge to center of fourth edge. Basting threads will cross at center; they will aid in blocking canvas after work is completed.

TO WORK NEEDLEPOINT: Cut strands into 18″ lengths. When starting first strand, leave 1″ of yarn on back of canvas unless otherwise directed and cover it as work proceeds; your first few stitches will anchor it in place. To end a strand or begin a new one, run strand under four or five stitches on back of work; do not make knots. Keep tension of stitches firm and even. Stitching tends to twist the working strand; now and then let needle and strand hang freely to untwist. Follow charts and individual directions to work each design, using continental or diagonal stitch shown opposite or stitches described in individual directions.

TO BLOCK NEEDLEPOINT

Materials: Softwood surface, such as pine or plywood. Brown paper. T- or carpenter's square. Rustproof thumbtacks.

Directions: Cover wood surface with brown paper. Mark canvas outline on paper for guide, making sure corners are square. Mark horizontal and vertical center lines on paper outline and on canvas. Place canvas, right side down, over guide. Match center markings on canvas with those on paper. Fasten canvas to wood with rustproof tacks; tack corners first, then the center of each side; continue placing tacks until there is a solid border of tacks around entire edge, dividing and subdividing spaces between thumbtacks already placed. Wet thoroughly with cold water; let dry. If piece is badly warped, block again.

Continental Stitch

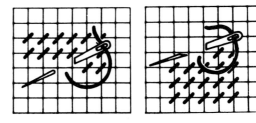

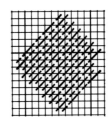

Mosaic Stitch

Diagonal Stitch

Note: If yarn is not colorfast, dissolve salt in cold water and block with salt water.

Crochet

CHAIN STITCH: To make first loop on hook, grasp yarn about 2″ from end between left thumb and index finger. With right hand, lap long strand over short end, forming a loop. Hold loop in place with left thumb and index finger. Grasp hook in right hand, insert hook through loop, catch strand with hook and draw it through loop. Pull end and long strand in opposite directions to close loop around hook.

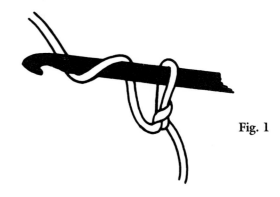

Fig. 1

Figure 1: To make your first chain stitch, pass hook under yarn on index finger and catch strand with hook.

Draw yarn through loop on hook. This makes one chain stitch. Repeat last step until you have as many chains as you need. One loop always remains on hook. Practice making all chains uniform.

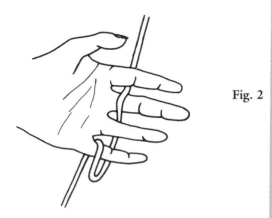

Fig. 2

Figure 2: Weave yarn through left hand.

SINGLE CROCHET:

Fig. 1

Figure 1: Insert hook in second chain from hook. Yarn over hook.

Fig. 2

Figure 2: Draw yarn through chain. Two loops on hook.

Fig. 3

Figure 3: Yarn over hook. Draw yarn through 2 loops on hook. One single crochet has been made.

Fig. 4

Figure 4: Work a single crochet in each chain stitch. At end of row, chain 1 and turn work around.

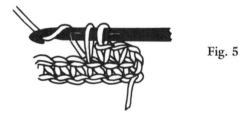

Fig. 5

Figure 5: Insert hook under both top loops of first stitch, yarn over hook and draw through stitch. Yarn over and through 2 loops on hook. Work a single crochet in same way in each stitch across row.

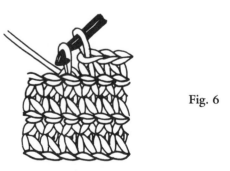

Fig. 6

Figure 6: To make a ridge stitch or slipper stitch, work rows of single crochet by inserting hook in back loop only of each single crochet.

HOW TO INCREASE 1 SINGLE CROCHET: Work 2 stitches in 1 stitch.

HOW TO DECREASE 1 SINGLE CROCHET: Pull up a loop in 1 stitch, pull up a loop in next stitch (3 loops on hook), yarn over hook, draw through all 3 loops at once.

SLIP STITCH: Insert hook in work. Yarn over hook and draw through both the stitch and the loop on hook. Slip stitch makes a firm finishing edge. A single slip stitch is used for joining a chain to form a ring.

HALF DOUBLE CROCHET:

Fig. 1

Figure 1: Yarn over hook. Insert hook in 3rd chain from hook.

Fig. 2

Figure 2: Yarn over hook, draw through chain. Yarn over hook again.

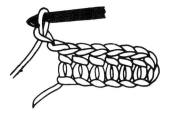

Fig. 3

Figure 3: Draw through all 3 loops on hook. One half double crochet has been made.

Fig. 4

Figure 4: Work a half double crochet in each chain across. At end of row, ch 2 and turn work.

DOUBLE CROCHET:

Fig. 1

Figure 1: Yarn over hook. Insert hook in 4th chain from hook.

Fig. 2

Figure 2: Yarn over hook. Draw through chain. There are 3 loops on hook.

Fig. 3

Figure 3: Yarn over hook. Draw through 2 loops on hook. There are 2 loops on hook. Yarn over hook.

Fig. 4

Figure 4: Draw yarn through remaining 2 loops on hook. One double crochet has been made. When you have worked a double crochet in each chain across, chain 3 and turn work. In most directions, the turning chain 3 counts as first double crochet of next row. In working the 2nd row, skip the first stitch and work a double crochet in the 2 top loops of each double crochet across. The last double crochet of each row is worked in the top chain of the chain 3 turning chain.

TREBLE OR TRIPLE CROCHET: With 1 loop on hook put yarn over hook twice, insert in 5th chain from hook, pull loop through. Yarn over and draw through 2 loops at a time 3 times. At end of a row, chain 4 and turn. Chain 4 counts as first treble of next row.

HOW TO TURN YOUR WORK: In crochet a certain number of ch sts are needed at the end of each row to bring work into position for the next row. Then work is turned so reverse side is facing the crocheter. Follow the stitch table below for the number of ch sts to make a turn.

Single crochet (sc)	Ch 1 to turn
Half double crochet (half dc or hdc)	Ch 2 to turn
Double crochet (dc)	Ch 3 to turn
Treble crochet (tr)	Ch 4 to turn
Double treble crochet (dtr)	Ch 5 to turn
Treble treble crochet (tr tr)	Ch 6 to turn

CROCHET ABBREVIATIONS

ch—chain stitch	sc—single crochet
st—stitch	sl st—slip stitch
sts—stitches	dc—double crochet
lp—loop	hdc—half double crochet
inc—increase	tr—treble or triple crochet
dec—decrease	dtr—double treble crochet
rnd—round	tr tr—treble treble crochet
beg—beginning	bl—block
sk—skip	sp—space
p—picot	pat—pattern
tog—together	yo—yarn over hook

MEASURING YOUR GAUGE: Most knitting and crochet directions include a stitch gauge. The stitch gauge gives the number of stitches to the inch with the yarn and hook or needles recommended in the pattern stitch. The directions are based on the given gauge. The gauge (or tension) at which you work controls of the size of each finished piece. It is therefore essential to work to the gauge given for each item if you want it to be the correct size. To test your gauge, cast on 20–30 stitches, using the hook or needles specified. Work in the pattern stitches for 3″. Smooth out your swatch and pin it down. Measure across 2″ and place pins 2″ apart. Count number of stitches between pins. If you have more stitches to the inch than directions specify, you are working too tightly; use a larger hook or needles. If you have fewer stitches to the inch, you are working too loosely; use a smaller hook or needles.

Most patterns give a row gauge, too. Although the proper length does not usually depend on the row gauge (directions usually

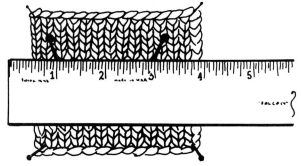

give lengths in inches rather than rows), in some patterns it is important to have the proper row gauge, too.

HOW TO FOLLOW DIRECTIONS: An asterisk (*) is often used in crochet directions to indicate repetition. For example, when directions read "* 2 dc in next st, 1 dc in next st, repeat from * 4 times" this means to work directions after first * until second * is reached, then go back to first * 4 times more. Work 5 times in all.

When parentheses ( ) are used to show repetition, work directions within parentheses as many times as specified. For example, "(dc, ch 1) 3 times" means to do what is within ( ) 3 times altogether.

"Work even" in directions means to work in same stitch without increasing or decreasing.

Knitting

CASTING ON: There are many ways of casting on stitches. The method shown here is only one of them. It gives you a strong and elastic edge.

Fig. 1

Figure 1: Allow enough yarn for the number of stitches to be cast on (about ½″ per stitch for lighter weight yarns such as baby yarns, 1″ per stitch for heavier yarns such as knitting worsted, more for bulky yarns on large needles). Make a slip loop on needle and tighten knot gently.

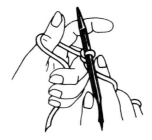

Fig. 2

Figure 2: Hold needle in right hand with short end of yarn over left thumb. Weave strand that comes from ball through right hand, over index finger, under second, over third, and under fourth finger.

Fig. 3

Figure 3: Bring needle forward to make a loop over left thumb. Insert needle from left to right in loop; bring yarn in right hand under, then over point of needle, and draw yarn through loop with tip of needle.

Fig. 4

Figure 4: Keeping right hand in same position, tighten stitch on needle gently with left hand. You now have 2 stitches on needle. Repeat Figures 3 and 4 for required number of stitches.

KNIT STITCH:

Fig. 5

Figure 5: Hold needle with cast on stitches in left hand and yarn in same position as for casting on in right hand. Insert point of needle from left to right in first stitch.

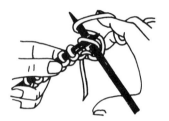

Fig. 6

Figure 6: Bring yarn under and over point of right needle.

Fig. 7

Figure 7: Draw yarn through stitch with point of needle.

Fig. 8

Figure 8: Allow loop on left needle to slip off needle. Loop on right needle is your first knit stitch. Repeat from Figure 5 in each loop across row. When you have finished knitting one row, place needle with stitches in left hand ready to start next row.

GARTER STITCH: If you work row after row of knit stitch, you are working garter stitch.

PURL STITCH:

Fig. 9

Figure 9: To purl, insert needle from right to left in stitch on left needle. Bring yarn over and under point of right needle. Draw yarn back through stitch and allow loop on left needle to slip off needle.

Purl Side

Knit Side

STOCKINETTE STITCH: If you work one row of knit stitch and one row of purl stitch alternately, you are working stockinette stitch.

REVERSE STOCKINETTE STITCH: If you work one row of purl stitch and one row of knit stitch alternately, you are working reverse stockinette stitch.

BINDING OFF:

Fig. 10

Figure 10: Knit the first two stitches. Insert left needle from left to right through front of first stitch. Lift first stitch over second stitch and over tip of right needle. One stitch has been bound off, one stitch remains on right needle. Knit another stitch. Again lift first stitch over second stitch and off right needle. Continue across until all stitches have been bound off. One loop remains on needle. Cut yarn, pull end through loop and tighten knot.

TO INCREASE ONE STITCH: There are several ways to increase a stitch.

Method 1 is illustrated. Knit 1 stitch in the usual way but do not slip it off left needle.

Bring right needle behind left needle, insert it from right to left in same stitch (called "the back of the stitch") and make another knit stitch. Slip stitch off left needle. To increase 1 stitch on the purl stitch, purl 1 stitch but do not slip it off left needle. Bring yarn between needles to back, knit 1 stitch in back of same stitch.

Method 2: Pick up horizontal strand between stitch just knitted and next stitch, place it on left needle. Knit 1 stitch in back of this strand, thus twisting it.

Method 3: Place right needle behind left needle. Insert right needle in stitch below next

stitch, knit this stitch, then knit stitch above it in the usual way.

TO DECREASE ONE STITCH: On the right side of work, knit 2 stitches together as in illustration, through the front of the stitches (the decrease slants to the right), or through the back of the stitches (the decrease slants to the left). On the purl side, purl 2 stitches together. Another decrease stitch is called "psso" (pass slip stitch over). When directions say, "sl 1, k 1, psso," slip first stitch (take it from left to right needle without knitting it), knit next stitch, then bring slip stitch over knit stitch as in binding off.

KNITTING ABBREVIATIONS

k—knit	psso—pass slip stitch over
p—purl	inc—increase
st—stitch	dec—decrease
sts—stitches	beg—beginning
yo—yarn over	pat—pattern
sl—slip	lp—loop
sk—skip	MC—main color
tog—together	CC—contrasting color
rnd—round	dp—double-pointed

MEASURING YOUR GAUGE: Most knitting and crochet directions include a stitch gauge. The stitch gauge gives the number of stitches to the inch with the yarn and hook or needles recommended in the pattern stitch. The directions are based on the given gauge. The gauge (or tension) at which you work controls the size of each finished piece. It is therefore essential to work to the gauge given for each item if you want it to be the correct size. To test your gauge, cast on 20–30 stitches, using the hook or needles specified. Work in the pattern stitches for 3″. Smooth

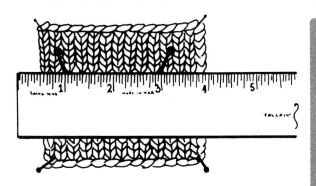

"(K 3, p 2) 5 times" means to do all that is specified in parentheses 5 times in all.

"Place a marker on needle" in directions means to place a safety pin, paperclip, or bought plastic stitch marker on the needle between the stitches. It is slipped from one needle to the other to serve as a mark on following rows.

out your swatch and pin it down. Measure across 2″ and place pins 2″ apart. Count number of stitches between pins. If you have more stitches to the inch than directions specify, you are working too tightly; use a larger hook or needles. If you have a fewer stitches to the inch, you are working too loosely; use a smaller hook or needles.

Most patterns give a row gauge, too. Although the proper length does not usually depend on the row gauge (directions usually give lengths in inches rather than rows), in some patterns it is important to have the proper row gauge, too.

HOW TO FOLLOW DIRECTIONS:

When parentheses ( ) are used to show repetition, work directions within parentheses as many times as specified. For example,

Quilting Stitch

Cut 18″ strand of thread. Knot one end. Bring needle up from lining through quilt top; give a little tug to thread so that knot passes through lining only and lies buried in batting. Sew on marked line with running stitch, making stitches as small and close as you can (5 to 10 per inch); space stitches evenly, so they are the same length on both sides of quilt. To end off, backstitch and take a long stitch through the top and batting only; take another backstitch and clip thread at surface; the thread end will sink into batting.

quilt top
batting
lining

Index